Transforming Understandings of
Diversity in Higher Education

Transforming Understandings of Diversity in Higher Education

Demography, Democracy, and Discourse

Edited by Penny A. Pasque, Noe Ortega, John C. Burkhardt, and Marie P. Ting

Foreword by Phillip J. Bowman

1996–2016 20TH ANNIVERSARY

PUBLISHING, LLC.

STERLING, VIRGINIA

COPYRIGHT © 2016 BY
STYLUS PUBLISHING, LLC.

Published by Stylus Publishing, LLC
22883 Quicksilver Drive
Sterling, Virginia 20166-2102

All rights reserved. No part of this book may be reprinted
or reproduced in any form or by any electronic, mechanical,
or other means, now known or hereafter invented, including
photocopying, recording, and information storage and
retrieval, without permission in writing from the publisher.

Library of Congress Cataloging-in-Publication Data
Names: Pasque, Penny A., editor of compilation.
Title: Transforming understandings of diversity in higher education: demography, democracy, and discourse / Penny A. Pasque [and three others]; foreword: Phillip J. Bowman.
Description: First edition.
Sterling, Virginia : Stylus Publishing, LLC, [2016] |
Includes bibliographical references and index
Identifiers: LCCN 2016004488 (print) |
LCCN 2016005427 (ebook) |
ISBN 9781620363751 (cloth : alk. paper) |
ISBN 9781620363768 (pbk. : alk. paper) |
ISBN 9781620363775 (library networkable e-edition) |
ISBN 9781620363782 (consumer e-edition) |
ISBN 9781620363775 (library PDF) |
ISBN 9781620363782 (e-book)
Subjects: LCSH: Minorities--Education (Higher)--United States. |
College students--United States--Social conditions.
Classification: LCC LC1099.3 .T725 2016 (print) |
LCC LC1099.3 (ebook) | DDC 378.008--dc23
LC record available at http://lccn.loc.gov/2016004488

13-digit ISBN: 978-1-62036-375-1 (cloth)
13-digit ISBN: 978-1-62036-376-8 (paper)
13-digit ISBN: 978-1-62036-377-5 (library networkable e-edition)
13-digit ISBN: 978-1-62036-378-2 (consumer e-edition)

Printed in the United States of America

All first editions printed on acid-free paper
that meets the American National Standards Institute
Z39-48 Standard.

Bulk Purchases

Quantity discounts are available for use in workshops and for staff development.
Call 1-800-232-0223

First Edition, 2016

We dedicate this book in the same spirit with which it was conceived: Each generation builds on the work of those who came before, especially in this challenging area of diversity scholarship, where doors and windows have been sealed shut for far too long. In addition to informing the many fields where diversity has become a topic of inquiry, each new contribution to our understanding of this topic also shapes the possibilities for those who will live in the world we are seeking to describe. Understanding that, we offer this book with the hope that all children and all grandchildren will awaken to a world of greater insight, greater justice, and the full appreciation of the abundant diversity that surrounds us all.

CONTENTS

Foreword   *xi*
   Phillip J. Bowman

Acknowledgments   *xvii*

Introduction   *1*
   Transforming Understandings of Diversity in Higher Education:
   History and Context
   John C. Burkhardt, Christina Morton, Marie P. Ting, Penny A. Pasque, and Noe Ortega

1. Color-Blind Ideology and the Disconnected Power-Analysis Frame   *21*
   Considerations for Historically Black Colleges and
   Universities' Diversification
   Uma M. Jayakumar and Annie S. Adamian

2. An Interview With Uma M. Jayakumar   *40*
   Social Agency and the Power of Resistance
   Diane M. Back

3. A Theory of Equity   *44*
   A Social and Legal Analysis of College Access for Low-Income Students
   Jarrett T. Gupton and Karen Miksch

4. An Interview With Jarrett T. Gupton   *54*
   The Value of Uncertainty and the Need for Nuance
   Sheela Linstrum

5. Lesbian, Gay, Bisexual, Transgender, and Queer Students on Campus   *57*
   Fostering Inclusion Through Research, Policy, and Practice
   Michael R. Woodford, Jessica Joslin, and Kristen A. Renn

6. An Interview With Michael R. Woodford 81
   Bringing Invisible Communities to Light: Disciplinary Norms, Collaboration, and the Quest for Legitimacy
   Timothy Hickey-LeClair

7. Racially and Socioeconomically Diverse Students' Pathways to College 88
   An Exploration of Latin@ Students
   Angela M. Locks, Dawn Person, Michelle Cuellar, Jeanette Maduena, and Melba Schneider Castro

8. An Interview With Angela M. Locks 118
   Understanding the Complexities of the College-Going Process
   James M. Ellis

9. Architecture of Diversity 123
   Using the Lens and Language of Space to Examine Racialized Experiences of Students of Color on College Campuses
   Michelle Samura

10. An Interview With Michelle Samura 144
    How the "Blue Wall" Changes Our Discourses on Race in Higher Education: Stepping Out of the Comfort Zone and Seeing Things in a Different Light
    Jimin Kwon

11. Including Disability in the Discourse 148
    Extending and Advancing the Definition of *Diversity* in Higher Education
    Allison Lombardi and Adam Lalor

12. An Interview With Allison Lombardi 163
    Including Disability in the Discourse
    Lloyd Edward Shelton

13. The Impact of Media Imagery on Academic Identity Development for Black Male Student Athletes 166
    LaVar J. Charleston and Jerlando F. L. Jackson

14. An Interview With Jerlando F. L. Jackson 177
    An Instrumental Diversity Researcher
    Carly Wegner

15. Racialized and Gendered Experiences of African American Female Faculty at Public Community Colleges 180
    Tamara Nichele Stevenson and Eboni M. Zamani-Gallaher

16. An Interview With Tamara Nichele Stevenson 202
    Surviving Racial Battle Fatigue: Cultivating Safe Spaces in
    Racialized Environments
    Tonya Kneff

17. Unpacking the Mandate Rhetoric of Historically Black Colleges and
    Universities' Diversity Discourses 207
    Courtney Carter

18. An Interview With Courtney Carter 218
    Unpacking the Mandate Rhetoric of Historically Black Colleges
    and Universities' Diversity Discourses
    Demar F. Lewis IV

19. Transforming Demography, Democracy, and Discourse Through 223
    Diversity in Education and Society
    John C. Burkhardt and Marie P. Ting

Contributors 230

Index 241

FOREWORD

Since 2005 the National Center for Institutional Diversity (NCID) at the University of Michigan (U-M) has evolved through three strategic stages: Agenda-Setting (2005–2009); Partnerships (2009–2013); and the current focus on Demography, Democracy, and Diversity (2013–present). As founding director of NCID, I worked very closely with Lester Monts, who was senior vice provost for academic affairs at the time, and other key U-M stakeholders, to refine the NCID mission to develop a strategic agenda and organize related strategic partnership activities around an evolving set of core priorities with growing national visibility.

During the Agenda-Setting stage, four major NCID programmatic advances were achieved. These included a systematic agenda-setting process guided by a reciprocal translation approach that linked exemplary diversity scholarship with multilevel engagement, innovation, and social change activities; the Postdoctoral Fellows Program, which awarded annually two exceptional early-career scholars the opportunity to be affiliated with NCID and a relevant U-M academic or research unit in residence; the National Diversity Scholars Network, which consists of Emerging Diversity Scholars (Exemplary Diversity Scholars, Exemplary Diversity Dissertation awardees, Visiting Diversity Scholars, and Faculty Associates); and the Diversity Research and Policy Program, which includes several collaborative Diversity Exemplar Evaluation Network projects and a mixed-methods study supported by the National Institutes of Health of exemplary research opportunity interventions that promote higher education and career diversity.

This exciting new book, *Transforming Understandings of Diversity in Higher Education: Demography, Democracy, and Discourse,* strategically builds on the National Diversity Scholars Network to break new ground in several pressing diversity areas that will continue to challenge scholars, students, educators, administrators, policymakers, and the general public as we move further into the twenty-first century. The book includes cutting-edge research on, but not limited to, transforming understandings; considerations for historically Black colleges and universities' (HBCU) diversification; equity and access for lesbian, gay, bisexual, transgender, and queer or questioning students' inclusion; exploration of Latin@ students; architecture of diversity;

advancing disability; media and Black student athletes; African American female faculty; HBCU diversity discourses; and the promise of diversity.

To place this unique book and these critical issues in a better context, I briefly highlight the National Diversity Scholars Network and the reciprocal translational approach that guided the development of this unique network of scholar activists whose exceptional contributions to this book reflect their strong commitment to bridging exemplary scholarship and multilevel engagement to address the complex challenges and opportunities of diversity in the twenty-first century.

National Diversity Scholars Network

The National Diversity Scholars Network, based at the NCID, continues to grow in interdisciplinary scope and national visibility. This national network of more than 350 scholars includes 157 Emerging Diversity Scholars, 158 Exemplary Diversity Scholars, 17 Exemplary Dissertation Scholars, 14 Postdoctoral Fellows, 4 Visiting Scholars, and more than 20 Faculty Associates engaged in collaborative NCID research activities at universities across the country. Each year, the NCID Postdoctoral Fellowship Program continues to grow in national prominence with outstanding Postdoctoral Fellows selected from an extremely competitive national pool of more than 100 applicants. This core NCID initiative was developed in 2008 to advance the center's national visibility; its national commitment to institutional diversity; and its strategic agenda to bridge exemplary scholarship with multilevel engagement, innovation, and social change. The growing success of the NCID Postdoctoral Fellows Program is based on strategic partnerships with U-M schools, colleges, and institutes as well as other universities in the United States and beyond. Building on the Michigan Society of Scholars Program model, NCID has been able to recruit outstanding young scholars as Postdoctoral Fellows with strong commitments to the NCID mission and who are also attractive as potential tenure-track faculty at U-M and other major research universities.

In addition to the Postdoctoral Fellows, the National Diversity Scholars Network includes a growing number of highly qualified, early-career scholar activists who received one of three other NCID citations: Exemplary Diversity Dissertations, Exemplary Diversity Scholars, or Emerging Diversity Scholars. It is important to note that the selection of NCID Postdoctoral Fellows is based not only on the quality and relevance of scholarship but also on each candidate's fit with relevant U-M academic departmental priorities during a particular year. A major goal is to identify early-career Diversity Scholars whose exceptional scholarship makes them attractive as potential faculty members at U-M and other peer institutions. Toward this end, application materials are reviewed by the NCID leadership to determine the fit among applicants' research, teaching, and multilevel engagement interests with the NCID's mission and priority areas. The most competitive applicants' materials are then forwarded to various U-M academic units for rigorous scholarly review to assess quality and fit with current department priorities. Based on this extensive review, all selected National Diversity Scholars Network citation recipients were rated as extremely impressive, with strong potential for successful academic careers at U-M and other major universities.

This book draws on the innovative diversity scholarship and multilevel engagement of a select group of scholar activists in the interdisciplinary NCID-based National Diversity Scholars Network who are engaged with an especially critical set of diversity issues in higher education. These higher education scholars bridge their cutting-edge scholarship with multilevel engagement, innovation, and social change activities to address a range of policy-relevant diversity challenges in higher education. Guided by a scholar activist approach, an especially innovative aspect of this book is the focus on the interplay among the themes of demography, democracy, and discourse in the cutting-edge diversity scholarship of these scholars on pressing issues of policy, programs, institutional type, immigration, race, class, sexual orientation, gender, and ability and disability.

Reciprocal Translation Approach

Rather than being detached scholars, the contributors represent exemplars of the National Diversity Scholars Network who personify the early NCID strategic agenda, including (a) innovative scholarship, research, or creative work on some aspect of diversity in the broadest sense; (b) the bridging of interdisciplinary scholarship with innovation to address pressing challenges and opportunities of diversity; and (c) the building of partnerships among scholars and policy-relevant leaders engaged in exemplary multilevel change activities at campus, institutional, local, state, or national, global levels. The National Diversity Scholars Network was systematically designed to attract exemplary scholar activists whose interests in diversity issues cross disciplinary boundaries in the evolving core NCID priority areas, including the current focus on demography, democracy, and diversity.

Reciprocal Translation Approach: Scholarship Engagement

Based on consultation with U-M–based and external stakeholders, NCID has supported a growing array of mission-driven collaborative initiatives and projects since 2006 with increasing national prominence. To further develop a distinctive national niche, a unique reciprocal translational agenda was developed at NCID between 2006 and 2009 to promote exemplary diversity scholarship, new mission-driven initiatives, and strategic partnership activities. For example, this reciprocal translational approach guided the development of the National Diversity Scholars Network and is reflected in the exceptional contributions in this book by the scholar activists whose research and career trajectories represent exemplars of reciprocal translation. As illustrated in Figure F.1, this reciprocal translational approach focuses on the benefits of bridging exemplary diversity scholarship with multilevel engagement (Bowman, 2013; Bowman & St. John, 2011). The left oval highlights the importance of exemplary scholarship to improve understanding of complex diversity challenges and opportunities, and the right oval highlights the importance of strategic partnerships to bridge exemplary diversity scholarship with multilevel engagement, innovation, and social change activities to address policy-relevant diversity challenges.

This focus in this unique translational approach promotes the reciprocal benefits of exemplary diversity scholarship and multilevel higher education; institutional and social change is reflected in the chapters by the various scholar activists. Consistent with the NCID mission, Figure F.1 highlights how the reciprocal translation of "exemplary scholarship" to "multilevel engagement" focuses on both the "traditional translation" of exemplary scholarship to guide multilevel engagement—and the "reverse translation" of multilevel activist engagement that can inspire new diversity scholarship—in addition to further supporting "multilevel social change," "best practices," and "national exemplars." This reciprocal translation approach also extends the classic adage by the eminent social psychologist Kurt Lewin (1952) that "there is nothing so practical as a good theory and nothing so theoretical as a good practice" (p. 169). As suggested in Figure F.1, in the best tradition of action research, such reciprocal links between theory-driven scholarship and policy-relevant practice can help resolve pressing diversity challenges at multiple levels: higher education, organizational or institutional, local or state, and national or international.

Demography, Democracy, and Discourse: Bridging Diversity Scholarship With Engagement

For each chapter in this book, the contributors were asked to submit new work that pushes the edge of our latest conceptualizations of diversity as organized around one or more of the core themes of demography, democracy,

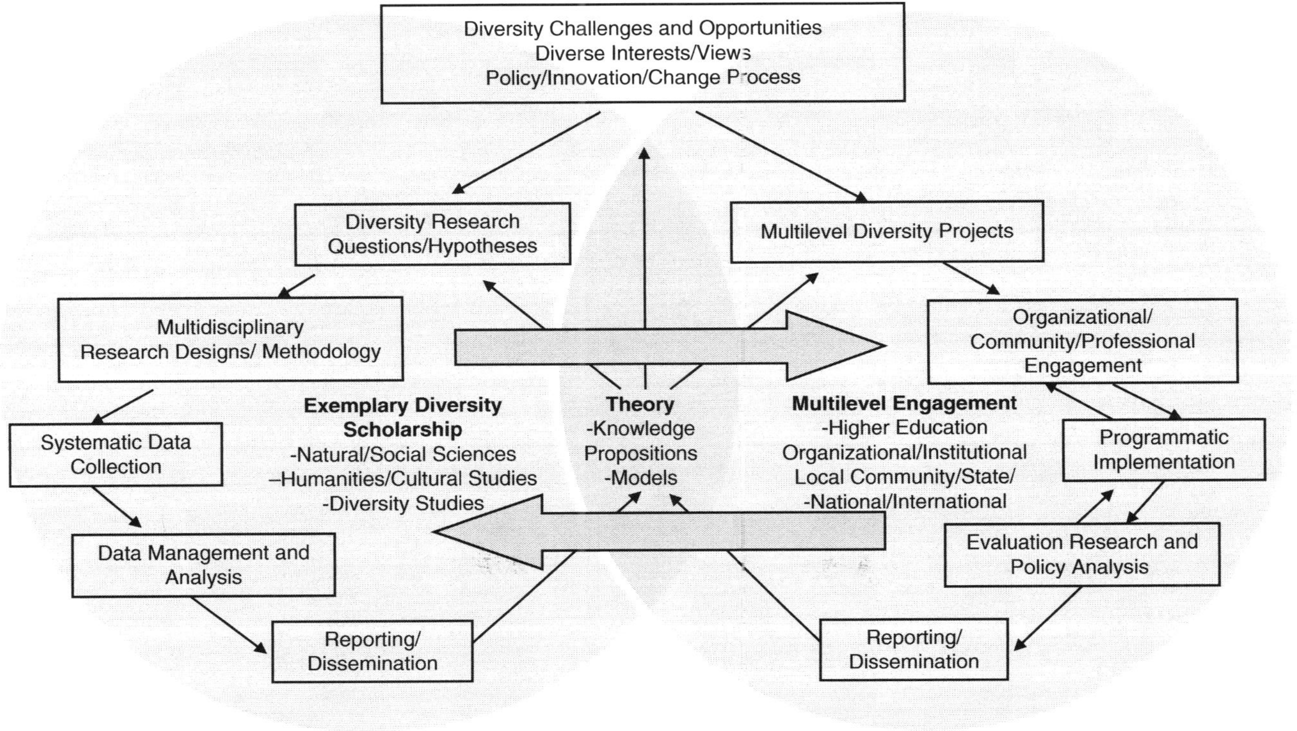

FIGURE F.1 Diversity Research and Policy Program: National Center on Institutional Diversity Bridging Exemplary Diversity Scholarship With Multilevel Engagement Reciprocal Translation Approach: Scholarship <–> Intervention and discourse. As a unique exercise in bridging scholarship and engagement, each contributor was asked to reflect on the paths his or her scholarship has taken as an assistant, associate, or full professor at institutions across the nation and share insights with the next generation of graduate students with similar career aspirations. I agree that this innovative approach makes this new book unique among a growing number of excellent books on diversity issues in higher education. Systematically converging the insights from a growing national diversity network of senior, midcareer, junior, postdoctoral, and graduate scholar activists should help to shape the next generation of scholarship and strategic action necessary to better understand and resolve the most pressing diversity challenges of the twenty-first century. In this sense, this new book makes a significant contribution to the NCID mission and reaffirms higher education's critical role in promoting knowledge, justice, and opportunity in a diverse democracy and global economy.

Phillip J. Bowman
Founding Director, NCID
University of Michigan

References

Bowman, P. J. (2013). A strengths-based social psychological approach to resiliency: Cultural diversity, ecological and life span issues. In S. Prince-Embury (Ed.), *Translating resiliency theory for application with children, youth and adults* (pp. 299–324). New York, NY: Springer.

Bowman, P. J., & St. John, E. (2011). Toward a 21st century meritocracy: Bridging scholarship, intervention research, and social change. In P. J. Bowman & E. St. John (Eds.), *Readings on equal education: Diversity, merit, and higher education: Toward a comprehensive agenda for the 21st century* (pp. 325–348). New York, NY: AMS Press.

Lewin, K. (1952). *Field theory in social science: Selected theoretical papers by Kurt Lewin*. London, UK: Tavistock.

ACKNOWLEDGMENTS

A book of this kind depends on contributions from many individuals, each who play important roles in its development. Lena M. Khader and Krystal Golding-Ross, graduate assistants at the University of Oklahoma, provided invaluable support for this project in their copyediting roles. Several University of Michigan graduate students and staff, including Carlos Robles, Demar Lewis, Charlotte Ezzo, and William Lopez, also provided significant assistance in verifying facts and checking citations. We would also like to thank Michael Betzold for copyediting aspects of this manuscript and for his helpful suggestions that resulted in a better, more clearly rendered manuscript.

In addition, we would like to thank John von Knorring and Sarah Burrows for their tireless efforts championing this book, which we believe furthers knowledge critical to the field of higher education. We also appreciate Alexandra Hartnett and the rest of the team at Stylus Publishing for providing hours of support with this manuscript.

We would also like to thank all the faculty, administrators, staff, graduate assistants, visiting scholars, and awardees who, over the past decade, have contributed to the success of the National Center on Institutional Diversity, based at the University of Michigan. Special recognition is due to Patricia Gurin and Phillip Bowman, the directors of the center whose vision sustained and influenced the center's work during its crucial formative years.

Finally, we would like to acknowledge the tireless dedication of the people who are committed to advancing opportunity and extending inclusive participation in higher education and throughout all societies. It is our sincere hope that this book offers them something of value and inspiration.

INTRODUCTION
Transforming Understandings of Diversity in Higher Education: History and Context

John C. Burkhardt, Christina Morton, Marie P. Ting, Penny A. Pasque, and Noe Ortega

Many terms and phrases in public discourse carry multiple meanings and lack specific definition. *Diversity* is certainly one such term. Because it has acquired an accepted connotation in popular use, it has received only occasional close examination in scholarship (Smith, 2009; Stulberg & Weinberg, 2011). In light of its contradictory meanings in the history of education and its rapidly expanding applications in educational research, policy, and rhetoric, there is an obvious threat of confusion that can jeopardize the desired ends associated with the use of this term. One of the intended contributions of this book is to further appreciation of diversity as text, in context, and within the many subtexts from which it derives its meanings.

Because the word *diversity* is not new in its general use but has taken on special meaning as it has come to be applied in social, cultural, and political contexts, it is not necessary to establish a full etymology of its use. Precisely because of the way that *diversity* has often become identified as a problem in education and society, it is worth noting that the use of the term in biblical translation is found in the Book of Exodus (31:5, Wycliffe Bible, early version), where it is used to describe the abundance of natural resources and the beauty available for use and enjoyment. Fast-forward to the eighteenth and nineteenth centuries and *diversity* was a term in frequent use in scientific work across many fields, generally referring to a desired aspect of the natural world and one of special value in the advancement of agriculture. The term found its way into descriptions of economic systems and technology during the twentieth century. As used popularly today and employed in many fields of study, the word *diversity* is used to describe an obvious aspect of many different parts of our lives. Gardeners take joy in it. Epicureans thrive on it. Investors depend on it.

In education, *diversity* has sometimes taken on a different and more ambiguous nature, suggesting an unmet challenge. This in itself is not unusual: When concepts and ideas are subjected to scholarly examination, and even more frequently when they become encoded for use in contested policy debate, they often become *problematized*, which is itself a term that could find acceptance only in the academy. Similar to terms such as *health care* or *social security*, which on first appearance are positive and desirable, diversity has become less a description of abundance, fascination, and promise and more an issue attendant with complications. There are now challenges associated with diversity; diversity is something we must cope with and respond to. The aim of achieving diversity fatefully implies there are shortages to manage, constraints to address, barriers to remove, and powerful forces that must be overcome in that pursuit. While the use of the term in that way accurately applies to the task of opening opportunity to *all* individuals and groups in our institutions and society, even when we do so we will not have achieved diversity; we will have recognized and responded to it, for it already exists everywhere we look. By making diversity a problem, we associate it with problems. Some problems are very real (i.e., racism, sexism, ableism, heterosexism, classism), but diversity itself is not a problem.

In introducing and framing the work reported in this volume, we begin by examining how some of these meanings of the term *diversity* have come into use and point out how they may be confounding the discourse and educational practice inside and surrounding the academy. In this book's concluding chapter, we suggest the need for a transdisciplinary consideration of diversity as one means of bridging divisions in understanding and applying this important—perhaps we should say life-sustaining—idea. We also describe how the National Center for Institutional Diversity (NCID), based at the University of Michigan, is hoping to provide support and leadership in this effort.

Difference and U.S. Higher Education: Historical Roots

Just as Harvard was founded to educate ministers for Congregational and Unitarian service in the early 1600s, a different denomination of Protestants, the Anglicans, established the second colonial college, William and Mary (Thelin, 2011). Other congregations and other colonial colleges followed similar patterns of differentiation in what was taught, who was taught, and who was allowed to teach. As new colleges were established westward across the continent, most were affiliated with a specific purpose derived from a religious tradition and supported by faithful sponsors who shared the defining belief. Some of these institutions were founded for the very purpose of responding to exclusion elsewhere or to guard an unpopular view. Today we can see this pattern: Wesleyans throughout the Midwest, Catholics where they were accepted (and especially where immigrant groups came to settle), Baptists and Methodists in the South.

The word *mission* persists in our description of an institution's core values and purpose even if its relationship to the word *missionary* has been obscured. From the beginnings of higher learning in our country, we have responded to differences in backgrounds, affiliations, and beliefs most frequently by creating new institutions. That pattern, largely unchanged and often unacknowledged, continues today.

When the idea of offering higher education opportunities to women was established, women's colleges were formed (Solomon, 1985). Sometimes these were established in the same communities where men's colleges already existed (a pattern that Catholic higher education later followed); however, when this occurred, efforts to maintain separation between students became something of an obsession. The curriculum in colleges serving men and those serving women differed as well, reflecting assumptions and biases of the times. Normal schools, established to prepare teachers, also followed the pattern of separation by gender with few exceptions. When groups that favored the abolition of slavery congregated, they founded colleges on this radical principle.

In *The Shape of the River*, Howard Bowen and Derek Bok (1998) cite the experiences of students from the North and South who studied and shared rooms at Harvard in the 1850s. In one example, Henry Adams was assigned to board with "Roony" Lee, the son of the Confederate Civil War general. Judged by today's measures, the two young men had much in common. But Adams related that "a thin edge of friendship" was sufficient to relieve them of the fate given to "mortal enemies" a few years later as they found themselves separated by a civil war (Bowen & Bok, 1998, p. 218).

Following that war, African Americans in very limited numbers were given access to college. This departure from practice was most often accommodated through the creation of new—and separate—institutions. In some cases, philanthropic support for these institutions was offered on the explicit agreement that instruction would be constrained to preparation in the trades and agriculture. This very issue resulted in a ferocious debate between W. E. B. DuBois and Charles S. Johnson over whether such an approach would inevitably limit newly freed Blacks to second-tier status in society. DuBois argued, presciently, that separating races for educational purposes would inevitably result in fewer opportunities for Black advancement and could lead to the creation of educational castes (Gasman, 2002).

We find similar patterns of institutional specialization and enforced distance each time U.S. higher education has encountered new student populations and occasionally when new professions and disciplines were introduced. This history may be noted, for example, in the ways we have accommodated Jewish students, Native American students, and students with various abilities and disabilities, and in fields as different from one another as the arts, medicine, and military leadership (see Table I.1).

In sum, higher education in our country has historically dealt with difference through a process of accommodation through separation, almost never through inclusion and transformation. We boast of the diversity that exists across the U.S. system of higher education, and it is diverse when viewed as a system. But at the institutional level, and often when we examine how different disciplines are regarded, diversity has never been a key feature. On the contrary, the effort to specialize and distinguish institutions based on what is taught and to whom it is taught has been the dominant model, even as we moved toward a concept of higher education as a public, as opposed to a private, undertaking. In some cases, this segregation model has eventually given way to more inclusive educational environments, which usually occurred through a process of accommodation of differences (intramural segregation). Only in rare instances has it been followed by a full transformation of policy, practice, and attitudes.

TABLE I.1
Higher Education Institutions' Responses to New Student Populations

Issue of Diversity and Inclusion	*Higher Education's Response*
Differences in religious beliefs	Denominational colleges, Catholic and Jewish institutions
Women attending college	Women's colleges
Students with physical limitations	Gallaudet University and schools for the blind
Blacks attending college	Segregated institutions
Technology and agriculture	Land-grant institutions
Preparing teachers	Normal schools
Nontraditional learners	Nontraditional environments
Geographic and cost constraints	Community colleges
Hispanic students	Hispanic-serving institutions

Access, Diversity, and Citizenship

The rise of public higher education is associated with the establishment of land-grant institutions, but this also coincided with the expansion of the political and geographic composition of the United States that occurred through the second half of the nineteenth century. We can see in the founding of public institutions the release of pent-up energy that had been constrained by the friction generated when the consideration of adding new states to the union was based on their identification with slavery or emancipation. Understood in that way, the growth of state-affiliated public colleges can be seen as a manifestation—state by state and institution by institution—of the racial and economic tensions that distorted and held back the spread of democratic participation for more than 100 years.

Consequently, expansion of state colleges and universities throughout the late nineteenth century and midway through the twentieth century did not translate into meaningful diversity on U.S. campuses. The apparent disconnection between institutions that had been established to serve the public and the fact that only some segments of the population were honestly considered for admission clarifies the meaning of *public* in this context. Logically (at least in terms of the prevailing logic at that time), public higher education was premised on a democratic ideal, and it derived its impetus from its role in preparing citizens and leaders for service in a democratic society. This was a participatory view of democracy, not an inclusive view of service to the public as it might have been more broadly described. Within that framework, the exclusionary practices of many public institutions, some maintained well into the 1970s (and some would argue continued today), reflected and served to reproduce the circumstances that defined democratic participation throughout the century.

Women were not given the vote until the 1920s, and while their influence on civic and even political democratic practices was notable (including organization of the suffrage movement with little male support), the argument that they should be prepared for full citizenship was not forcefully evident until the first two decades of the twentieth century (Alemán & Renn, 2002). After the 19th Amendment, but not because of it, women started to enter large public universities (admittedly as co-eds, not eds) between the wars and in greater numbers following World War II (Solomon, 1985). Today, of course, women constitute the majority of U.S. college students, but they are far from the majority of faculty, top administrative leaders, or students in high-paying fields such as science, technology, engineering, or math (Allan, 2011; Pasque & Errington Nicholson, 2011).

Where African Americans exercised voting rights in the North, they were, on occasion, admitted to colleges but still not guaranteed inclusion

(Thelin, 2011). They were expressly prohibited by law from attending college in many southern states. While we should be quick to point out that the argument for democratic preparation was as much a rationalization as it was a reason, it is consistent with a pattern in which democratic access and educational access have been connected in policy and practice.

The current battle over the admission of undocumented immigrant students to colleges and universities fits this historical pattern. Despite the fact that many states actually invest less in student support to higher education (and might presumably relinquish some influence over institutional policies), legislative prohibitions explicitly bar access through admission to college in 13 states, and several more states even prohibit the use of private scholarship funds to undocumented students (Burkhardt et al., 2012). This pattern has become so prevalent that it almost seems logical: Noncitizens should not be given access to higher education because it is a right reserved for those who have earned democratic privileges. The fact that many public institutions were established in states before they were states, or that we educate thousands of international students every year, is not inconsistent with the prevailing pattern. Access to higher education has traditionally followed voting rights, not preceded it, and sometimes after some gap in time. The contemporary case of undocumented students, not unlike the surcharge paid by out-of-state or international students, is consistent with a view of public higher education as an earned right of citizenship. The argument that access to public higher education is earned by contributing through taxes to the state has been eroded. The fact that the related practices and policies continue to persevere offers some insight into a historical pattern and a persistent defensive logic for this form of exclusion.

Sinister, With Ongoing Implications

In the 1920s and throughout the decades that followed, Ivy League institutions acted to increase the diversity of their undergraduate student bodies, but their reasons for doing so were less than honorable even by the standards of those times. As reported by Karabel (2005), a concern was raised about the increasing number of Jewish students who were finding spots in the freshmen cohorts at Harvard, Yale, and Princeton. This trend represented a threat to the cherished patterns of campus life. A disturbing letter, addressed by an alumnus to President A. Lawrence Lowell of Harvard, blatantly argued,

> The Jew is undoubtedly of high mental order, desires the best education he can get CHEAPEST, and is more persistent than other races in his

endeavor to get what he wants. It is self-evident therefore, that by raising the standards of marks he can't be eliminated from Harvard, whereas the same process of raising the standard "White" boys ARE eliminated. And this is to go on? Why the Psychology test if not to bar those not wanted? (p. 117)

It was not hard to determine where these new students were originating: It was the cities of the east coast of the United States that had attracted immigrants from Europe in the later years of the nineteenth century and throughout World War I. Admissions officers at Harvard, Princeton, and Yale moved to diversify their enrollments by recruiting students from other parts of the country. Diversity, in this context, meant an optimal geographic mix, and geography was meant to ensure that "red-blooded American boys" would find their ways to these elite institutions. The so-called character test remained in use at Princeton through the mid-1960s (Karabel, 2005).

At this same time, and seemingly based on similar motives of intentional exclusion, class sizes were limited, and explicit targets were set for the percentage of Jewish students in each class (10% at Yale). In the process of attempting to shape entering classes in these elite schools, three related concepts were introduced into higher education that continue to influence practices today.

First, the argument for selectivity in admissions became accepted and associated with elite institutions. Second, the use of standardized testing as a means of determining eligibility for admissions took root. This mechanism was almost a foregone requirement if admissions committees were to diversify enrollments outside a traditional geographic area and known candidates from a few private preparatory schools. But as the crude but prescient observation made in the preceding letter suggests, the use of testing as a factor in admissions was not without bias from its very beginning.

Third, and in contrast to the contention that testing offered a new form of objectivity in determining who should be given access to college, even these decidedly anti-Semitic practices left something behind for the future consideration of diversity in college and university admissions. To circumvent the unintended effect of standardized testing and the use of high school grades to determine admissions, but without sacrificing the virtue of selectivity (on whatever basis), admissions officers began to incorporate noncognitive factors into their consideration of candidates. The admissions profession, as it originated in these schools and under these circumstances, adopted the practice of *shaping* a freshman class. The values that shaped the class included some that were obviously despicable, but the recognition that factors beyond those measured by tests or prior achievement might be considered in admissions is still relevant. Standardized testing has always been and continues to be a confounding challenge to understanding and advancing diversity in concept and practice in higher education (Brittain & Landy, 2014; Guinier, 2015; Soares, 2012).

When judging the implications of any systematic process that shapes or constrains the characteristics of students admitted to a given institution based on some definition of *diversity*, we might always remember this example of how Jewish students were considered at elite institutions during the two decades after World War II. How different might it have been if the nation's leaders during World War II had been educated under different circumstances and with different assumptions?

Diversity as a Term of Use in the Civil Rights Era

There are two historical representations of the civil rights movement. One begins with the organization of workers and those excluded from the labor force in the 1930s, and the other is associated with efforts to secure voting, housing, and educational access for racial minorities and women in the years following World War II. Neither of these long struggles were really premised on an argument for diversity as such. More accurately, these were related efforts to ensure recognition of social and economic rights and were waged to address long-standing distortions in power held in U.S. society. They were conjoined in their premise of economic justice, basic human rights, and protection from unfair treatment (Williams, 2005). They shared tactical approaches and some notable alliances in leadership. The union movement and the civil rights movements, whether viewed separately or as aspects of a single struggle, were meant to be disruptive. We sometimes characterize those who opposed these historic efforts as being *ignorant* or unabashedly *racist*, and certainly those terms do apply in some cases. But the prospect and implications of diversifying schools, workplaces, or communities were viewed as an attempt to disrupt a way of life. There was no shortage of outright racism and classism at work in the opposition to these movements either in the North or the South, but the manipulation of the fears associated with diversifying social and institutional patterns inspired violent resistance and fueled claims of unfathomable upheaval.

Whatever the social forces at work, these were not diversity movements at their core. Although the term *integration* was adopted by those in the movements, women did not need to be integrated into most places in society (corporations, board rooms, legislatures, and private clubs were obvious exceptions), and more African Americans were seeking fair treatment and opportunity than the distant vision of full social integration.

In a keynote speech presented to educators at the Union Institute in Cincinnati, Ohio, Betty Overton-Atkins (2015) observed that Reverend Martin Luther King Jr. did not mention the term *diversity* in any of his major speeches or letters. While this observation is difficult to verify given the breadth of King's public communication, we find no evidence to contradict it. The point is that while King spoke about the dignity of all men and women, including the poor and our international enemies, his appeals were based on a moral and ethical foundation. Diversity is neither moral nor ethical per se; it is natural, scientific, artistic, and many other things. It was not a central theme of the civil rights era even if that era resulted in social and judicial changes that led inevitably to the consideration of diversity as a societal objective.

In a rather unexpected way, the term *diversity* did make an appearance at the end of this momentous period. The context in which it appeared gave further evidence of the historic approach taken to serving new populations through differentiation and exclusion, which we described earlier. In 1971 the College Entrance and Examination Board and the Educational Testing Service formed a commission to examine approaches to serve nontraditional students, at that time the most recent outlier group claiming a place in higher education. After a 2-year study, the commission issued its report titled "Diversity by Design" (1973) and suggested that the particular needs of this population merited specialized instruction and perhaps even the formation of a new national university to serve them. It is remarkable that the term *diversity* was employed with no reference to women, people of color, or economic class at the time of the commission's deliberations ending in 1973.[1]

Diversity as a Desired Objective and a State Interest

The civil rights era and the increasing expectations of Americans to participate in economic and civic life set the context for a discussion of a concept like diversity (by whatever name it would be given) in our educational institutions and ultimately in the courts. It required at least a nominal inclusion of different participants in our community, educational, and cultural lives before we might begin to even partially comprehend the meaning and importance of what has now been framed as the concept of diversity.

Obviously this could not mean that diversity did not exist prior to the changes in American society in the past half century. As suggested earlier in this chapter, such a characterization would be absurd on its face. Only in breaking down walls that previously obstructed our awareness and understanding of diversity in its many forms could we open ourselves to seeing and appreciating what has arguably always been present in our lives. Recognizing this pattern, seeing that partial acceptance (even by exception) must precede a greater appreciation and further insistence of full inclusion, has set the stage for contemporary discussions about diversity as a desirable objective, rather than a descriptor in educational policy and in the courts.

The fact that higher education institutions, and shockingly many faculty members and scholars, had overlooked or actively resisted diversity as a basic reality of the natural world is a testament to prejudice and ignorance. The further realization that exploitive scientific experimentation and theories of eugenics originated, perpetuated, or advanced in the academy well into the twentieth century is horrifying (Kevles, 1985; Reverby, 2009). But the concept of diversity took shape in the nexus between higher education and the courts, beginning with challenges to affirmative action practices in the 1970s.

When the U.S. Supreme Court handed down a decision in *Regents of the University of California v. Bakke* (1978), it began a series of long judicial cases that are still reshaping practices in colleges and universities. In an opinion by Justice Lewis J. Powell, the court established diversity as a legitimate state interest, and by consequence, a reasonable objective in college admissions. Paraphrasing a previous opinion on the subject of academic freedom by Justice Felix Frankfurter, Powell stated, "The atmosphere of 'speculation, experiment and creation'—so essential to the quality of higher education—is widely believed to be promoted by a diverse student body," and he went on to state that a diverse student body "clearly is a constitutionally permissible goal for an institution of higher education" (p. 438).[2]

The *Regents of the University of California v. Bakke* (1978) decision set the stage for a series of subsequent cases in which the court considered and generally limited the approaches taken by colleges and universities to achieve the interests cited and legitimized in *Bakke*. In two cases involving the University of Michigan, *Grutter v. Bollinger* (2003) and *Gratz v. Bollinger* (2003), the court's decisions recognized the benefits of diversity as important to fulfilling the educational mission of the university. In issuing its findings, the court commended the research presented by the institution attesting to the effects of diversity on student learning.

Naming a state interest in creating diverse educational environments in higher education is a long way from requiring states (or universities) to actively seek diversity or to make it meaningful in interactions between students. In this respect, the past 30 years might be characterized as a game of hide-and-seek between colleges and the courts as the means for achieving diversity are tested even if the end itself remains elusive. Later court decisions have served to limit approaches taken by colleges and universities to diversify their student bodies and suggested that only reasonable administrative efforts are needed to do so.

Justice Sandra Day O'Connor, in writing the majority opinion in the *Gratz v. Bollinger* (2003) case, reaffirmed the state's interest in promoting diversity in education and in society. In articulating her position she cited the historical patterns of exclusion especially related to issues of race. She also took note of the ability of U.S. society and its institutions to rectify past injustices over time. On that basis, she suggested that diversity was a goal that was to be achieved perhaps in 25 years (and then presumably henceforth taken for granted). In stating that policies to ensure diversity in colleges and universities "must be limited in time," she stipulated that "the Court expects that 25 years from now, the use of racial preferences will no longer be necessary to further the interest approved today" (p. 539).

Even in this opinion, provided by perhaps the central actor in the nation's highest court, we find the seeds for further confusion related to the argument underpinning diversity as a defensible social and governmental interest. Are we to expect that once some element of representation along racial lines has been achieved, presumably within 25 years, institutional efforts and protection from the courts will no longer be required? Do other forms of diversity, such as those based on sexual orientation, ability, or economic status, deserve similar treatment, and if so, are those limited in time as well?

Why Do the Meanings We Assign to Diversity Matter to Practitioners?

In introducing his opinion in the 1978 *Regents of the University of California v. Bakke* decision, Powell quoted Supreme Court Justice Oliver Wendell Holmes in a very interesting passage. In *Towne v. Eisner* (1918), Holmes made an observation about the contextual nature of language:

> A word is not a crystal, transparent and unchanged, it is the skin of a living thought, and may vary greatly in color and content according to the circumstances and the time in which it is used. (cited in Holbrook, 1923, p. 1)

Over a period of about 20 years, the word *diversity* has been repurposed as an objective rather than a basic and accepted element of our social and natural order. In this transition the word has taken on the notion of a category, a collection, a special subset of human identities and conditions.

It has been associated with its own agenda and accorded new status as a value. The *diversity agenda* (if that term even makes sense) has been reconstructed to include race, religious belief, gender, sexual orientation, ability, economic class, and the interests and concerns of first-generation students. This convening of what are otherwise separate and very different groups may be a legitimate way to describe and manage the claims of different deserving interests without the risk of exclusion, and in that way it serves several different political and institutional ends. But, as Young (2011) stated, this not only comes at the cost of logic and precision but also confuses the central issues and quite frequently crosses the line of insensitivity. Not to quibble with Justice Holmes, but this has become a case where the changing context in which a term is used has introduced significant and perhaps unintended implications.

Technically and syntactically, defining the concept of diversity seems to be a nominal problem, but in this case nominal does not mean small or only a question of semantics. Serious implications stem from the drift in associated meanings; some affect scholarship, some limit practical application of the term in the context of practice, some raise legal questions, and all of them frustrate the underlying goals that have become associated with the idea of diversity in higher education and society.

The various chapters in this volume, if read as a collection, demonstrate this point. Each contribution has been well conceived, making use of a particular understanding of diversity as a concept and as a theme in contemporary U.S. higher education. Appropriate methods of scholarship have been employed to illuminate important questions stemming from the definitions adopted by the contributors in the context of their disciplines and their areas of professional practice. Conclusions are drawn from the findings of each study, all of which are well focused and quite helpful. In reviewing the book as a whole, we believe that it meets the test of providing an original and meaningful constellation of perspectives on one of the most important topics under discussion in our field. But as we have implied, it is a constellation. It is not a representation of the universe.

When elementary school students construct their three-dimensional models of the planets in our solar system, they take great pains (or their parents do at least) to get the size, color, and relative position of the planets right. But what would easily win a top prize at the annual science fair would be a way of showing how the universe is expanding and what this means for those of us living on one of the smaller and more vulnerable planets orbiting around one sun. We face a similar challenge for a book of this design. Each of the chapters offers something unique to understanding the complexities of diversity in higher education and society. In addition, the chapters written by graduate students were based on their interviews with award-winning authors and offer insight (or foresight) of special importance. But the challenge to practitioners in higher education settings is not unlike the problem faced by parents the day after the science fair. We have a model, and it incorporates examples and it suggests relationships, but now what do we do with it?

Like the science experiment, the term *diversity* itself has become too precious to discard and too important to leave undefined in professional or scholarly use. It does not pay for those of us who have been charged with pursuing a mandate for greater inclusion and opportunity in our institutions and in society to settle for an ill-considered answer to such a central concept.

The Chapters

With these thoughts in mind, we draw the reader's close attention to the various chapters in this volume. Based on the goals of the book, we contacted previous NCID award-winning scholars (outlined in the foreword by Phillip J. Bowman), whose research has opened up new understandings of the complexities of diversity in higher education. The scholars were asked to contribute their most innovative thinking, drawing on their current and cutting edge research agenda. Some of the scholars chose to cowrite with researchers, practitioners, or graduate students. We sought original material that relates to the book's themes and shows the scholar's progress in continuing study of the topic. Given the importance of diversity in their work and the many contexts and meanings associated with the concept, we asked the contributors the following question: What would you write if you had one chance to tell the world what diversity means to you in your scholarship at this point in your life?

During the time the scholars were writing their contributions, graduate students interviewed the NCID award-winning scholars about their research and career trajectory and then wrote a chapter based on their own reflections of this interview. This was a wonderful way to engage graduate students in the writing process of this book as well as to support intergenerational discussions about the importance of academic careers based on diversity, demography, democracy, and discourse. The interview chapters immediately follow the chapters written by the NCID scholar (i.e., interviews are the even-numbered chapters) and were written by Diane M. Back (Chapter 2), Sheela Linstrum (Chapter 4), Timothy Hickey-LeClair (Chapter 6), James M. Ellis (Chapter 8), Jimin Kwon (Chapter 10), Lloyd Edward Shelton (Chapter 12), Carly Wegner (Chapter 14), Tonya Kneff (Chapter 16), and Demar F. Lewis IV (Chapter 18).

It is important to note that the scholars represent various institution types from across the country and at various levels of the tenure and promotion process (i.e., assistant professor, associate professor, full professor). This publication, further illuminated by the interviews, provides a unique contribution regarding the latest thinking on diversity as well as strategies to navigate the tenure and promotion process while focusing on research often marginalized yet touted in the academy. It also provides an important opportunity for graduate students to connect directly with national scholars who received recognition from NCID and who have dedicated their careers to diversity, demography, democracy, or discourse in a way that may illuminate what may often be hidden to people interested in navigating academic careers.

Chapter 1 begins with an exploration of the implications of diversifying historically Black colleges and universities (HBCU) given the prevalence of color-blind racial primes among Whites entering college today and the established harms of color-blind ideology on the education of Black people. Contributors Uma M. Jayakumar and Annie S. Adamian clearly describe Bonilla-Silva's theory of color-blind ideology and his analysis of data on White students at predominantly White institutions (PWI) as they provide a comparative analysis of color-blind frames among White students at HBCUs in their own data set. This exploratory analysis suggests that color-blind frames evolve and adapt to more racially conscious contexts yet continue to perpetuate color blindness. Notably, they offer a fifth frame of color-blind ideology: the disconnected power-analysis frame.

Chapter 3 by Jarrett T. Gupton and Karen Miksch explores the tensions between democracy and meritocracy in educational discourse and how this relates to college access. The chapter sheds light on the critical need to focus on social and legal equity when discussing low-income students and diversity in higher education. The authors do so by addressing the place of merit in a democratic society and the ways the legal system has rationalized discrimination based on social class. Consistent with our observations related to previous court cases, it raises the following critical question: Is preserving access to higher education for low-income students a compelling government interest?

Michael R. Woodford, Jessica Joslin, and Kristen A. Renn in Chapter 5 also probe the implications of changing concepts of diversity that tends to be understood as racial and ethnic diversity and, at times, relates to gender, yet not often enough do concepts of diversity include sexual orientation, gender identity, or gender expression. The authors discuss the state of the field of lesbian, gay, bisexual, transgender, and queer or questioning (LGBTQ) scholarship in higher education and bring attention to the experiences of university community members who identify as LGBTQ. In addition to critically assessing the body of scholarly literature in this area, they propose a model that integrates our LGBTQ community members to more effectively inform policy and practice to foster LGBTQ student success and well-being.

The collaboration in Chapter 7 of Angela M. Locks, Dawn Person, Michelle Cuellar, Jeanette Maduena, and Melba Schneider Castro offers two related research studies that explore important policy conversations occurring at federal, state, and local levels regarding college access, college attendance, and student learning outcomes in postsecondary environments. In our dynamic sociopolitical environment, which more often than not emphasizes accountability, understanding how students get to college and what they learn in college is critical for higher education scholars, practitioners, and leaders. This chapter focuses on a praxis-driven assessment and evaluation model for the Gaining Early Awareness and Readiness for Undergraduate Program and provides an overview of empirical findings on how low-income Latin@[3] students develop their college aspirations, behaviors, and attitudes in middle and high school environments.

Michelle Samura in Chapter 9 artfully examines the experiences of college students of color, which are complicated in the current U.S. racial climate, particularly when there are disconnects between the rhetoric and reality of racial diversity on campuses: a promotion and celebration of the idea, on the one hand, and the ways in which students experience it, on the other hand. Samura argues that the lens and language of space offer researchers and practitioners an updated approach to understand students' racialized experiences in depth. This spatial approach sheds light on race relations and racial structures in tangible campus environments. She draws on her research on Asian American college students and discusses how a spatial lens locates larger racial meanings in students' lived experiences, concrete environments, and social relationships. It is important to note that she addresses how a spatial approach provides an accessible language to discuss experiences of racialization, race making, and racism in higher education.

In Chapter 11 Allison Lombardi and Adam Lalor shift attention to the rapid increase in the enrollment of students with disabilities at U.S. colleges and universities. The authors examine the essential scholarship on disability-related issues and draw attention to the lack of knowledge about disability in higher education. To be sure, disability is an identity that for some can change over a lifetime yet is omitted far too often from the discourse on demography and diversity.

LaVar J. Charleston and Jerlando F. L. Jackson's Chapter 13 examines how the mainstream and social media perpetuate a narrow stereotypical representation of Black male student athletes. With results from a qualitative study, their chapter explores the extent to which Black male student athletes' development of their academic identity is influenced by media messages. Further, they explore how the involvement of Black male student athletes in intercollegiate athletics has been blamed for stunted development academically.

In Chapter 15 Tamara Nichele Stevenson and Eboni M. Zamani-Gallaher explore the dynamic and complex intersection of two enduring yet consistently ignored components of American higher education: African American female faculty and public community colleges. Notably, persistent segmentation and low numbers of African American women characterize the faculty ranks across institutional type. This chapter highlights findings drawn from a larger exploratory study of the racialized and gendered experiences of African American female public community college faculty. Stevenson and Zamani-Gallaher seek to understand the extent to which participants experience racial battle fatigue because of racial microaggressions (i.e., the exchange and response to race-related mental, emotional, and physical tensions) and the racialized stressors associated with their faculty role.

In Chapter 17 Courtney Carter seeks to shift the national discourse on diversity from one that focuses largely on the experiences of students at PWIs to one that looks more closely at HBCUs. Drawing from statements made by HBCU insiders, including Black school administrators, advocates, consultants, and scholarly experts, Carter argues that diversity is conceptualized as a way to deal with challenges of institutional viability and legitimacy.

In conclusion, NCID director John C. Burkhardt and NCID associate director Marie P. Ting reflect in Chapter 19 on contributions to this volume as they envision what it would mean to transform understandings of diversity in higher education, including the interconnections between demography, democracy, and discourse. They describe the ongoing initiatives for NCID that serve at the nexus of research, policy, and practice. Burkhardt and Ting expand our understandings beyond higher education as they consider the academy's dynamic relationship with society as a whole. The chapter centers on how the phrase *increasing diversity* is not enough to change and ultimately transform institutions and society in a way that is inclusive and sustainable.

Diversity as Text and Context

Looking at how we have viewed diversity for periods of 10, 20, or even 50 years gives us sufficient insight to offer a very simple typology that combines elements of time and motion and can be helpful in taking scholarship into everyday practice. This typology (see Table I.2) roughly follows the historical evolution and the expansion of arguments made in defense of diversity in our colleges, universities, and society as a whole.

It is a working heuristic, nothing more, and one we use at NCID to foster discussion, not to preempt it. While the typology we offer is generally

TABLE I.2
Understanding Diversity as a Dynamic Interest in Education and Society

Arguments for Diversity in Higher Education and Society as Related in Context (Time)	Representative and Responsive Actions to Changing Meanings of Diversity (Motion)
Moral and philosophical	Marches, demonstrations, church activism
Legal and political	Enforcement of voting rights, Affirmative Action, discrimination lawsuits, identification of protected classes, Title IX, Americans with Disabilities Act
Economic and competitive	Workforce preparation, workplace diversity training, international comparisons
Educational and mission–related	Educational benefits of diversity; science, technology, engineering, and mathematics programs; higher education as a vehicle for social transformation
Democracy– and constituency–driven	Access for immigrants, 10% plans, shifting costs to students and families

derived from an analysis of public discourse, we believe implications can be derived from it for professional practice, especially in educational settings.

As the model suggests, for more than a half century various arguments have been put forth in favor of greater diversity and inclusion in higher education and society. The term *diversity* itself might not have been present in each previous era, but the concepts of inclusion, fairness, equity, participation, and opportunity associated with it were evident and articulated. Each argument ties diversity to a pairing of broader educational and social values, each attracts a particular supporting rationale, each has its own proponents; and over time as an argument ages in public discourse, opposing arguments and opponents are generated as well. Some of the arguments have resulted in positive changes that seemed to further the goal of increased diversity as it was articulated in a given context; some did not. Of course given the observation that diversity is in itself a given state of the unencumbered world—the goals of inclusion, respect, and opportunity are really at stake—the thought of achieving diversity is not the real outcome but a phrase adopted to stand for a broader set of aspirations and values.

Rather than one argument (along with its counterarguments) replacing another, these positions add up and overlap. Changes in societal contexts favor or introduce bias against certain views, and over time educational, political, and public discourse has become crowded with a complex and often internally inconsistent host of arguments, claims, counterclaims, and outright disagreements. Not surprisingly, some of these arguments are more closely associated with certain groups and constituencies than others. While that fact might lend momentum to broader social movements (e.g., commitments on behalf of all people of color or all poor people), more often it has led to competition, political divisions, and stalemates.

This book offers an opportunity to explore the ways a definition of this important concept—*diversity*—might be approached. It has been written by a group of esteemed scholars who represent many academic disciplines across U.S. higher education. In each of the chapters, diversity is explored through the lens of a different perspective and frequently through the use of different tools of inquiry. Not surprisingly, the contributors offer us contrasting ideas to consider as we attempt to clarify and specify the meanings of such a concept so important to the work of colleges and universities.

In that sense, this book offers a contribution toward efforts to make better sense of an important idea. In doing so, we do not aim to preemptively eliminate differences in perspective or to arrive at one uncontested definition of a complicated term. It is our hope that we might further enrich an important and ongoing discussion in higher education, one that ultimately shapes issues placed before our courts, the general public, and all of us in education and policy-setting roles. The diversity of the contributors and the differences across their various approaches to scholarship help to ensure that goal.

The intention of bringing together different and emerging views of this concept prompted the very question put to these scholars as we started the task of designing and editing this book. As previously mentioned, we asked each potential contributor, What would you write if you had one chance to tell the world what diversity means to you in your scholarship at this point in your life?

The chapters that follow offer lessons in perspective along with insight into how scholars are defining a term that is centrally important to their profession, their scholarship, their praxis, and themselves. A special feature of this volume is that it also considers the satisfactions and tensions these scholars have experienced in their research and educational practice. Many of these challenges can be traced to the dynamic but unsettled nature of the key concept that binds their scholarship, but their reflections presented in the interviews with graduate students also tell us something about the ways research related to diversity is understood and regarded within the academy. The need to balance scholarly commitments with professional successes and impediments is important to have acknowledged as we attempt to associate the frequently stated value of diversity with greater specificity and measurability.

The observations offered by these researchers, and those of the graduate students who interviewed them, are therefore especially insightful and telling. They provide another reminder that scholarship of this sort is difficult to situate as a core pursuit in an academic career. That fact prompts even greater appreciation for the scholars who have contributed their work and the ideas that have been captured in this volume. It also pushes us all to redouble our efforts and to find new ways of supporting and encouraging the next generation of colleagues as they pursue their interests and their convictions with courage.

Notes

1. It is worth noting that even at the end of this significant period of change in higher education and society, the 27 members of the commission included three women, three African American, and no Latin@ members.
2. In the same opinion, Powell praised the admissions process at Harvard for expanding its use of geography as a means to increase diversity by considering race as a supplemental factor as well, a somewhat ironic endorsement of Harvard's earlier efforts to achieve diversity described earlier in this chapter.
3. We use Latin@ throughout this book to reflect inclusivity of women, men, and transgender people. In this way, Latin@ does not privilege one gender over another.

References

Alemán, A. M. M., & Renn, K. A. (2002). *Women in higher education: An encyclopedia*. Santa Barbara, CA: ABC-Clio.

Allan, E. J. (2011). Women's status in higher education: Equity matters. *ASHE Higher Education Report, 37*(1).

Bowen, W. G., & Bok, D. (1998). *The shape of the river: Long-term consequences of considering race in college and university admissions*. Princeton, NJ: Princeton University Press.

Brittain, J., & Landy, B. (2014). Reducing reliance on testing to promote diversity. In R. D. Kahlenberg, (Ed.), *The future of Affirmative Action: New paths to higher education diversity after Fischer v. University of Texas* (pp. 160–174). New York, NY: Century Foundation.

Burkhardt, J. C., Ortega, N., Vidal Rodriguez, A., Frye, J. R., Nellum, C. J., Reyes, K. A., & Hernandez, J. (2012). *Reconciling federal, state, and institutional policies determining Educational access for undocumented students: Implications for professional practice*. Ann Arbor, MI: National Forum on Higher Education for the Public Good.

Gasman, M. (2002). W. E. B. DuBois and Charles S. Johnson: Differing views on the role of philanthropy in higher education. *History of Education Quarterly, 42*(4), 493–516.

Gould, S. B. (1973). *Diversity by design: Commission on non-traditional study.* San Francisco, CA: Jossey-Bass.

Gratz v. Bollinger, 123 S. Ct. 2411 (2003).

Grutter v. Bollinger, 539 U.S. 306 (2003).

Guinier, L. (2015). *The tyranny of the meritocracy: Democratizing higher education in America.* Boston, MA: Beacon Press.

Holbrook, E. (1923). The change in the meaning of consortium. *Michigan Law Review, 22*(1), 1–9.

Karabel, J. (2005). *The chosen: The hidden history of admission and exclusion at Harvard, Yale, and Princeton.* New York, NY: Houghton Mifflin Harcourt.

Kevles, D. J. (1985). *In the name of eugenics: Genetics and the uses of human heredity.* Boston, MA: Harvard University Press.

Overton-Atkins, B. (2015, January). *Intersectionality and the King legacy: The complex dynamics of leadership and social justice.* Keynote address presented at the Martin Luther King Jr. Legacy Lecture, Union Institute & University, Cincinnati, OH.

Pasque, P. A., & Errington Nicholson, M. (2011). Preface. In P. A. Pasque & M. Errington Nicholson (Eds.), *Empowering women in higher education and student affairs: Theory, research, narratives and practice from feminist perspectives* (pp. xv–xxi). Sterling, VA: Stylus.

Regents of the University of California v. Bakke, 438 U.S. 265 (1978).

Reverby, S. (2009). *Examining Tuskegee: The infamous syphilis study and its legacy.* Chapel Hill: University of North Carolina Press.

Smith, D. G. (2009). *Diversity's promise for higher education: Making it work.* Baltimore, MA: Johns Hopkins University Press.

Soares, J. A. (2012). *SAT wars: The case for test-optional college admissions.* New York, NY: Teachers College Press.

Solomon, B. M. (1985). *In the company of educated women: A history of women and higher education in America.* New Haven, CT: Yale University Press.

Stulberg, L. M., & Weinberg, S. L. L. (Eds.). (2011). *Diversity in American higher education.* New York, NY: Routledge.

Thelin, J. R. (2011). *A history of American higher education.* Baltimore, MA: Johns Hopkins University Press.

Towne v. Eisner, 245 U.S. 418 (1918).

Williams, C. (2005). The racial politics of progressive Americanism: New deal liberalism and the subordination of Black workers in the UAW. *Studies in American Political Development, 19*(1), 75–97.

Young, I. M. (2011). *Justice and the politics of difference.* Princeton, NJ: Princeton University Press.

1

COLOR-BLIND IDEOLOGY AND THE DISCONNECTED POWER-ANALYSIS FRAME

Considerations for Historically Black Colleges and Universities' Diversification

Uma M. Jayakumar and Annie S. Adamian

Conversations about diversification have expanded beyond the traditionally White institutional context to include historically Black institutions. Multiple factors, including financial hardships, court mandates, and an interest in the potential educational benefits of increasing diversity, have led many historically Black colleges and universities (HBCU) to expand recruitment strategies to target Black and non-Black students (Arroyo, Palmer, & Maramba, 2015; Stewart, 2012; Stuart, 2013). Most of this expansion has been in a growing White student population (Butrymowicz, 2014). Some HBCUs have high populations of White students, such as Kentucky State University with 26% and Bluefield University with 85%, but the overall percentage of White students attending HBCUs nationally is roughly 15% (Butrymowicz, 2014). What these shifting demographics, demography, and diversification trends will mean for the historical legacy of providing racially affirming environments and climates that counter societal racism for Black students is yet to be determined.

We would like to acknowledge Andrew Arroyo, assistant professor of interdisciplinary studies at Norfolk State University, for collaborating with us in 2014–2015 on collecting these data and specifically for conducting all interviews.

It is crucial to understand whether color-blind frames are prevalent among White students at historically Black institutions, particularly given the prevalence of color-blind ideological frames among Whites in segregated precollege neighborhoods and schooling environments, and the documented harms of color blindness on students of color at traditionally White institutions (TWI; Lewis, Chesler, & Forman, 2000). Color-blind ideology has a stereotyping effect on students of color and contributes to a hostile learning environment (Lewis et al., 2000). It also legitimizes Black subordination and educational disparities (Williams & Land, 2006). Further understanding and identifying color-blind ideology in college can facilitate educational programming and proactive efforts to address the problem and foster humanizing learning environments where students of color can thrive.

In this chapter we suggest that color-blind ideology is a concern not only at TWIs, where previously documented (Bonilla-Silva, 2010; Lewis et al., 2000; Spanierman, Neville, Liao, Hammer, & Wang, 2008; Warikoo & de Novais, 2014), but also at HBCUs, as we begin to document here. Furthermore, White students' color-blind frames seem to have adapted and thus appear more nuanced and advanced with the passage of time and within the HBCU context. To illustrate both points we provide examples from our own data set with White students at HBCUs exhibiting frames of color-blind ideology in contrast to the examples from Bonilla-Silva's (2010) book that describe White students at TWIs collected almost two decades ago. In addition to the evolving language and nature of color-blind ideologies found across time and institutional contexts, we find an emerging and pervasive new frame of color-blind ideology, which we describe in closing. But before focusing on the higher education context and analysis, the next section provides a foundational theoretical understanding of what color-blind ideology is and why it is a pressing social problem that will need to be addressed to advance racial diversity and equity.

Color-Blind Ideology: Bonilla-Silva's Theory and Its Connection to Racial Inequality

Color-blind racism emerged from the civil rights era as the new dominant racial ideology that covertly enables the contemporary reproduction of racial inequity through subtle means that appear nonracial (Bonilla-Silva, 2010). Racial inequality today is covertly reproduced and normalized through common-sense tactics (e.g., racial profiling, urban planning, inequitable schooling, segregation, school closures, college admissions, and hiring practices) that are supported by the logic of color-blind frames. Hence, as Bonilla-Silva (2010) proclaims, "despite its suave, apparently nonracial character, the new racial ideology is still about justifying the various social arrangements and practices that maintain white privilege" (p. 211). This assertion, and more specifically, the evolving nature of racism and its present day manifestation, is supported by the theoretical contributions of numerous scholars (Alexander, 2011; Bobo & Kluegel, 1997; Burke, 2012; Kovel, 1985; López, 2014; Thomas, 2000; Wellman, 1993). We focus on Bonilla-Silva's (2010) theory of color-blind ideology and its connection to reproducing inequality for the following reasons: (a) The grounding of his analysis and work on higher education issues and policies makes it particularly accessible for the audience we seek to inform, and (b) his theory uniquely identifies and outlines four central frames that are foundational to understanding how color-blind ideology is embraced and enacted by Whites who are not necessarily overtly or even intentionally racist.

Whereas racial inequalities were historically created and sustained by overtly racial policies and institutional structures, today they are sustained through covert mechanisms such as seemingly nonracial practices and policies. For example, during the Jim Crow era, the legal system provided explicit permission for law enforcement to target people on the basis of race for the purpose of segregating people of color into lower social status positions. Doing so now is technically against the law and more socially unacceptable. However, it continues to occur through socially sanctioned policies and practices justified by language and rationales that claim to be nonracial but nonetheless legitimize the subordination of Black people and other people of color (Williams & Land, 2006). For example, New York City's stop-and-frisk law allows police officers to stop, interrogate, and search individuals on the basis of reasonable suspicion. Since 2002, "Nearly nine out of 10 stopped-and-frisked New Yorkers have been completely innocent," according to the NYPD's [New York Police Department's] own reports (New York Civil Liberties Union, 2014, para. 1). Of the stops reported in 2014, 80% were Blacks and Latin@s (New York Civil Liberties Union, 2014). Additionally, Arizona's Senate Bill 1070 gives police officers the authority to stop individuals to check their immigration status at any time (Small, 2011). Opposition to the bill sparked national discourse about racial profiling, yet a Rasmussen Report poll showed that 70% of Arizona voters agreed with the bill (Small, 2011). While racial inequality after the passage of civil rights legislation continues to be explained as the outcome of nonracial dynamics, unconscious ideological frames aligned with maintaining the racial order are shaping individuals' sociopolitical inclinations and actions (Bonilla-Silva, 2010; Feagin, 2010).

The reliance on dominant ideologies shaped by oppressive sociopolitical policies and practices that reproduce inequality is known as *common sense* (Gramsci, 1971; Kumashiro, 2009). Common-sense thinking and practices refer to the ways oppressive systems are first normalized through habits of mind and actions. Indeed, color-blind ideology relies on the commonsensical ways of thinking about race and racism in the United States today that feels nonracial and is facilitated by accessing one's own internalized color-blind frames or "*set paths for interpreting information*" (emphasis in original; Bonilla-Silva, 2010, p. 26). Consequently, color-blind frames support a hegemonic culture by normalizing, shaping, and influencing everyday thoughts, actions, practices, and policies that create and reinforce negative outcomes for people of color. These frames include cultural racism, naturalization, minimization of racism, and abstract liberalism. Bonilla-Silva (2010) contended that these four frames contribute toward the development and perpetuation of color-blind racism wherein "whites rationalize minorities' contemporary status as the product of market dynamics, naturally occurring phenomena, and Blacks' imputed cultural limitations" (p. 2). Next, we briefly summarize each frame and the ways they contribute to the performances of color-blind ideology.

The cultural racism frame of color-blind ideology replaces genetic inferiority rationales for racial disparities with cultural ones. According to Bonilla-Silva (2010), the cultural racism frame "relies on culturally based arguments . . . to explain the standing of minorities in society" (p. 28). The rejection of racist beliefs in regard to the genetic inferiority of people of color creates a framework for what constitutes racism and absolves people from colluding in systems of oppression. Through falsely attributing cultural deficits to people and communities of color as an explanation for current gross inequities, racism can be rationalized as a thing of the past and human suffering as a consequence of cultural practices.

The naturalization frame "allows whites to explain away racial phenomena by suggesting natural occurrences" (Bonilla-Silva, 2010, p. 28). Within this frame, people deracialize oppressive practices, systems, and social constructs such as segregation and poverty, believing they are the result of the choices and natural manifestations of individuals detached from systemic inequities.

The minimization of racism frame "suggests discrimination is no longer a central factor affecting minorities' life chances" (Bonilla-Silva, 2010, p. 28). This frame relies on language that individualizes racialized stories to stay disconnected from institutional racism. By individualizing racialized stories, White people attempt to dismantle discourse about the systemic oppression of people of color. For example, by claiming to know a person of color who has "made it," one can minimize the structural and racial dynamics that create barriers to success for people of color.

The abstract liberalism frame supports and reproduces the maintenance of the status quo while allowing the user to appear race-neutral and morally and racially just. In this sense, people who operate from an abstract liberalism frame view the world through a lens that affirms a belief that the United States systemically functions to provide equal opportunity for everyone—politically, economically, and socially—and that institutional racism is a thing of the past. They can do so while acknowledging the existence of current-day discrimination and prejudice. Bonilla-Silva (2010) asserts that abstract liberalism is the foundational frame of color-blind ideology. It is also the least straightforward, and, thus, we discuss it in greater detail.

Bonilla-Silva (2010) defines *abstract liberalism* as a frame that "involves using ideas associated with political liberalism and economic liberalism in an abstract manner to explain racial matters" (p. 28). Political liberalism is the idea that the government should not intervene in social-justice–based policies. Economic liberalism is rooted in capitalist notions of working hard and you-can-be-anything-you-want-to-be meritocracy, and the American dream. The abstract liberalism frame allows one to take the firm stance that the United States is the land of equal opportunity and use this abstract position and morally framed rationale to reject race-based policies or practices that could actually lead to reducing racial inequality. Racist actions that are justified through abstract liberalism co-opt the same language of freedom and equal opportunity once used by activists to support civil rights legislation (Bonilla-Silva, 2010). By using the language of equal opportunity in the abstract, White people can reject race-based policies such as Affirmative Action while simultaneously appearing as though they were in support of, and even passionate about, reducing racial inequality. Through this frame, they can acknowledge that discrimination exists while they reject actions intended to address the issue based on an adherence to liberal values.

The four frames of color-blind ideology outlined here enable individuals who would theoretically, morally, and otherwise object to racism and racial injustice feel justified in participating in supporting the status quo. Moreover, they provide a comfortable personal distance from the participation that allows individuals to disassociate from their complicity and potentially even remain unaware of it. A person can, then, not feel like a racist and not be perceived as such. Thus, the function of this new racial ideology, like those preceding it, is to provide a logical framework that justifies existing racial hierarchies and the societal structures and policies currently in place that legitimize Black subordination and reinforce racial inequality.

Comparing White Students' Color-Blind Frames Across Institutional Types

We know that White college students are increasingly entering postsecondary institutions after having mostly interacted in segregated environments and with color-blind racial primes (Smith, 2004). Studies have documented the persistence of these frames among White students at TWIs (Lewis et al., 2000), even when a campus has a strong diversity infrastructure (Warikoo & de Novais, 2014). Additionally, continued opportunities for White racial isolation in which color-blind primes and frames are often developed and strengthened (Bonilla-Silva, 2010; Smith, 2004) are more readily available at TWIs (e.g., Greek life) and are associated with maintaining a postcollege color-blind orientation (Jayakumar, 2015). While there is some documentation of the problem of color-blind racial frames among White students at TWIs (Bonilla-Silva, 2010; Spanierman et al., 2008; Warikoo & de Novais, 2014) and its potential negative impact on the educational experiences of Black college students (Lewis et al., 2000), research has not yet explored whether the issue persists in historically Black institutions where we are seeing a trend of pressure toward diversification and increased White student enrollment.

In the previous section, we established the significant harms of color-blind ideology on the lives of people of color. A noteworthy and common feature across all four frames underlying the ideology is that they allow strategically evading or inadvertently failing to acknowledge structural racism, oppression, power and privilege, and systemic explanations for the persistence of racial inequity. Thus, we wondered: Would these color-blind frames and the comfort they provide be disrupted in a traditionally Black and more racially conscious environment where one is presumably more likely to face viewpoints and knowledge that challenge the color-blind racial frames of the White students who are increasingly entering college? Would such challenges promote greater awareness and accountability for current inequities? Or might the challenges lead to the further justification and preservation of color-blind frames and the harmful ideology and racial injustice they support? In our data set on White HBCU graduates, we overwhelmingly observed the latter scenario. We elaborate on this phenomenon through an exploration that builds on Bonilla-Silva's (2010) analytical and theoretical work.

The following provides a comparative example of the four color-blind frames—cultural deficiency, naturalization, minimization of racism, and abstract liberalism—as expressed by White students across institutional contexts. We build on Bonilla-Silva's (2010) analysis (based on data collected from 1997 to 1998) and provide comparative examples of our more recent data collected almost two decades later. Our purpose is to demonstrate the evolving nature of color-blind frames toward even more complex and problematic forms. Given the space limitations of what we may offer in this chapter, drawing directly from White college student data cited and discussed in Bonilla-Silva's (2010) book, we hope to create an avenue for the practitioner to have access to a more in-depth analysis and explanation of the complex contours of color-blind ideology that go beyond the central frames we focus on here to explore color-blind frames in the HBCU context.[1]

In particular, Bonilla-Silva (2010) uncovers and details various linguistic maneuvers and tactics White participants employ to avoid appearing racist while using color-blind frames. We incorporate some discussion of these where relevant, but we strongly encourage and invite the reader to refer to Bonilla-Silva's (2010) book for more in-depth explanations and examples. For each of the frames we begin our comparison with an example of the TWI college student data collected and used by Bonilla-Silva to develop his theory of color-blind ideology. Thereafter, we build on Bonilla-Silva's (2010) analysis and offer an analogous usage of the frame from data on a sample of 13 White students who attended one of three HBCUs with 80% to 90% Black enrollment in the mid-Atlantic and northeast regions of the country.[2]

Cultural Deficiency Frame

White students who exhibit a cultural deficiency and minimization of racism frame in either traditionally White or Black institutional contexts offer explanations disconnected from structural and systemic racism. However, the students in the more racially conscious HBCU environment seem to have to exert a greater effort to maintain color-blind frames. This exertion may be because they encounter direct challenges to core assumptions underlying the frames that can cause dissonance, defensiveness, and discomfort, which make the frames vulnerable to being dismantled. The following examples show how White students engage with the topic of racial disparities across contexts. This set of comments reflects a similar usage of both the cultural deficiency and the minimization of racism color-blind frames, and they both draw on story lines of "exceptional Blacks" to avoid appearing racist.

In the following comment from a White student at a TWI, the participant provides his rationale for achievement and wealth disparities:

> Hmm, I think it's due to lack of education. I think because if they didn't grow up in a household that afforded them the time to go to school and they had to go out and get jobs right away, I think it is just a cycle [that] perpetuated things, you know. I mean, I can't say that blacks can't do it

because, obviously there are many, many of them [who] have succeeded in getting good jobs and all that. (Bonilla-Silva, 2010, p. 41)

This student, Jay, draws on the culture of poverty argument for explaining racial disparities. In doing so he minimizes the impact of racism and overlooks the connection between racial and class privilege. His framing is deficit-oriented but allows him to steer away from the uncomfortable topic of race. The last part of the quote is a semantic move that allows the participant to bring up, dismiss, and disassociate himself from an argument that he perceives as problematic and even racist.

It was clear in our interviews from the HBCU context that participants were exposed to critical dialogues about topics such as slavery, reparations, and structural inequality. Thus, students in an HBCU setting were more likely to encounter alternative explanations for inequality that challenged the cultural deficiency frame. In the following comment, Carly, a White female student who attended an HBCU, exemplifies having a cultural deficiency frame challenged. She states,

> The whole class was one sided . . . everything viewed from the African American's view. . . . This was hard for me as I was not instilled with that view. . . . I did so much research . . . and interviewed African Americans . . . [and] I found it upsetting that the undertone of the class focused on being paid back . . . someone owing a group. . . . My girlfriend who is black and from LA . . . [is] educated, . . . [her] son went to Norfolk Academy, . . . [she] shook her head over the structure of the class, . . . she said this is why so many White people think the way they do about Black people. . . . She told me I earned my Black card as I received an A in the class.

This particular student conveyed a strong cultural deficiency frame. Throughout her interview, she expressed deficit views of her Black peers and consistently dismissed classmates' emotions, language, and knowledge while elevating her own contributions. In this particular passage she dismisses her Black classmates and the focus of the class by selectively and strategically giving authority of determining what is or is not racially problematic to a Black girlfriend who supports her cultural deficiency perspective.

Jay and Carly make reference to the story line of the exceptional Black to maintain their own positions and deflect the perception of appearing racist. The student in the first example, Jay, also minimizes racism and uses the cultural racism frame. However, he uses a general example and overall is not as defensive. Carly has access to knowledge about inequality and because she personalizes and takes offense to this understanding, she attempts to dismantle it with affirmation from her exceptional Black friend. Carly is more complicated because she acknowledges a systemic or structural understanding but then moves forward to defend and maintain her cultural deficiency frame. Her discussion is more personalized, and she exhibits more defensiveness, because unlike Jay, she is in a context where White discourse and practices are not centered within her experience.

Most notably, both students are saying disparaging things about Black people; however, Carly exhibits greater discomfort and has to make a greater effort to resist seeming racist. She is made aware of an alternative lens, and given her apparent lack of openness to having her prior position challenged, she has to work twice as hard with what she is saying to preserve her cultural deficiency frame and avoid sounding racist.

Naturalization Frame

In line with color-blind ideology, students in both institutional contexts made sense of racial phenomena, such as segregation, as natural occurrences that reflect personal choices and values. This was particularly the case when rationalizing the racial isolation of Whites, further justified by referencing the same behavior by people of color. We include one representative example provided by Bonilla-Silva (2010) from a White female student at a TWI and two from White students who attended a historically Black college. The main difference is that the latter two feel more of a need to justify their answers whether talking about their own behavior or that of a White peer, whereas the TWI student's response appears more relaxed and less defensive. Sara, the White student who attended a TWI, states,

> Hmm, I don't really think it's a segregation. I mean, I think people, you know, spend time with people that they are like, not necessarily in color, but you know, their ideas and values and you know, maybe their class has something to do with what they're used to. (Bonilla-Silva, 2010, p. 37)

In accordance with the naturalization frame, Sara explains segregation as a result of individual choices that have nothing to do with racial preference. She seems to casually offer the rationale that people probably just naturally "spend time with people that they are like." She concedes that social class may have something to do with what people value or perhaps with what feels natural, but more important, she does not acknowledge the intersectionality of race playing a role.

The following HBCU students' usages of the naturalization frame similarly portray segregation as a natural choice. In the following, Sandra, a White female HBCU graduate, responds to a question about who she is friends with:

> I mean I was really friends with most of the Caucasian girls just because they were either athletes or I just knew 'em because I, I mean they were usually athletes because I helped bring them in, to recruit, so I mean I knew of their experiences and for the most part I think they had a positive experience overall.

Even though she is at an institution where she has greater access to Black peers than to White peers, Sandra justifies having all White friends as a nonracial choice. Interestingly, she provides an extensive justification and explanation of the circumstances that may have led to this outcome, although segregation was not a topic that was brought up by the interviewer, who only asked who she hung out with. Her offering of a rationale suggests her awareness that she is segregating (with all White people) and that she feels some tension and the need to justify her behavior.

Mark, another White student from the HBCU context, who strongly critiqued Black students for attending HBCUs to self-segregate, later grappled with the idea that White students attending traditionally White universities could similarly be viewed as intentionally choosing to self-segregate. Nonetheless, he resolved this dissonance and maintained the naturalization frame. Mark rationalizes,

> You know, the people that choose to, you know, go to a, and it is, you know, it is kind of hard to say this as a White person, because no matter what we choose to do it's, you know, it's usually going to be within our own race. And if you say, "I'm going to go to, I'm going to go to Kent State University [a TWI]." So, it's easy to say that but, you know, and look at it and say like, "Gosh, you chose to self-segregate." Yeah, but, I don't know, it's hard to jump in someone else's shoes.

Unlike earlier in the interview where Mark states that Black people go to HBCUs in order to self-segregate, he said that with White people going to TWIs, we don't know if their being there is a result of making random choices that are natural and color-blind. There is some truth to this statement and the acknowledgment of White privilege in the sense of stating that White people, regardless of what choices they make and without having to be intentional, have a greater choice in opting in and out of traditionally White spaces. Nonetheless, he does not fully go there, and instead makes a semantic move in the direction of holding on to the idea of White people's choices being color-blind, natural, or not determinable. Thus he arrives at a discrepancy or dissonance from his own competing stances on whether race plays a determining role (which seems to vary based on the racial identity of those involved), and while he struggles, he ultimately maneuvers to maintain White privilege.

Minimization of Racism Frame

The minimization of racism frame was prevalent throughout the 13 White HBCU student participants in our data set, and, more generally, it often occurred in conjunction with the other three frames. Thus, we selected comparative example comments where participants directly used the minimization of racism frame to dismiss racial disparities in job placement and promotion. For example, Janet, who is from the traditionally White institutional context, dismissed racial disadvantage in hiring by saying,

> I would say that's a bunch of crap [laughs]. I mean, if [you're] qualified they'll hire you and if you are not qualified, then you don't get the job. It's the same way with, once you get the job, if you are qualified for a promotion, you'll get the promotion. It's the same way with white, Blacks, Asians, whatever. If you do the job, you get the job. (Bonilla-Silva, 2010, p. 45)

Mark, the student from a historically Black institutional context, was more explicitly dismissive of institutional racism and privilege. He personalizes his answer, although, when asked about whether race plays a role in shaping opportunities generally, he says,

> You know, I, I haven't seen it. You know, everything, everything I've gotten to this point, I've gotten through hard work. I wish I could say there was some, something I could just point to and identify like, "Man, that was the color of my skin . . . that was a give me." You know what? I would take a give me. I did, I have never, it's never once occurred to me to say, "Gosh, I don't have to try hard. I'll get this with my Whiteness." I mean, it's just . . .

Mark not only personalizes his response and comes across as more defensive but also reveals an awareness of Whiteness and yet still dismisses institutional racism and White privilege. His language, in using the term *Whiteness*, indicates that he has an awareness of privilege that he is defending. Interestingly, although the White male interviewer does not probe, his answer conveys a frustration or perception about being called out on his privilege as he exhibits a high degree of defensiveness. Given that the White interviewer does not make comments to elicit such a response or posture, we suspect it may have something to do with his institutional experience and environment. It seems that a level of personalization and defensiveness is associated with preserving color-blind frames within a more racially conscious context.

Abstract Liberalism Frame

The abstract liberalism frame allows individuals to present themselves as fair and just while opposing policies, practices, and actions that promote racial equity. Kay, a White student at a TWI, objected to the hypothetical scenario of a company hiring an equally qualified Black applicant over a White applicant in the interest of increasing diversity. Kay reasoned,

> Well, I guess if I was, like, put in the situation and like, I think about if I was in that situation, if I was the applicant, I would be very upset. If I found out that was the reason. Just because, you know, we have lack of diversity. I mean, you need, I don't know [laughs] I'll just shut up [laughs]. (Bonilla-Silva, 2010, p. 137)

Although Kay claimed to be in support of Affirmative Action in college admissions, when asked the question in terms of job placement where the circumstances perhaps more closely resembled a scenario that she could experience and be negatively affected by in the future, her stance changed. She provides a rationale that allows her to maintain her racially progressive posturing. More specifically, she claims that supporting the hypothetical hiring of an equally qualified Black applicant over the White applicant would end up harming the Black applicant.

Similarly, in the following statement drawn from a White female HBCU student, Nancy claims to support equality but rationalizes a lack of support for action with the potential for reducing racial disparities by advancing people of color. She also offers the story line of racial preferences as being harmful to people of color. In this comment and throughout her interview, Nancy exhibited a great deal of rhetorical incoherence, which occurs when Whites discuss racial matters that make them uncomfortable, and they become less comprehensible in their speech (e.g., incomplete sentences, multiple digressions, repetitive and tangential; Bonilla-Silva, 2014). We use boldface for ease of reading but otherwise kept her response intact. In the following, Nancy, a White female HBCU graduate, explains where she stands in regard to understanding racial inequities and race-conscious policies:

> **Of course, but I also feel like if you can truly understand, but then understand to the point where you're not making excuses for that race to not progress** cause I've met other people, I've met one other person

who, he had some, he grew up in like in a poor, I guess like in a poor neighborhood somewhere in Texas and he was constantly with minorities and was just a white guy from Texas who joined the Black Panthers he was just like really into stuff but his identity was: I'm a part of this black movement and everything with him, if it was anything you could "pull under a hat" he considered racist and his dynamic was—there was also another girl who was from Gambia and she looked at it as you know she's African American, born in America, went to a TWI—and he looked at her like why didn't you go to an all-black school? So I feel like sometimes, going to [the HBCU she attended], I could understand where she was coming from, I didn't judge her, that's also like something that I learn from [the HBCU she attended] like people make choices, but sometimes, you know other white minorities or other white people can understand but I feel like some people will try to then, **it's the same thing like being fanatic like going against another race and I feel like as a minority that doesn't make excuses for another race like I can understand** cause sometimes I'll just feel like oh I get, **I get why certain things in the community aren't like this and I understand why African Americans have gone through this, this, and this, I understand it completely and I feel like that makes me a minority sometimes**. I'm like oh ok I get it **but I also understand that, in explaining where I understand, there's room** for people, there's **room for me to say there's certain can be excused as far as the actions of African Americans in today's society,** if that makes any sense. (emphasis in original)

Nancy, who self-identified as White and is also ethnically Albanian, feels that it's okay for "White minorities and other White people" to be understanding about Black people's circumstances based on a history of injustice, but she equates taking action today to "making excuses." Moreover, she piles on various story lines and justifications for her stance, all the while maneuvering to avoid appearing racist. The rhetorical incoherence is prominent throughout our HBCU interview data, particularly for those White students attending HBCUs who predominantly use the abstract liberalism frame and have an awareness of structural racism. The levels of incoherence within our overall data far exceed the preceding examples.

Introducing the Fifth Frame of Color-Blind Ideology: Disconnected Power Analysis

In addition to the four frames of color-blind ideology outlined by Bonilla-Silva (2003, 2010, 2014), our data on White HBCU students revealed an emerging fifth frame that was distinct from the existing frames. While the essence of the abstract liberalism frame is the ability to use the notion of equal opportunity and fairness in the abstract to oppose actions that could tangibly promote more racially just outcomes, the essence of the disconnected power-analysis frame is the ability to align oneself with racially progressive conceptual understandings of structural racism, Whiteness, and counternarratives that challenge racial hierarchy while disconnecting one's own story, personal experiences, and actions from this understanding and critical analysis. We define this new frame and provide an example from our data to demonstrate how it is used to preserve privilege and protect the status quo, while avoiding the label of appearing racist and internalizing White guilt.

Disconnected Power-Analysis Frame

Related to the usage of an abstract liberalism frame within the HBCU context, we found that students seemed more likely to have a theoretical understanding of structural inequality and privilege; however, this often did not align with their own personal actions, which stood in contrast to their espoused stance. For example, Rachel, a White HBCU graduate, conveys some understanding of structural racism, power, and privilege in the following:

> I keep using the term *structural racism*, but, like, just everywhere in everything, just the opportunities afforded, you know, for everything from, you know, job opportunities to educational opportunities and I just, like, know in the same way I think that people have this sort of veil over their eyes I think that I have this magnifying glass on where I am hyper-sensitive almost, maybe not hyper-sensitive, but hyper aware, not sensitive, aware of all of those things being, um, perpetrated or, like, perpetualized I don't know, um throughout, like, every layer of everything I look at when I, especially, like, when I'm, like, in the hospital when I'm, um, I work at a shelter and just seeing like the just how, like, the Black American experience is just so influenced by, like, all of these things just pushing people in certain directions and they're so invisible and so you have to, like, really educate or you have to be educated to these things to [be] able to recognize them or you just, like, totally miss it, you know, and even I recognize that ignorance now in my friends and family the things that they say I just, like, can't believe just sort of this it's just, like, over the head, you know, so, one of that. (emphasis added)

Rachel demonstrates some rhetorical incoherence, suggesting her discomfort with her new understanding about structural racism and its insidious nature. Most notably, her awareness and understanding of structural racism allow her to claim an increased *race cache* or legitimacy that benefits her by enabling her to not appear to be racist in the racially conscious institutional context while simultaneously undermining or not supporting actions that could potentially lead to change. This understanding, awareness, and hypercritique that surface even more when evaluating other Whites are not used when sharing her own experiences with running for student president of her HBCU. In recalling other students' concerns, Rachel stated,

> *But there was a minority* that, like, the, the words that came out of the one girl's mouth that had, like, kind of started the conversation was, like, very, like, I don't wanna, umm, misquote her but it *was something along the lines of, umm "You just don't have what a strong Black woman has." Like, just, just sort of these things that are very, like, like, it didn't matter what I had done, what my plan was or anything. It was just related to the fact that she didn't want to be represented, she didn't perceive me as being able to represent her well.* Umm. But I think it was just a couple of people and there was also, umm, a couple people brought up in class. I don't know if they felt this way or what it was but, like, you know, we were at an HBCU and this was, like, I was going to be making money in this. *Well, I was going to be representing the school in this role and, like, I was taking a spot away from someone who is Black and that they didn't feel comfortable supporting that and that part of their interest in being at an HBCU was, umm, you know supporting their race. Like, that's why they went there and I was encumbering that so. I don't know, but that was just, like, a couple people*, I don't mean.

Her statement of the concerns seems matter of fact and she seems to minimize the amount of dissent she experienced. In other words, she is quick to be dismissive of her Black peers' concerns about her assuming this role. Rachel further provided her rationale for dismissing the views of some of her classmates in stating the following:

> And also, you know, just with the role of student government. In student government, like, it was like a pretty big thing of, like, how we represented the students and, umm, so I think they felt like they needed someone who understood everything. And *I just talked a lot about how, like, you know, you hire someone to do a job, they don't nece[ssarily]—you know, you don't hire a lawyer that, like, went through the same crime you went through. You hire someone that, like, understands it and can represent you well and that cares* and—well, I don't know, that cares. But that'll do a good job but maybe the lawyer thing doesn't work but that I care and that I had a, you know, good advocacy background and that type of stuff.

Notably, Rachel minimizes her classmates' desire to have a Black peer represent them, although she herself explained (see her initial quote) how different it is to experience life as a Black person in the United States and how more people should be sensitive to the reality of structural racism.

The important point here is not whether it is a problem for a White student to hold this leadership position but that Rachel's disconnected power-analysis frame allowed her to unconsciously preserve her privilege by neglecting to consider the structural argument to which she adamantly claimed to adhere and that she uses to evaluate the behaviors of other Whites she encounters and knows. Having a disconnected power-analysis frame allows Rachel to believe she is racially progressive and committed to eradicating structural inequities, and as she says, she is "hyper-aware" and vigilant while she holds on to and even bolsters her White privilege. Rachel understands and can problematize how the dominant story and society are stacked in favor of Whites. She can point out how it plays out in real-time scenarios and acknowledge institutional racism as something that is still affecting people's life chances and opportunities today. However, she does not see herself as an actor in it.

The disconnected power-analysis frame also allowed White students who were relatively more conscious of racial inequality to more comfortably interact with, fit into, and benefit from the traditionally Black and more racially progressive environment in which their racial identity and privilege were more salient and more vulnerable to being challenged. It facilitates refuge from White guilt and shame, which were more prevalent for White students who exhibited a disconnected power-analysis frame in comparison to those who relied on the other four frames. Moreover, and most unfortunately, it allowed for engagement with Black peers and in the environment without increasing cross-cultural empathy and understanding that could lead to allyship and solidarity, and without personal accountability or commitment toward challenging racism and White privilege in any real way.

Conclusions and Implications for Research and Practice

In this chapter, we explore the implications of diversifying HBCUs given the prevalence of color-blind racial primes among Whites entering college today and the established harms of color-blind ideology on the education of Black people. We summarize Bonilla-Silva's (2010) theory of color-blind ideology and his analysis of data on White students at TWIs collected almost two decades ago; thereafter, we provide evidence of color-blind frames among White students at historically Black institutions in 2015. Our preliminary analysis suggests that color-blind frames evolve and adapt over time and within more racially conscious contexts and that there is a fifth frame of color-blind ideology at work, which we labeled the *disconnected power-analysis frame.*

Further research will be necessary to validate our assertions and to more thoroughly understand the pervasiveness of color-blind ideology and its implications for Black students attending HBCUs. This line of inquiry might explore how color-blind ideology undermines the educational tradition and mission of HBCUs. It will also be important for scholars to document and learn from instances in which White students' precollege racial primes are dismantled in service of developing antiracist frames in solidarity with communities of color. Overall, we echo Lewis and colleagues' (2000) call for placing a greater onus and analysis on the problematic role of White students who are, although not intentionally but certainly based in part on their internalized racial primes, level of racial awareness, and racial frames, contributing to the racial isolation and negative climate experienced by Black students at TWIs and potentially by Black students at HBCUs.

As HBCUs continue to face financial pressures and legal mandates to increase diversity, especially when White student percentages at these institutions rise, it is critical that conversations and institutional efforts toward diversification are not mapped after the integration approaches of TWIs. The integration of TWIs required dismantling an embedded institutional system and culture rooted in relegating Blacks and other people of color to second-class citizenship set up by court-mandated segregation and dehumanizing practices. Historically, Black colleges are not, and have never been, in a position of power to exclude White people in the same way or to relegate them to an inferior status.

Administrators of historically Black institutions seeking to diversify will need to address the broader societal and racial contexts in which they are situated. We hope that HBCUs such as Acorn State, which is creating institutional infrastructures and offices dedicated to diversity and inclusion, are doing more than their stated goal of ensuring their new minorities are not isolated and ignored. Based on our research and emerging findings, we recommend for diversity programming at HBCUs to include facilitated critical spaces for White students to grapple with and address their color-blind frames.

Notes

1. The data are from the 1997 Social Attitudes of College Students Survey (Bonilla-Silva, 2003), which includes 627 participants from 3 different major universities.

His analysis, summarized in this chapter, is based on a 10% random sample of 41 White students from the data set.
2. This qualitative data was collected in collaboration with Andrew Arroyo, assistant professor at Norfolk University in 2014–2015, for his emerging work exploring non-Black students' reasons for attending HBCUs and our forthcoming work on color-blind ideology that we build on in this chapter.

References

Alexander, R. (2011). *Marketing Whiteness: Geographies of colorblind liberalism.* Retrieved from escholarship.org/uc/item/8gt8w8fp

Arroyo, A. T., Palmer, R. T., & Maramba, D. C. (2015, December). Is it a different world? Providing a holistic understanding of the experiences and perceptions of non-Black students of historically Black colleges and universities. *Journal of College Student Retention: Research, Theory, & Practice,* 1–23.

Bobo, L., & Kluegel, J. R. (1997). Status, ideology, and dimensions of Whites' racial beliefs and attitudes: Progress and stagnation. In S. Tuch & J. Martin (Eds.), *Racial attitudes in the 1990s: Continuity and change* (pp. 93–120). Westport, CT: Praeger.

Bonilla-Silva, E. (2003). *Racism without racists: Color-blind racism and the persistence of racial inequality in the United States.* Lanham, MD: Rowman & Littlefield.

Bonilla-Silva, E. (2010). *Racism without racists: Color-blind racism and the persistence of racial inequality in the United States.* (3rd ed.). Lanham, MD: Rowman & Littlefield.

Bonilla-Silva, E. (2014). *Racism without racists: Color-blind racism and the persistence of racial inequality in the United States.* (4th ed.). Lanham, MD: Rowman & Littlefield.

Burke, M. (2012). *Racial ambivalence in diverse communities: Whiteness and the power of color-blind ideologies.* Lanham, MD: Lexington Books.

Butrymowicz, S. (2014). *Can historically Black colleges serve mostly White students?* Retrieved from hechingerreport.org/can-historically-black-colleges-serve-mostly-white-students-2

Feagin, J. (2010). *The White racial frame: Centuries of racial framing and counter-framing.* New York, NY: Routledge.

Gramsci, A. (1971). *Selections from the prison notebooks.* New York, NY: International Publishers.

Jayakumar, U. M. (2015). The shaping of postcollege colorblind orientation: Residential segregation and campus diversity experiences. *Harvard Educational Review,* 85(4), 609–645.

Kovel, J. (1985). *White racism: A psychohistory.* New York, NY: Columbia University Press.

Kumashiro, K. (2009). *Against common sense: Teaching and learning toward social justice.* New York, NY: Routledge.

Lewis, A. E., Chesler, M., & Forman, T. A. (2000). The impact of "colorblind" ideologies on students of color: Intergroup relations at a predominantly White university. *Journal of Negro Education, 69*, 74–91.

López, H. (2014). *Dog whistle politics: How coded racial appeals have reinvented racism and wrecked the middle class.* Oxford, England: Oxford University Press.

New York Civil Liberties Union. (2014). *Racial justice: Stop-and-frisk data.* Retrieved from www.nyclu.org/content/stop-and-frisk-data

Small, J. (2011). *Arizona's controversial immigration legislation has deep roots.* Retrieved from www.ncsl.org/research/immigration/a-special-report-immigration-and-the-states.aspx

Smith, W. A. (2004). Black faculty coping with racial battle fatigue: The campus racial climate in a post–civil rights era. In D. Cleveland (Ed.), *A long way to go: Conversations about race by African American faculty and graduate students at predominantly White institutions* (pp. 171–190). New York, NY: Peter Lang.

Spanierman, L. B., Neville, H. A., Liao, H. Y., Hammer, J. H., & Wang, Y. F. (2008). Participation in formal and informal campus diversity experiences: Effects on students' racial democratic beliefs. *Journal of Diversity in Higher Education, 1*(2), 108–125.

Stewart, P. (2012). *Three Mississippi HBCUs finding diversity fuels their mission.* Retrieved from diverseeducation.com/article/48872

Stuart, R. (2013). *HBCUs looking beyond Black students to stay competitive.* Retrieved from diverseeducation.com/article/57952

Thomas, M. (2000). Anything but race: The social science retreat from racism. *African American Research Perspectives, 6*(1), 79–96.

Warikoo, N. K., & de Novais, J. (2014). Colour-blindness and diversity: Race frames and their consequences for White undergraduates at elite U.S. universities. *Ethnic and Race Studies, 38*(6), 860–876.

Wellman, D. (1993). *Portraits of White racism.* Cambridge, England: Cambridge University Press.

Williams, D. G., & Land, R. R. (2006). The legitimization of Black subordination: The impact of color-blind ideology on African American education. *Journal of Negro Education, 75*, 579–588.

2

AN INTERVIEW WITH UMA M. JAYAKUMAR
Social Agency and the Power of Resistance
Diane M. Back

The first time I met Uma M. Jayakumar was in the fall of 2012 when she spoke at a University of Michigan event called "The Supreme Court and Affirmative Action in the 21st Century: Michigan, Texas, and Beyond," featuring a prestigious panel moderated by Patricia Gurin and organized by Phillip Bowman, director of the National Center for Institutional Diversity. She was invited based on her work cited in numerous Supreme Court briefs, including one submitted to the court by the Civil Rights Project, the American Educational Research Association, American Psychological Association, National Women's Law Center, 17 U.S. senators, and the Asian American Center for Advancing Justice. Despite her impressive work, I was struck by how approachable Uma was when I introduced myself then and when I met her again in the winter of 2014. On both occasions, Uma came across as extremely kind and relatable as well as a strong advocate for students; a sentiment confirmed through further exploration.

I had the opportunity for a second meeting and to have an extended discussion with Uma when she returned to the University of Michigan to participate in a panel discussion hosted by the School of Education alongside civil rights activist Bob Moses and Elizabeth Birr Moje to commemorate Martin Luther King Jr. That conversation was to encompass "diversity, equity, access to higher education and the role that schools play in educational opportunity and attainment" and also featured an introduction by the university's senior vice provost, Lester Monts. In the forum, Uma described higher education as "a critical sight for the contestation of institutional forces that reinforce societal hegemonic structures." She also emphasized that all scholarship, regardless of whether it is acknowledged as such, is political in that it has social implications for either reproducing or challenging the status quo. Further, she poignantly noted that "we as actors within higher education can actively choose to either be part of the problem or a part of the solution." These values of having personal and social responsibility were illustrated by Uma's passionate retelling of a movement among students, faculty, and community members to successfully challenge a decision by her institution's leadership that would have resulted in evicting an Upward Bound program that was one of the oldest and largest in the country and had successfully served students facing the greatest barriers to college access for more than 44 years. The impact she had was described by her University of San Francisco faculty colleague and associate dean, Elena Flores, in the following way:

> Not only did Jayakumar speak up, which is admirable for a non-tenured faculty member and someone so new to the institution, but she did it in a way that brought people together and was the beginning of a movement that ultimately saved the program.

Similarly, it was clear in our discussion that her dedication to diversity work was driven by a deeply held conviction to support institutional change.

Uma's current work explores choice, access, and racial equity in higher education; the roles that social agency and transformative resistance play in admissions, access, and retention; and the need to address equity and diversity in short-term climate fixes and long-term cultural and institutional shifts simultaneously. Her social consciousness was reinforced not only by spending most of her childhood summers in India, where she witnessed and questioned poverty and social-class inequality, but also in response to surviving personal trauma and nurturing her own agency.

However, during her undergraduate years at the University of California, Los Angeles (UCLA), her personal interest in social justice and capacity for resistance was met with an emerging critical consciousness about racial inequality. At this time, while taking classes in education and being involved in the Career Based Outreach Program, she began to understand what she called the "caste-like" racial inequalities that exist in the United States. This marked a major turning point in which she resolved to move beyond a sense of guilt and frustration to more substantially commit to an antiracist agenda and not being complicit in the problem. She felt betrayed by false notions of meritocracy, the American dream, and higher education as the great equalizer, and she said she awakened to how such ideologies were oppressive to her own and other communities of color. The importance of looking at the root of problems became necessary in her evolution of moving beyond the simple naming of inequality and toward a greater exploration and understanding of how it is embedded in our culture and institutions. She viewed graduate school as the next step in building a foundation of tools to further identify and better understand these problems and to work toward institutional change. She earned her master's and doctoral degrees in higher education and organizational change at UCLA, as an advisee of Alexander Astin and Walter Allen.

Uma describes her dissertation work as following in the footsteps of one of her academic and personal heroes, Patricia Gurin, whose expert testimony before the Supreme Court in *Grutter v. Bollinger* (2003) inspired Uma's scholarship before she even had the opportunity to meet Pat. Ten years later, Uma's own scholarship contributes to shaping policy and theoretical perspectives on Affirmative Action and access to higher education. Her research on the educational benefits of diversity "addresses policy-relevant questions with the intention of informing litigation and retaining affirmative action, while we also work toward more radical change." In Jayakumar (2008), cited in numerous Supreme Court briefs, she empirically demonstrated the mediating effects of campus racial climate on student body diversity and cross-racial interactions on college campuses. In another strand of her work, Uma seeks to inform strategies and frameworks for transforming college access and opportunity structures toward education for liberation. In Jayakumar, Rican, and Allen (2013), she documents counternarratives of community agency and resistance to exclusionary schooling practices and their subsequent impact on the college-going processes of Black students and other students of color. She described the alternative model they present as one that is

> rooted in community and student resistance, that is a humanizing pathway nurtured by a liberatory college-going culture, where community cultural wealth is a catalyst for cultural integrity and transformative resistance and ultimately allows students of color to enter college as a challenge to social reproduction. (p. 572)

At the point of wrapping up the interview, I asked Uma what else she would want others to know about her. Most apparent are her humility and desire to acknowledge those who have supported her. Further, she gave credit to the key people whose support and belief in her gave her the ability to realize her own capabilities. The mentors she emphasized and whom she asked that I acknowledge here are Walter Allen, Patricia Gurin, Phillip Bowman, James Jackson, Alexander Astin, Tyrone Howard, and Gregory Hancock.

Her gratitude to those who came before her and believed in her is shown by the honor and respect she has for the work of her elders. In addition, she has a desire to pay this forward by encouraging those who may look to her scholarship as well. Evidence of Uma's commitment can be seen with her current students, one of whom describes Uma in the following:

> Having Dr. Jayakumar as my mentor has made the impossible possible. Working alongside her is inspiring, energizing, and healing. She has taught me the ins and outs of scholarly writing, research, teaching, and learning toward social justice. Simultaneously, during this process she has supported me in healing from my own insecurities of feeling like a fraud in academic spaces, toward believing that I have something important to contribute. She has supported me in dismantling barriers that were keeping me from being of service in ways that I used to only feel in my heart and imagine in my mind.

References

Grutter v. Bollinger, 539 U.S. 306 (2003).

Jayakumar, U. M. (2008). Can higher education meet the needs of an increasingly diverse and global society? Campus diversity and cross-cultural workforce competencies. *Harvard Educational Review, 78*(4), 615–651.

Jayakumar, U. M. (2012, October 18). Higher education versus higher "schooling": Challenging the reproduction of inequality. In E. E. Chairperson (Chair) *The Supreme Court and Affirmative Action in the 21st century: Michigan, Texas, and beyond*. Symposium conducted at the School of Education, University of Michigan, Ann Arbor.

Jayakumar, U. M., Rican, V., & Allen, W. R. (2013). Pathways to college for young Black scholars: A community cultural wealth perspective. *Harvard Educational Review, 83*(4), 55–579.

3

A THEORY OF EQUITY

A Social and Legal Analysis of College Access for Low-Income Students

Jarrett T. Gupton and Karen Miksch

In the wake of the Great Recession, a national conversation about inequality and social mobility began. President Barack Obama (2013) declared that economic inequity was the "defining challenge of our age" and made a commitment to using the rest of his term in office to reducing inequality and improving upward mobility. First Lady Michelle Obama and the president announced initiatives to help control college costs and expand higher education opportunities for low-income students. While this desire to increase access aligns with the democratic values of U.S. higher education, it is sometimes at odds with its meritocratic values. Supreme Court decisions indicate a weakening of the social contract based on distributive justice and the rise of a contract based primarily on merit.

Given the focus on higher education as a means of social mobility for low-income students, this chapter explores the tension between democracy and meritocracy in the discourse on diversity. We frame our analysis with social contract theory, a conceptual tool that helps us frame the relationship between the public and institutions of higher education. To that end, this chapter addresses the following question: What is merit in a democratic society? Further, we discuss the ways broad policy trends and the legal system have rationalized discrimination based on social class and confront whether preserving access to higher education for low-income students is a compelling or legitimate government interest. This chapter calls attention to the need for a specific type of diversity discourse related to low-income students within higher education, one that is critically and intentionally focused on equity in social and legal arenas.

Social Contract Theory and Higher Education

Under basic social contract theory, individuals relinquish certain liberties, and in return society or government protects their rights (McDowell, 2001). However, in discussing the social contract's role in higher education, analysis moves beyond moral and political theory as established by Locke, Hobbes, and Rousseau. Among many social contract theories, we use John Rawls's (1971) concept of "justice as fairness" (p. 5) to ground our analysis for three reasons. First, Rawls's theory is a hybrid of the works of Locke and Rousseau, linking and extending various strands of social contract theory to a more modern context. Second, justice as fairness not only is a political theory but also helps frame the moral responsibilities of higher education. Third, it is an equity-based theory. Rawls's theory rests on two guiding principles: liberty and equality. The liberty principle suggests that all individuals have an equal right to certain basic inalienable freedoms (Freeman, 2007). The equality principle sets the foundation for Rawls's idea of distributive justice, the notion that society should be structured to maximize opportunities for the least advantaged. While the full theory is more complex, it provides a useful framework to ground our analysis. In the higher education literature, the relationship between an individual and society governs the relationship between the university and the public, often represented by various stakeholders.

A Tale of Two Policy Eras

The social history of higher education in the United States is the story of an ebb and flow between the values of meritocracy and democracy. Higher education policy has evolved through distributive and regressive eras. In terms of access for low-income students, the first era encompasses the expansion of public higher education and programs to maintain affordability. The second, more recent, era features increased costs for college and fewer needs-based financial supports, increased competition for admission, and the expansion of private for-profit higher education.

The Distributive Era, 1862 to 1979

Access to higher education for low-income students has its roots in nineteenth-century policy reform efforts to establish a set of colleges for the public (Kezar, 2010). In the early nineteenth century, the United States had a number of colonial colleges, which were religious institutions for the sons of the wealthy. As the century progressed, the democratic ideals of Thomas

Jefferson and Andrew Jackson began to take hold. In particular, Jefferson and Jackson stressed antielitism, the right to education, and the right of the common man (White male farmers) to fully participate in a democratic society (Keyssar, 2000). By the mid-nineteenth century, many people were requesting the formation of agricultural colleges, which in turn led to the Morrill Act of 1862 (also known as the Land-Grant College Act) and the Morrill Act of 1890 (also known as the Agricultural College Act). The Morrill Acts of 1862 and 1890 established new colleges and universities focused on providing science, engineering, and technology training (Brubacher & Rudy, 2002). Land-grant universities focused on agricultural and applied sciences, while more established private and public universities focused on liberal arts education and research. Moving into the twentieth century, the mass expansion of higher education continued with the formation of community colleges and municipal or city colleges, providing access to industrial training in low-income urban areas (Kezar, 2010). Higher education continued to become more accessible to low-income students until the last two decades of the twentieth century.

In 1947 the Truman Commission released *Higher Education for American Democracy*, a report that helped establish a network of community colleges and recommended increased amounts of student aid. In 1949 Congress passed the GI Bill, allowing returning veterans to subsidize their college education, leading to massive increases in enrollments. In the 1960s Lyndon Johnson's Great Society agenda aimed to reduce racial and economic inequities. In 1964 Johnson declared a war on poverty and signed the Economic Opportunity Act, which led to the creation in 1968 of the Special Services for Disadvantaged Students, now known as the TRIO programs (Council for Opportunity in Education, 2015; McElroy & Armesto, 1998). In 1965 Congress passed the Higher Education Act (HEA) to "strengthen the educational resources of our colleges and universities and to provide financial assistance for students in postsecondary and higher education" (Higher Education Act, 1965, p. 1219). The HEA created multiple college grant and loan programs including Pell grants, which addressed the Truman Commission Report's call for the federal government to help keep tuition affordable (Thelin, 2004). During this era the expansion of higher education increased access for low-income students and, along with other social policies, helped reduce the country's income gap. As Tierney (1997) states, these policies did not define "*public higher education* in this century in terms of merit—that is, who deserves to attend—but in terms of access—that is, how to enable the broad public to attend" (p. 173, emphasis added). Thus, U.S. public higher education in the twentieth century operated, in policy and practice, on a theory of distributive justice (Tierney, 1997, 2007; Young,

1990). The income gap in the country decreased until it started widening again in the 1980s (Thomas & Bell, 2008).

By the middle of the twentieth century, American society was addressing issues of racial and gender inequity. Desegregation and the civil rights movements had a profound effect on higher education. Issues of class inequities moved to the background, while race and gender took the foreground. As this occurred, the era of distributive justice soon gave way to a regressive policy era.

The Regressive Era, 1980 to Present

Several policy reforms of the 1980s ushered in the regressive policy era (Mortenson, 2015), which featured a decline in state support for higher education and a change from a focus on need to merit. The increasing necessity of a college degree and great increases in tuition (Thomas & Bell, 2008) have contributed to a rapid growth of economic inequity (Noah, 2012; Wilson, 2012). Low-income students can no longer afford college without incurring large amounts of debt.

One of the significant trends of the past 30 years is the decline of state funding for higher education (Bergeron, Baylor, & Flores, 2014). Many institutions have increased tuition to offset these cutbacks, shifting a greater portion of the cost of college onto students and their families. In many states the decrease in funding for higher education has adversely affected low- and middle-income households (Bergeron et al., 2014). Many colleges and universities have started to cut need-based grants to students in favor of more merit-based scholarships (Drew, 2012; Long & Riley, 2007). Colleges and universities are focusing more on admitting students who meet a rigid set of academic standards and less on students with unmet financial need.

With the decline of social distributive policies of the previous era, the country's income gap has widened. In the current regressive era, families have less money to pay for college, and fewer forms of need-based aid are available. In one generation, higher education has made the transition from being affordable and accessible to a luxury item available mostly to the best and the brightest (Kezar, 2010; Thomas & Bell, 2008).

These tragic shifts in higher education have some roots in the distributive era. As the country created new types of colleges and universities after World War II, older institutions began to separate themselves as unique. The creation of land-grant colleges helped spur the creation of research universities that shifted to admitting academically elite students. As Nidiffer and Bouman (2004) noted, elite universities changed from admitting the poor to conducting research on the poor. The expansion of higher education allowed a small subset of the most elite private and public universities to restrict opportunities for admission. The unintended consequence of the postwar expansion of higher education was that it allowed private and certain public universities to focus on academic merit narrowly quantified by grade point averages and standardized test scores, chasing greater prestige and excluding low-income students.

The premium placed on a college education, along with increased competition for admission, led to the creation of university rankings for public consumption (Alon, 2009; Alon & Tienda, 2007). In the distributive era access to higher education exceeded the demand, but in the regressive era access is constricted. Instead of inclusivity, many colleges and universities now choose exclusivity and the lure of prestige and high ranking (Thomas & Bell, 2008). In this light, the regressive era represents a revision of the social contract between the public and higher education. The ideals of distributive justice are dwindling. Illustrating the difference between the two eras is the growth of for-profit education. The regressive era has seen the privatized for-profit sector grow and expand (Thelin, 2004) to take on more of the task of providing access for low-income students.

While the distributive era featured overt discussions about diversity (Reconstruction, the civil rights movement, and desegregation), the regressive era features a more covert diversity discourse. While prior generations solidified the legal rights of underrepresented groups, many forms of institutional discrimination still exist. Affirmative Action was already challenged in the mid-1970s and has experienced further challenges as the regressive era continued. Title IX was implemented, although it was not always acted upon. Class issues in higher education have remained unaddressed. While it seems many people have tired of discussing race and ethnicity, many colleges still struggle with the issue of income. As higher education no longer operates with a distributive philosophy, the discussion of access for low-income students comes at a time when colleges and universities are lacking resources because of cuts in state funding.

The Legal Context

Legal discourse initially paralleled the developing higher education focus on racial and gender inequities (Guinier, 1997; Klarman, 2004). Litigants challenged segregated postsecondary institutions, and Affirmative Action was designed to be a remedy to eliminate inequality on the basis of race and sex as well as to deal with the legacy of slavery (Lawrence, 2001). With the 1978 *Regents of the University of California v. Bakke* decision, the Supreme Court provided specific guidelines: In finding that Affirmative Action could not be used to redress past inequality, the court narrowed how race and ethnicity could be considered. In particular, Justice Lewis F. Powell's opinion highlighted the educational benefits of diversity, establishing a philosophy that continues to drive education discussions today. In essence, the Supreme Court's decision to limit Affirmative Action in higher education to the diversity rationale in *Bakke,* the subsequent Michigan cases (*Gratz v. Bollinger,* 2003; *Grutter v. Bollinger,* 2003), and most recently *Fisher v. University of Texas* (2013) has controlled the debate over Affirmative Action in college admissions and whether there is a fundamental right to postsecondary access.

In *San Antonio School District v. Rodriguez* (1973), the Supreme Court had to decide whether the poor are a "suspect class" (p. 408) and whether education is a fundamental right under the U.S. Constitution. The plaintiffs were Mexican American parents whose children attended public schools in Edgewood, one of the poorest districts in Texas. The Texas system of financing public schools, as in many states, relies on local property taxes to supplement state and federal funds provided to school districts. Because property values vary by district, the amount of per-pupil expenditure varies, resulting in unequal funding. The decision before the court was whether this public school financing system discriminated against the poor. The court ruled that "where wealth is involved, the Equal Protection Clause does not require absolute equality or precisely equal advantages" (p. 24). In refusing to declare unequal funding unconstitutional, the court distinguished between unconstitutionally denying education and providing a poorer quality of education, which the majority determined was not an equal protection violation.

As the appellees correctly argued, equal protection applies when a state has deprived its members of a fundamental right. The *San Antonio School District v. Rodriguez* (1973) majority, however, ruled "the importance of a service performed by the State does not determine whether it must be regarded as fundamental for purposes of examination under the Equal Protection Clause," p. 30). The court rejected the appellees' argument that education has a close relationship to the "effective exercise of First Amendment freedoms and to intelligent utilization of the right to vote" (p. 35) and decided education is not a fundamental right.

We contend that we must address the question of merit in a democratic society and contest current policies that focus on test scores as the arbiter of meritocracy. Further, legal advocates and policymakers must amend the ways the legal system has rationalized discrimination based on social class. Legal and education policy experts have severely criticized *San Antonio School District v. Rodriguez* (1973). Goodwin Liu (2004) argues that real access to higher education requires overturning that decision. We contend that in addition to challenging the court's opinion that the poor have not faced a history of oppression in the United States, we must also contest the notion that education is not a fundamental right.

The legal discourse on diversity obfuscates income inequality. In the social sciences, researchers recognize that race and class are linked. Although race, place, and class are intertwined, most courts consider each aspect separately. As Morgan (1998) points out, "Unfortunately, for the most part, neither federal nor state courts have taken this confluence of circumstances into account in deciding education litigation cases" (pp. 279–280). This leaves low-income students relegated to the margins of discussion.

Conclusion

The social contract has shifted in a manner that marginalizes discussion of college access for low-income students. In the distributive era, legal and social policies were based on an ethos of distributive justice (Tierney, 2007). These policies protected and promoted access to higher education for low-income students. But the social contract has shifted away from distributive justice and toward a focus on competition and merit. The discourse on access has also changed to focus more on racial and gender inequality than income inequality. In the regressive era, the discourse on access to higher education has become narrow and fragmented. Recent renewed discussion of access for low-income students has been difficult to fit within the confines of traditional diversity discourse.

The Limits of Our Discourse

Social class constitutes a social identity. Class groupings can be drawn along economic lines. But how do individuals in a social class see and understand themselves and create a form of group solidarity? Do low-income individuals see themselves as part of a collective group? Missing in the discourse on access for low-income students is a clear understanding of this process of forming group solidarity.

Many racial and ethnic groups invoke a shared ancestry and common experiences of oppression that create bonds of solidarity and a group identity. Race, gender, and sexual orientation rely on some form of conscious collectivity; social class and income status seemingly do not. Although racial and ethnic, gender, and sexual orientation categorizations are complex and controversial, they help underrepresented groups form collective communities and devise strategies for social and political action. However, social class seems to operate as an unconscious collective (Bottero, 2004). Many members of various income groups are not conscious of being members of those groups. How do we generate a new discourse on an unconsciously experienced collectivity? We need to answer that question to change the diversity discourse to recognize class and income inequality as a main component of identity.

The Meaning of Equity

We contend that equity in a democratic society must include some level of distributive justice. During the distributive era, higher education functioned as a driver of social mobility by providing access to many. In the current regressive climate, the focus on narrow measures of academic merit benefits a privileged few. Equity in the regressive era means maximizing human development with limited support for public systems such as higher education. Regressive-era policies favor a focus on the individual but not necessarily the broader society. What we are suggesting is a way of thinking about equity that is focused not just on individuals but on the responsibility of a democratic society to foster social mobility.

While we do not know what will shape the next era of higher education, we suggest policymakers, along with colleges and universities, address four imperatives. First, assert that education is a fundamental right, and access to quality education is foundational to sustaining a democratic society. Overturning the *San Antonio School District v. Rodriguez* (1973) decision is a start in that direction. Second, there must be a discussion on whether social class constitutes a protected class under the Equal Protection Clause (U.S. Const. amend. XIV). Recognizing social class legally would help make more people aware of their income status as a shared collective experience. Third, develop a language for the discussion of diversity that recognizes the unique way social class identities are formed in a manner less conscious than race, gender, or sexual orientation. And fourth, redefine merit beyond the limited scope of standardized tests and grade point averages. Equity does not mean eroding academic excellence nor rewarding the academically mediocre. Equity in a democratic society entails actions to preserve and promote the fundamental rights of all to access quality public services. Education is one of those rights, and individuals of all income levels are entitled to it.

References

Agricultural College Act of 1890, 7 U.S.C. § 321 (2015).

Alon, S. (2009). The evolution of class inequity in higher education: Competition, exclusion, and adaption. *American Sociological Review, 74*, 731–755.

Alon, S., & Tienda, M. (2007). Diversity, opportunity and the shifting meritocracy in higher education. *American Sociological Review, 72*, 487–511.

Bergeron, D., Baylor, E., & Flores, A. (2014). *A great recession, a great retreat: A call for a public college quality compact*. Retrieved from www.americanprogress.org/issues/higher-education/report/2014/10/27/99731/a-great-recession-a-great-retreat

Bottero, W. (2004). Class identities and the identity of class. *Sociology, 38*, 985–1003.

Brubacher, J. S., & Rudy, W. (2002). *Higher education in transition: A history of American colleges and universities* (4th ed.). New Brunswick, NJ: Transaction.

Council for Opportunity in Education. (n.d.). *TRIO: History*. Retrieved from www.coenet.us/coe_prod_imis/COE/TRIO/History/COE/NAV_TRIO/TRIO_History.aspx?hkey=89b3a80a-3a9e-4580-9fda-38156b9318f8

Drew, C. (2012, July 12). Help for the not so needy. *New York Times*. Retrieved from www.nytimes.com/2012/07/22/education/edlife/a-rise-in-students-receiving-merit-awards.html

Education Amendments of 1972, U.S.C. 20 § 1681 (1986).

Fisher v. University of Texas at Austin, 570 U.S. (2013).

Freeman, S. (2007). *Rawls*. New York, NY: Routledge.

Gratz v. Bollinger, 539 U.S. 244 (2003).

Grutter v. Bollinger, 539 U.S. 306 (2003).

Guinier, L. (1997). Reframing the affirmative action debate. *Kentucky Law Journal, 86*, 505–525.

Higher Education Act of 1965, 20 U.S.C. § 1001-1155 (2015).

Keyssar, A. (2000). *The right to vote: The contested history of democracy in the United States*. New York, NY: Basic Books.

Kezar, A. (Ed.). (2010). *Recognizing and serving low-income students in postsecondary education: An examination of institutional policies, practices, and culture*. New York, NY: Routledge.

Klarman, M. J. (2004). *From Jim Crow to civil rights: The Supreme Court and the struggle for racial equality*. New York, NY: Oxford University Press.

Lawrence, C. R. (2001). Two views of the river: A critique of the liberal defense of Affirmative Action. *Columbia Law Review, 101*, 928.

Liu, G. (2004). Race, class, diversity, complexity. *Notre Dame Law Review, 80*, 289–302.

Long, B. T., & Riley, E. (2007). Financial aid: A broken bridge to college access. *Harvard Educational Review, 77*(1), 39–63.

McDowell, G. (2001). *Land-grant universities and extension into the 21st century: Renegotiating or abandoning a social contract*. Ames: Iowa State University Press.

McElroy, E. J., & Armesto, M. (1998). TRIO and Upward Bound: History, programs, and issues-past, present and future. *Journal of Negro Education, 67*, 373–380.

Morgan, D. C. (1998). Less polite questions: Race, place, poverty and public education. *Annual Survey of American Law, 59*(267), 477–494.

Morrill Act of 1862, 7 U.S.C. §301 (2015).

Mortenson, T. (2015, February). State investment and disinvestment in higher education. *Postsecondary Education Opportunity: The Pell Institute for the Study of Opportunity in Higher Education, 272*, 1–24. Retrieved from www.pellinstitute.org/downloads/newsletters-PEO_Number_272_February_2015.pdf

Nidiffer, J., & Bouman, J. P. (2004). The university of the poor: The University of Michigan's transition from admitting impoverished students to studying poverty, 1870–1910. *American Educational Research Journal, 41*(1), 35–67.

Noah, T. (2012). *The great divergence: America's growing inequality crisis and what we can do about it*. New York, NY: Bloomsbury Press.

Obama, B. (2013). *Remarks by the president on economic mobility*. Retrieved from www.whitehouse.gov/the-press-office/2013/12/04/remarks-president-economic-mobility

Rawls, J. (1971). *A theory of justice*. Cambridge, MA: Harvard University Press.

Regents of the University of California v. Bakke, 438 U.S. 265 (1978).

San Antonio Independent School District v. Rodriguez, 411 U.S. 1 (1973).

Servicemen's Readjustment Act of 1944, 38 U.S.C. §3301-3325 (2012).

Thelin, J. R. (2004). *A history of American higher education*. Baltimore, MD: Johns Hopkins University Press.

Thomas, S. L., & Bell, A. (2008). Social class and higher education: A reorganization of opportunities. In L. Weis (Ed.), *The way class works: Readings on school, family, and the economy* (pp. 273–287). New York, NY: Routledge.

Tierney, W. G. (1997). The parameters of Affirmative Action: Equity and excellence in the academy. *Review of Education Research, 67*(2), 165–196.

Tierney, W. G. (2007). Merit and Affirmative Action: Promulgating a democratic public culture. *Urban Education, 42*, 385–402.

U.S. Const. amend. XIV.

Wilson, J. W. (2012, July 10). The great disparity. *Nation*. Retrieved from www.thenation.com/article/168822/great-disparity

Young, I. M. (1990). *Justice and the politics of difference*. Princeton, NJ: Princeton University Press.

Zook, G. F. (1947). *Higher education for American democracy: A report* (Vols. 1–6). Washington, DC: Government Printing Office.

4

AN INTERVIEW WITH JARRETT T. GUPTON
The Value of Uncertainty and the Need for Nuance

Sheela Linstrum

Jarrett Gupton's academic trajectory is a testament to his curiosity. Jarrett admits that his interest in diversity scholarship arose almost by accident; he simply "fell into it." Despite somewhat aimless beginnings as a graduate student at the University of Southern California (USC), Jarrett soon specialized in college access for low-income and homeless students, an area he continues to explore. Jarrett's work is sophisticated and nuanced, reflecting his passion for helping homeless youths pursue postsecondary education.

In the early years of his doctoral work at USC, Jarrett worked with his adviser, William G. Tierney, on a research project about the challenges of college access for low-income students in the Los Angeles area. This research included examining the availability of financial aid, school and state policies that influence low-income students, and experiences that influence students' educational choices. During this research project, his adviser suggested that Jarrett consider studying postsecondary access for homeless youths. Jarrett had entered USC with the intention of studying race and ethnicity in higher education and decided to focus on this area and develop his own research agenda.

Jarrett's research extended far beyond the typical course work and dissertation research. He spent 2 years tutoring homeless youths, becoming acquainted with the complexities of homelessness, recalling it was "fascinating to hear about their living situations." Some students, he learned, enjoyed attending school as a form of psychological relief from their daily lives. Others, he observed, struggled to conform to a formalized school environment.

Jarrett also noticed the personal development of the homeless students, some of whom seemed quite mature because of the challenges they had already faced. Some impressed him with their reflections on their family situations and their critiques of society. Jarrett invested a significant amount of time getting to know these students and sought to understand their perspectives. Too often, their voices are ignored, although they articulate well the challenges of being homeless. Jarrett said his volunteer work with them was "a great way of learning."

This connection to the human element of homelessness is evident in Jarrett's graduate dissertation, *Pathways to College for Homeless Adolescents* (2009). In it, he undertakes an ethnographic study of 11 college or college-bound homeless youths, examining the barriers they face to postsecondary access. By fusing the cultural narratives of these 11 students (which Jarrett calls "the participants' stories of their lives and educational experiences") with their cultural repertoires (or, he says, "their strategies for persisting through educational systems"), Jarrett explores the complexities of studying homeless youth. He links the experiences of his student subjects to a broader conversation about postsecondary access for homeless youths. Jarrett's scholarship reflects his appreciation for the human aspect of research; it is marked by his insistence that readers scrutinize these narratives and resist the temptation to oversimplify the individual experience and hastily impose a theoretical framework.

While theories are intended to guide discussion and help explain behavior, too strong a reliance on theory runs the risk of overlooking the important ways individuals and their experiences differ. Jarrett constructed heartfelt narratives that exposed the specific situations, psychological realities, and unique challenges of these students, often adding his own voice. These students were not just subjects but individuals with rich experiences and personalities whom Jarrett greatly respects.

Since receiving his PhD from USC, Jarrett has continued to study postsecondary access for low-income populations as an assistant professor at the University of Minnesota. Drawing on the lessons learned from his extensive research in the Los Angeles area, Jarrett is currently resuming his work on barriers to postsecondary education for homeless youths around Minneapolis and St. Paul. So far, his work is revealing new challenges for the students, including a more geographically diffuse population of homeless students and families as well as problems such as sex trafficking, which is prevalent in the region. Jarrett hopes his work will help inform state policymakers and human service organizations about ways to address the challenges faced by homeless youths and to inform interventions that attempt to create educational pathways for this population.

Although Jarrett has found his academic niche, he attributes part of his success in academia to keeping an open mind. Having observed his peers in graduate school, and now, as an adviser to graduate students of his own, he has noticed a tendency to stay with a research area that is a natural fit. But he cautions against blindly imitating trends: "Don't follow the party line." Jarrett thinks there is tremendous value in uncertainty at early stages of graduate study; he discourages young academics from narrowing their academic interests too early, reducing vital exploration. As a younger scholar, it is a challenge to find one's own voice and academic passion in the face of research topics that are currently in vogue. Although critical race theory and deficit modeling are especially popular at the moment, for example, he encourages young academics to allow for some uncertainty and search for ideas that exist outside the mainstream. To conform to academic trends would be an easier but perhaps less rewarding path for not only the academic but also the advancement of the field.

In fact, Jarrett expresses some concern over developments in diversity scholarship today, emphasizing that the "discourse needs to become more nuanced." Diversity scholarship tends to represent individuals as members of a single subgroup, but this often leads to harmful oversimplifications. The study of homeless youths, Jarrett notes, does not begin to capture the incredible diversity of homeless individuals. While homeless individuals often (although not always) share socioeconomic characteristics, the homeless population also encompasses many non-White individuals and members of the lesbian, gay, bisexual, transgender, and queer community. Problems of classification can be complicated, because *homelessness* has a variety of definitions; living conditions and paths to homelessness can vary tremendously. Jarrett believes that the study of homelessness, as well as diversity scholarship more broadly, needs to become more nuanced to account for these variations.

References

Gupton, J. (2009). *Pathways to college for homeless adolescents* (Doctoral dissertation). Available from ProQuest Dissertations and Theses database. (UMI No. 3368700)

5

LESBIAN, GAY, BISEXUAL, TRANSGENDER, AND QUEER STUDENTS ON CAMPUS

Fostering Inclusion Through Research, Policy, and Practice

Michael R. Woodford, Jessica Joslin, and Kristen A. Renn

It is commonly accepted that diversity among the students, staff, and faculty in the university community is critical to providing high-quality education. However, diversity tends to be understood as racial and ethnic and, at times, sex or gender diversity.[1] To bring attention to the experiences of lesbian, gay, bisexual, transgender, and queer (LGBTQ) university community members, a growing scholarship addresses issues of sexual orientation and gender identity and expression in higher education. In addition to increasing scientific knowledge, this research is critical in informing the development of responsive policies and programs that promote LGBTQ students' inclusion, well-being, and success. Much of this scholarship examines the campus climate for LGBTQ students, especially their perceptions and experiences. Although this work promotes understanding of the experiences of LGBTQ students, several issues and gaps exist, thereby limiting the information available. For example, minimal attention has been given to student outcomes and resilience. To create inclusive campus environments for LGBTQ students, it is necessary to address various aspects of the campus climate as well as the mechanisms of student engagement in promoting positive change (Hurtado, Carter, & Kardia, 1998).

In this chapter we build on the work of other scholars (Hurtado et al., 1998; Rankin, 2005, 2006) and discuss the field of LGBTQ research addressing student inclusion, success, and well-being in higher education. Because of its relevance to these broad outcomes, we critically assess the body of scholarly work addressing LGBTQ campus climate. In response to our analysis and to promote research that more effectively informs policy and practice, we present a conceptual model that integrates higher education theory on campus climate and student success with social psychology theory on minority stress and resilience. We begin by providing background information about the systems of oppressions affecting LGBTQ people and the meaning of key identity terms. We also give an overview of the history of LGBTQ policy, practice, and research in higher education and describe the current policy environment concerning LGBTQ students, which is part of the overall context in which LGBTQ students and universities exist.

Background

The social organization of sexuality and gender reflects systems of power (Eichstedt, 1996) that operate within and in conjunction with other systems of power, including those concerning race, ethnicity, ability, social class, sex, religion, and other individual and social identities. Systemic power imbalances in all these areas are oppressive. Heterosexism and genderism are complex phenomena that marginalize and oppress LGBTQ people while privileging heterosexual and cisgender identities (Bilodeau, 2009; Woodford & Bella, 2003).

Sexual orientation is multifaceted; it can involve sexual, emotional, or relational attractions toward others and is typically defined by one's gender and the gender or genders of those to whom one is attracted (Moradi, Mohr, Worthington, & Fassinger, 2009). Lesbian, gay, bisexual, pansexual, asexual, and heterosexual are examples of sexual orientation. *Gender identity* refers to the "conscious claiming and expression of gender as related to the self" (p. 6), and *gender expression* includes the outward manifestation of one's identity through personal characteristics and behaviors. By *transgender* we mean "anatomy, appearance, identity, beliefs, personality characteristics, demeanor or behavior [that] diverges from or is perceived to diverge from prevailing social norms about gender" (Currah & Minter, 2000, p. 17). Some transgender individuals identify as heterosexual; thus, we do not include transgender individuals in the category of sexual minorities. We also use *queer* in an inclusive way to mean a sexual or gender identity outside dominant standards (Beeman & Eliason, 1996). Throughout this chapter, we use the abbreviation LGBTQ to be inclusive of sexual minority and gender minority students; however, where necessary, we focus on particular groups in this category.

LGBTQ people have faced hostility, discrimination, and violence in K–12 and postsecondary educational settings. In the 1950s and 1960s, and in some places well into this century, school and university administrators used long-standing antisodomy statutes to fire employees and control and expel students suspected of being homosexual (Blount, 2005; Dilley, 2002). Until the American Psychiatric Association eliminated its categorization of homosexuality as a mental disorder in 1973, some student affairs personnel tried to treat and "cure" students believed to have same-sex desires (Dilley, 2002). Throughout most of the twentieth century, this persecution helped create a culture of invisibility and silence among sexual (and gender) minority people in education (Marine, 2011). With the 1969 Stonewall rebellion in New York City and the emergence of a fledgling gay liberation movement on college campuses, sexual minority students and faculty began a campaign for visibility, resistance, and activism in the 1970s and 1980s (D'Emilo, 1992; Marine, 2011). The 1980s also saw empirical investigations of gay, lesbian, and bisexual students' experiences on campus and studies of students' attitudes toward gay men and lesbians (Herek, 1988, 1993). In the late 1980s and early 1990s, colleges and universities became sites for AIDS activism and responses to waves of antigay violence sparked by the AIDS crisis (Duggan, 2002; Marine, 2011). Institutional responses to activism included acknowledging gay student organizations, establishing campus resource centers, and adding sexual orientation to institutional nondiscrimination policies. These responses were not universal, but higher education, public and private, seemed to have turned a corner on sexual orientation identities by the late 1990s and early 2000s, with growing attention to gender identity and expression on campuses during the past decade.

Even though progress toward equality has been made in a number of public policy areas, especially in the past few years (e.g., sexual minorities openly serving in the military, federal recognition of same-sex marriage), sexual prejudice still exists among a sizable proportion of the general public (Saad, 2012), and LGBTQ people often experience discrimination and mistreatment (Marzullo & Libman, 2009). At the time of writing this chapter, U.S. federal law does not prohibit employment and education discrimination based on sexual orientation and gender identity (Human Rights Campaign, 2014). Increasingly, municipalities and states have included sexual orientation in antidiscrimination laws, as have K–12 and higher education institutions. However, far fewer prohibitions of discrimination based on gender identity or expression exist in these systems. There is no uniform protection for LGBTQ college students, staff, or faculty. Even if a federal law were enacted to provide such protection, LGBTQ members of the university community would likely continue to be marginalized in one way or another, given the pervasive and resistant nature of heterosexism and genderism.

The State of LGBTQ Campus Climate Research

Throughout the United States, heterosexism, genderism, and trans/bi/homophobia manifest themselves on university campuses through discrimination and social norms that marginalize LGBTQ people. A growing body of work suggests that in addition to facing the typical challenges of college, LGBTQ students often feel unsafe on campus and experience harassment and discrimination because of their sexual orientation, gender identity, or gender expression (e.g., Rankin, 2003; Rankin, Weber, Blumenfeld, & Frazer, 2010). Although these studies provide important insights into the nature of campus climates for LGBTQ students, several critical issues and gaps exist, resulting in limited empirical understanding that can inform higher education policy and practice.

The general tendency has been to focus on LGBTQ students' experiences and needs, often highlighting disparities between LGBTQ students and other students, while overlooking the forces contributing to these disparities (e.g., Oswalt & Wyatt, 2011). For example, researchers of campus climate have given little attention to a critical component: how and why members of the majority non-LGBTQ group practice heterosexism/genderism. Specifically, few studies (Jewell & Morrison, 2010; Woodford, Howell, Kulick, & Silverschanz, 2013) examine the antecedents of heterosexist behaviors among college students. Likewise, although a plethora of studies examine anti-LGBTQ bias among college students (especially studies assessing sexual prejudice toward gay and lesbian people), most studies include limited samples, such as psychology undergraduates (exceptions include Brown, Clarke, Gortmaker, & Robinson-Keilig, 2004; Holland, Matthews, & Schott, 2013; Woodford, Silverschanz, Swank, Scherrer, & Raiz, 2012; Yost & Gilmore, 2011), and thus these studies do not provide insights about the perceptions of the general student body. Moreover, some studies (e.g., Brown et al., 2004; Holland et al., 2013; Yost & Gilmore, 2011) address attitudes that are no longer prevalent or in fashion, such as morality-based objections to same-sex sexuality (Morrison, Morrison, & Franklin, 2009; Walls, 2008), and then conclude that low levels of prejudice exist. Anti-LGBTQ prejudice, like other biases, has become increasingly subtle and nuanced throughout the years (Morrison et al., 2009; Walls, 2008), but attitudinal research conducted as climate research has not necessarily kept up with these changes. Additionally, campus climate researchers have not examined attitudes toward transgender individuals or subpopulations in the LGBTQ community (e.g., queer people of color). Finally, few scholars (Brown et al., 2004) have attended to faculty attitudes toward LGBTQ individuals or subpopulations, with some studies focusing on the attitudes of faculty in particular fields, such as social work (Chonody, Woodford, Brennan, Newman, & Wang, 2014; Woodford, Brennan, Gutiérrez, & Luke, 2013).

An increasing number of studies focus on the experiential and psychological climate for LGBTQ students. Although scholars have established that campus climate regarding race and sex affects student outcomes, including persistence to degree and a host of noncognitive attitudes, behaviors, and characteristics (e.g., political attitudes, civic engagement, health and mental health; see Hurtado, Griffin, Arellano, & Cuellar, 2008; Hurtado & Ponjuan, 2005; Pascarella & Terenzini, 2005), little is known about the consequences of campus climate for LGBTQ students. Much of the research on their experiences and perceptions is descriptive in nature (e.g., Brown et al., 2004; Rankin, 2003; Rankin et al., 2010; Yost & Gilmore, 2011), with some studies comparing the perceptions of sexual minority students and heterosexual students (Brown et al., 2004; Rankin et al., 2010; Yost & Gilmore, 2011). Existing outcome studies, often conducted by scholars concerned with mental health outcomes, generally demonstrate that an unwelcoming or hostile campus climate can have a negative impact on sexual minority students' well-being (Reed, Prado, Matsumoto, & Amaro, 2010; Silverschanz, Cortina, Konik, & Magley, 2008; Waldo, Hesson-McInnius, & D'Augelli, 1998; Woodford, Han, Craig, Lim, & Matney, 2014; Woodford, Howell, Silverschanz, & Yu, 2012; Woodford, Krentzman, & Gattis, 2012; Woodford, Kulick, & Atteberry, 2014; Woodford, Kulick, Sinco, & Hong, 2014). A few scholars (Silverschanz et al., 2008; Woodford & Kulick, 2015) have examined the academic impacts of a hostile climate. To the best of our knowledge, researchers have not examined the relationship between campus climate and outcomes among transgender students.

Existing outcome studies are also limited in that they tend to address only experiential climate (exceptions being Reed et al., 2010; Woodford & Kulick, 2015; Woodford, Kulick, & Atteberry, 2015), which is the anti-LGBTQ or supportive behaviors of others toward LGBTQ people; however, psychological climate (how groups on campus relate to one another) is also a critical part of campus climate and has been shown to be related to student outcomes among other minority students, such as students of color (Hurtado et al., 2008). In regard to experiential climate, until recently researchers focused mainly on overt assaultive behaviors (e.g., verbal and physical threats), overlooking everyday forms of mistreatment and microaggressions (e.g., antigay slurs, dirty looks) as well as ambient heterosexism in the social environment, such as hearing gay jokes or witnessing other students experience heterosexism (exceptions being Silverschanz et al., 2008; Woodford, Chonody, Kulick, Brennan, & Renn, in press; Woodford, Han, et al., 2014; Woodford, Howell, et al., 2012; Woodford & Kulick, 2015;

Woodford, Kulick, Sinco, et al., 2014). Contemporary biases toward marginalized groups, including sexual and gender minorities, are commonly manifested in covert ways, some of which may be unintentional (Franklin, 2000; Gomez & Trierweiler, 1999; Nadal, Rivera, & Corpus, 2010), in society and on college campuses (Rankin et al., 2010; Woodford et al., in press; Woodford, Han et al., 2014; Woodford, Kulick, Sinco et al., 2014). Recently, calls have been made for minority-stress researchers to examine the effects of subtle discrimination on LGBTQ people (Meyer, Ouellette, Haile, & McFarlane, 2011).

In understanding the role of contemporary discrimination on LGBTQ college students' well-being and development, it is critical to examine the effects of microaggressions and everyday discrimination, as well as indirect exposure to mistreatment (e.g., witnessing heterosexist harassment). Research suggests that heterosexist harassment and incivility, direct and indirect (Silverschanz et al., 2008; Woodford, Han et al., 2014; Woodford, Krentzman, et al., 2012), and sexual orientation microaggressions (Woodford et al., in press; Woodford, Kulick, Sinco, et al., 2014), including use of the microaggression expression "That's so gay" (Woodford, Howell, et al., 2012), can increase the risk for negative outcomes among sexual minority students.[2] Although these and other studies have contributed to knowledge about campus climate for sexual minority students, large-scale national studies focused on transgender students are crucial, yet largely absent from the literature.

Protective Factors, Resilience, and Identity Development

In addition to remediating negative campus climate, to promote LGBTQ students' well-being and academic achievement it is critical to give empirical attention to the role of protective factors, LGBTQ identity development, and intersecting identities, all of which are sizable gaps in existing outcome studies. Also generally missing are studies that account for differences among sexuality and gender subgroups among LGBTQ students (Beemyn, Curtis, Davis, & Tubbs, 2005; Hurtado et al., 1998).

While growing attention is being given to protective factors in health disparities research, their role in buffering LGBTQ students from the effects of a negative campus climate has been overlooked (Sanlo, 2004; exceptions being Woodford & Kulick, 2015; Woodford, Kulick, & Atteberry, 2014; Woodford, Kulick, Sinco, et al., 2014). We advocate taking a strengths-based, antideficit approach to understanding LGBTQ student outcomes. Understanding how the psychosocial strengths and resources of LGBTQ students can promote their resilience in the face of heterosexism and discrimination should be a key goal of contemporary research on LGBTQ students. For example, how might identity pride reduce the effects of daily microaggressions on academic success? How might self-esteem or personal resilience moderate the effects of negative campus climate on mental health outcomes?

Alongside exploring these and other individual-level protective factors, it is important to examine the role of potential moderators or mediators within the social environment, including relationships and institutional factors (Renn, Woodford, Nicolazzo, & Brazelton, 2014). A study of LGBTQ student leaders (Renn, 2007), for example, found that involvement in campus activism promoted identity development and led to increased engagement on campus, career exploration, and other activities that lead to positive student outcomes. LGBTQ students who participated in qualitative interviews conducted in 2013 as part of the National Study of LGBTQ Student Success (www.lgbtqsuccess.net) reported that faculty and peers provided critical support inside and outside the classroom (Linley et al., under review; Nguyen et al., 2014). Students also reported that institutional policies, programs, and curricula supported their academic development and integration (Pitcher, Camacho, Renn, & Woodford, 2014). At all levels of the environment, from individuals to peers, faculty, and institutions, LGBTQ identities can lead to positive engagement in ways that buffer students and support academic, social, and personal development and well-being.

There is a fairly robust literature on how college students develop lesbian or gay identities (Bilodeau & Renn, 2005), with fewer studies on bisexual identities (King, 2011) and even fewer concerning transgender identities (Beemyn & Rankin, 2011; Bilodeau, 2009). Many identity development theories suggest that development occurs in an ordered and linear fashion: Initially, individuals realize they are different from the heterosexual or cisgender majority and then go through a series of disclosures about their sexual orientation or gender identity to others (typically defined as *coming out*), ultimately emerging into a stage of identity pride and perhaps identity integration (see Bilodeau & Renn, 2005). Campus climate researchers and scholars of identity development have rarely connected the two concepts; that is, little is known about how students' sexual orientation and gender identity development interact with their campus experience (exceptions being Garvey & Rankin, 2015; Renn, 2007). Renn's (2007) qualitative study of LGBT student leaders suggested that the more individuals were "out" on campus, the more hostility *and* support they experienced. More recently, using quantitative data from Rankin and colleagues' (2010) national study of LGBT campus climate, they found that greater levels of outness among *queer-spectrum* and *trans-spectrum* students (see pp. 375–376 for an explanation of their terminology) were associated with lower perceptions of institutional campus responses to sexual and gender identity issues and lower perceptions concerning the importance of LGBTQ campus resources but were not associated with campus or classroom climate. Additional research is needed that considers how campus climate influences LGBTQ identity development and how LGBTQ identity development influences campus climate in regard to experiences and perceptions.

In considering answers to these questions, it is vital to consider the diversity among LGBTQ students. Intersectionality has gained significant traction in research on diversity (Cole, 2009), and research underscores the important influence of multiple categories of race, gender identity, and gender expression on LGBTQ students' experiences and perceptions of campus climate (Rankin et al., 2010; Woodford, Kulick, Sinco, et al., 2014). Scholars also argue for the importance of considering identity saliency when examining multiple identities (Goode-Cross & Tager, 2011). Yet, Renn (2010) noted that LGBTQ campus climate studies that examine student outcomes tend not to assess the role of intersecting identities or how multiple identities (e.g., sexual orientation, race, gender, gender expression) work simultaneously to produce an interlocking web of oppression that may affect health and well-being in distinct ways (Collins, 2000). To develop culturally competent programs to support diverse LGBTQ students, it is critical to examine outcomes for specific groups and compare groups across multiple identity categories. This task could be accomplished using a lens of intersectionality or multiple social identities to design research that addresses campus climate, LGBTQ identity development, and student outcomes of most interest.

LGBTQ Policies and Programs on Campus

Nationwide, colleges use various policy and program interventions as a way to create accepting and inclusive environments that support LGBTQ students' development and well-being. Generally, policy interventions include sexual orientation (and gender identity, in some cases) in institutional antidiscrimination policies and housing policies. Programs can include those that target LGBTQ students (e.g., coming out groups) and others that aim to foster a safe and accepting environment for LGBTQ students (e.g., speaker panels, LGBTQ ally programs). The Consortium of Higher Education LGBT Resource Professionals (www.lgbtcampus.org) offers a best practices resource for policy, programming, and practice (http://architect.lgbtcampus.org), although few of these practices are empirically evaluated. Concerns have been raised that LGBTQ initiatives on campuses tend not to be evaluated and are often developed without a comprehensive, systematic understanding of the climate for LGBTQ students, which can undermine program effectiveness (Draughn, Elkins, & Roy, 2002).

In addition to these issues, policy and program interventions do not necessarily reflect the nature of contemporary LGBTQ discrimination. For instance, antidiscrimination policies tend to address only blatant discrimination. Subtle discrimination, such as derogatory comments and negative slights, are more common today than acts of outright discrimination (Rankin et al., 2010; Woodford, Kulick, Sinco, et al., 2014) and they can negatively affect students (Woodford, Kulick, Sinco, et al., 2014). Student codes of conduct should address heterosexism and genderism, especially in their covert forms. Likewise, campus awareness programs need to include content on everyday forms of anti-LGBTQ prejudice and their negative impacts on students.

We also have concerns about educational programs that aim to create inclusive campuses for LGBTQ students. These initiatives tend to focus on building awareness and creating a network of allies able to support LGBTQ students (Draughn et al., 2002). These outcomes are critical, but it is also essential to educate allies to interrupt and eliminate systems of oppression (Draughn et al., 2002; Woodford, Kolb, Durocher-Radeka, & Javier, 2014).

A conceptual model is needed to guide research on campus climate and outcomes for LGBTQ students. Although the model we now present has not been empirically tested, we maintain that research informed by it would have a considerable impact.

Understanding LGBTQ College Students' Health and Academic Success: A Conceptual Model

As illustrated in Figure 5.1, the proposed model reflects socioecological theory (Bronfenbrenner, 1994) and an inputs-environment-outcomes approach (Astin, 1977) to student experiences and development.[3] It is also informed by theories concerning campus climate (Hurtado, Alvarez, Guillermo-Wann, Cuellar, & Arellano, 2012; Milem, Chang, & Antonio, 2005), institutional departure (Tinto, 1988, 1993), and minority stress (Meyer, 2003). Astin's (1977) input-environment-output (I-E-O) framework is central to the model; it maintains that although students' inputs directly affect their academic achievement and other outcomes, they are mediated by the college environment.

FIGURE 5.1. National, State, and Local Socio-Cultural-Historical Context for LGBTQ People

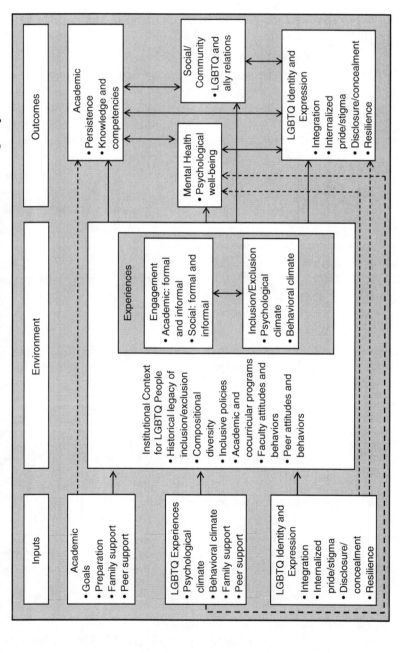

In the environment part of our model, campus climate and institutional departure are central. The model addresses institutional context, including history, student body composition and organization, and psychological and behavioral climate (Hurtado et al., 2012; Milem et al., 2005). Also, at the individual level (which we refer to as *experiences*), we integrate concepts from Tinto's (1988, 1993) work that suggest that students' integration or sense of belonging depends on their social and academic engagement on campus.

Minority stress theory (Meyer, 2003) underpins the entire model. According to this theory, besides the normative stressors all individuals encounter, LGBTQ individuals experience additional chronic and systemic stress because of LGBTQ-related prejudice, discrimination, and stigma, putting them at increased risk for negative outcomes (Meyer, 2003). Minority stress theory also suggests that protective factors can increase resilience to minority stressors. Meyer's (2003) theory specifically addresses resources on the individual (e.g., positive coping skills) and group (e.g., connections with the LGBTQ community) levels; we also consider the wider ecology and institutional resources.

National, State, and Local Socio-Cultural-Historical Context for LGBTQ People

In the model we propose inputs, environments, and outcomes are located in national, state, and local socio-cultural-historical context(s) for LGBTQ people, reflecting the influence of the macrosystem and exosystem (Bronfenbrenner, 1994). Basically, the larger society affects opportunities for LGBTQ people. Although people in the United States have become increasingly accepting of gay and lesbian people, acceptance is not universal (Andersen & Fetner, 2008). Further, research suggests that the larger social climate—laws and perceptions of the environment—can affect LGBTQ youth (Hatzenbuehler, 2011; Oswald & Holman, 2013). Regional support for LGBTQ identities is also quite variant. Moreover, higher education reflects and is shaped by culture and politics, and the external environment can affect institutional policies and practices, especially the development of LGBTQ policies and resources. Some institutions work toward LGBTQ student inclusion under opposition by external forces. In short, the larger context has an important impact.

Inputs

Inputs are the characteristics, demographics, and experiences students bring with them to the educational environment (Astin, 1977). In addition to demographic characteristics or identities (e.g., race, class, ability, gender, sexuality) and precollege (or pregraduate school) academic goals, preparation, and experiences, LGBTQ students' inputs include unique experiential and identity factors before entry into the academic environment. Demographic and experiential inputs can intersect and overlap. It is important to examine how intersecting identities affect students' inputs, environments, and outcomes in order to understand the influence of power and privilege (Renn, 2010).

Academic inputs. Among all students, precollege academic factors are a key determinant in academic outcomes, including grades, persistence, degree completion, and career or graduate school intentions and commitments (Pascarella & Terenzini, 2005; Tinto, 2005). An academically strong student is likely to have developed higher academic self-efficacy, which will interact with factors in the postsecondary environment to shape experiences and outcomes (Pascarella & Terenzini, 2005). Family, peer, and high school teacher or counselor support for higher education is also influential (Tinto, 1993).

There are also LGBTQ-specific academic inputs, such as K–12 experiences of harassment and bullying; support from teachers, guidance counselors, and peers; and involvement in gay/straight alliance organizations (Kosciw, Greytak, Palmer, & Boesen, 2014). These experiences shape students' expectations of college as well as their health and well-being (D'Augelli, Pilkington, & Hershberger, 2002). A longitudinal qualitative study conducted as part of the National Study of LGBTQ Student Success (www.lgbtqsuccess.net) suggests that LGBTQ students bring expectations to college based on prior experience with LGBTQ groups (e.g., high school gay/straight alliances or LGBTQ community youth groups). These expectations may influence which college is selected and how the student seeks LGBTQ resources on campus.

LGBTQ experiences (nonacademic). Prior to college, LGBTQ students also have a number of experiences in home and community settings. Psychological inputs include mental well-being and personal resilience. Given the pervasive nature of heterosexism and genderism, LGBTQ youth may suffer from discrimination by their families, peers, and others, which may threaten their mental health (D'Augelli et al., 2002; Meyer, 2003). However, some LGBTQ students may enter college with affirming experiences, such as supportive friends and family or participation in LGBTQ communities and groups (Kosciw et al., 2014). These experiences likely shape LGBTQ students' psychological well-being as well as their identity development.

LGBTQ identity and expression. It is beyond our scope to provide a description of sexual orientation and gender identity development models, but it is important to understand that a student's LGBTQ identity development before college can make a difference in the experience of higher education and in LGBTQ identity after college. A number of models consider disclosure or concealment of LGBTQ identity as a marker of development, with increasing disclosure (coming out) indicating advancement (see Bilodeau & Renn, 2005, for a synthesis of LGBT identity development models). Participation in an LGBTQ community is another common marker of development (Bilodeau & Renn, 2005). Connected to this, internalized stigma is an influential risk factor in minority stress theory (Meyer, 2003). Most models of LGBTQ identity formation end with *integration* of LGBTQ identity with other salient aspects of the self and relationships with family, friends, and community (Bilodeau & Renn, 2005). Precollege students (and college students) may be at any point in LGBTQ identity development. The extent to which they are out, participate in LGBTQ communities, form intimate relationships, and experience identity pride or stigma is crucial input as they enter and experience higher education.

Finally, personal resilience is a key input that can shape experiences and outcomes. LGBTQ youth may exhibit psychological resilience developed in parallel with their identity development (Mayer, Garofalo, & Makadon, 2014). Coping with anti-LGBTQ climates in school and possibly also at home and in the community provides a foundation for developing resiliency to overcome obstacles that may be placed in their way in college (Russell, 2005).

Summary. These academic, experiential, and identity-based inputs are part of LGBTQ students' foundation for college; they are the *person* elements of Bronfenbrenner's (1994) person-process-context-time model. There are, of course, innumerable other inputs, including other social identities and their concomitant privileges and disadvantages. These factors all shape the college experience, are shaped by it, and affect outcomes.

Environment

The college environment includes the institutional context for sexual and gender minorities and the experiences of LGBTQ students in college (i.e., climate). Our model holds that the environment has a direct effect on students' outcomes and can mediate the effects of inputs.

Institutional context for LGBTQ people. In our model, institutional context for LGBTQ people includes elements such as campus policies, faculty and peer attitudes and behaviors, academic and cocurricular programs, student body diversity, and the history of inclusiveness for LGBTQ people (Hurtado et al., 2012). A number of institutions across the country have a long and well-documented commitment to welcoming LGBTQ people. Such campuses have policies, programs, and inclusive curricula, such as LGBTQ studies courses, inclusion of gender identity and expression in antidiscrimination policies, gender-inclusive restrooms, mixed-gender housing options, LGBTQ support groups, and educational awareness programs promoting LGBTQ students' inclusion and development. Other institutions have much less support for LGBTQ people historically. For instance, although changes are occurring at some conservative religious colleges (O'Loughlin, 2013), a number of these institutions have policies that exclude LGBTQ students from fully participating in campus life; some even threaten to expel or otherwise punish students who are transgender or who engage in a same-sex relationship (see Jaschik, 2014).

Campus diversity and the attitudes and behavior of faculty and peers also influence LGBTQ students' experience. Ample evidence suggests that diversity—including among faculty—helps promote successful learning environments (e.g., Gurin, Dey, Hurtado, & Gurin, 2002; Hu & Kuh, 2003; Hurtado, 2001; Hurtado et al., 2012), and LGBTQ students likely also benefit. However, negative perceptions of LGBTQ people (Woodford, Silverschanz, et al., 2012), heterosexist behaviors (Rankin et al., 2010; Woodford, Kulick, Sinco, et al., 2014), and faculty who hold negative views of LGBTQ people (Brown et al., 2004; Chonody et al., 2014; Woodford, Brennan, et al., 2012) can contribute to a hostile campus environment.

Throughout the twentieth century, higher education institutions excluded and were hostile toward sexual orientation and gender minorities (see Marine, 2011). The process of overcoming this legacy has varied by campus, and evidence of past heterosexism, homophobia, and transphobia is ingrained in campus folklore, traditions, and symbols. LGBTQ students live and learn in physical and symbolic spaces that carry this history into the present. Heteronormative traditions, such as Girls Round Up Boys (GRUB) parties at sororities, ring-day dances where women are expected to wear white dresses and bring male dates, "smear the queer" activities during fraternity inductions, and binary-gendered campus mascots (e.g., the Minutemen and Lady Minutemen, or Volunteers and Lady Vols), continue to permeate student culture.

Experiences. In the proposed model, we divide LGBTQ college student experiences into two categories: engagement and inclusion or exclusion. Tinto's (1988, 1993) student retention model proposes that to persist in college, students need to be engaged on multiple levels, academically in their courses and informally through interacting with faculty and college staff as advisers and mentors. They can also be engaged socially through formal cocurricular groups and activities and informally through day-to-day relationships and conversations with their peers. Tinto argued that when students are engaged in each of these four ways, they are more likely to stay in school.

Our model recognizes that Tinto's four aspects of engagement are important to LGBTQ college students; however, their experiences of engagement are deeply affected by their campuses' psychological and behavior climates and whether they feel included or excluded on campus. Unfortunately, the climate on many campuses is often unwelcoming to them (Rankin et al., 2010). LGBTQ students' overall perception of their campus as homophobic or supportive may influence their ability to engage with faculty and peers formally and informally.

The relationship between LGBTQ students' engagement and their feelings of inclusion is not one-directional. Certain formal and informal academic environments can affect behavioral and psychological climates, and students' feelings of inclusion or exclusion. Research conducted with sexual minority students suggests that positive instructor relations and LGB friends can promote students' academic and social integration, but they do not protect students from the negative effects of a hostile campus climate (Woodford & Kulick, 2015). Likewise, participating in LGBTQ-inclusive courses and connecting with LGBTQ and allied faculty can lead LGBTQ students to feel more included on campus (Linley et al., under review). Engaging in other formal and informal social environments may shape LGBTQ students' feelings of inclusion. For example, fraternities can be powerful places of support, but their acceptance and treatment of LGBTQ people are crucial (Anderson, 2008).

Summary. Although we have tried to provide a comprehensive list of factors that shape institutional context and student experiences, the breadth and diversity of postsecondary institutions mean there are undoubtedly other aspects to be considered. The factors we list, however, are crucial to any examination of LGBTQ student experiences. They are shaped by what students bring to college, and they in turn shape student outcomes.

Outcomes

In our model, student outcomes apply across four categories: academic, mental health, social/community, and LGBTQ identity and expression. All the outcomes are interconnected, represented in our model through two-directional arrows.

Academic. We divide academic outcomes into two areas: persistence and knowledge or competencies. As we noted earlier, academic inputs affect academic outcomes, which are also influenced substantially by the level of support or challenge students receive (Sanford, 1966) from faculty, peers, and others in the college environment (Pascarella & Terenzini, 2005; Renn et al., 2014; Woodford & Kulick, 2015). Terenzini and Reason (2010) argued that *persistence*, defined as continued enrollment toward the degree (or other academic goal), can be considered an academic outcome and is influenced by input characteristics and the quality of interactions students have with academic content, faculty, and peers. They further argued that the quality of learning—the change in net knowledge during college—has similar influences. Pascarella and Terenzini's (2005) synthesis of the effects of college on students provides abundant evidence that increased knowledge and intellectual competencies are the result of engagement in the academic and cocurricular environment in college.

Mental health. Whether LGBTQ students find support for their identities in their college environment can influence their psychological well-being (Meyer, 2003), as can precollege inputs, although resilience may increase during college. If students experience college as a place where heterosexist behavior and attitudes are tolerated and expressed regularly, then their well-being may be at risk (Silverschanz et al., 2008; Woodford, Han, et al., 2014; Woodford, Kulick, & Atteberry, 2014; Woodford, Kulick, Sinco, et al., 2014). Of course, mental health is deeply connected with a number of other factors. For example, students' perceptions that they have been supported and appropriately challenged academically may influence their psychological well-being and postgraduation intellectual confidence (Woodford & Kulick, 2015).

Social/community. LGBTQ students' experiences of inclusion or exclusion on campus—including engagement in LGBTQ groups—may shape their sense of connection to the broader LGBTQ community. Students who are exposed to course material about LGBTQ history and contemporary issues may leave college feeling connected to community-based LGBTQ groups (Dessel, Woodford, & Warren, 2011). In contrast, those who experienced hostility and isolation—for example, students who were closeted and not involved in LGBTQ groups—may depart college without ties to the broader LGBTQ community. Of course, many factors, such as personality and the availability of LGBTQ resources on campus, are influential in shaping these outcomes.

LGBTQ identity and expression. The four LGBTQ identity and expression inputs carry through as outcomes. How students experience their identity before and during college is likely to influence their LGBTQ identity after college. We propose that LGBTQ students' level of resilience before and during college also shapes their expression of LGBTQ identity after college. For example, a student who encountered challenges to LGBTQ identity might respond through self-advocacy or through internalizing the discrimination; the response in turn could influence LGBTQ identity after college. The combination of precollege identity and expression with institutional context and in-college experiences can lead to a range of postcollege LGBTQ identity expressions. This identity and its expression interact with the other outcomes (academic, mental health, social/community) within the larger socio-cultural-historical context.

Summary. The four outcomes in our model influence one other and are influenced by the inputs and campus environment. These interrelated elements continue to shape one another after a student leaves college.

In developing this model, we aim to further the inclusion, success, and well-being of LGBTQ college students by presenting a framework to inform future studies examining outcomes among LGBTQ students. Because of the focus on outcomes, the model does not seek to understand the nature of anti-LGBTQ attitudes and behaviors on campuses, although these are critical aspects of campus climate. We encourage LGBTQ campus climate researchers to undertake studies addressing these topics to comprehensively understand heterosexism and genderism on campuses. Given the often covert nature of contemporary prejudices (Nadal et al., 2010), we suggest these studies should investigate the types of heterosexism and genderism that are less blatantly hostile toward LGBTQ people than fear- and avoidance-based attitudes formerly more prevalent (Morrison et al., 2009; Walls, 2008). Studies on the perpetuation of anti-LGBTQ behaviors on campus should include a range of overt and covert behaviors. We also suggest that these studies should address positive behaviors of allies toward LGBTQ people, including supporting LGBTQ peers, interrupting instances of LGBTQ discrimination, and advocating for LGBTQ inclusion. Where feasible, these studies should engage students, staff, and faculty.

Conclusion

Many universities throughout the country are committed to promoting safe spaces for LGBTQ students and supporting their development and health. While many studies examine campus climate for LGBTQ students, significant gaps remain regarding student outcomes and resilience. Policies and programs aiming to foster LGBTQ students' inclusion, academic development and success, and well-being must be informed by research that addresses these and other limitations. These studies must be grounded in relevant social science theories. To advance the field and address many of the shortfalls in the extant literature, we drew on theories of student development and engagement, campus climate, and minority stress to propose a multidimensional conceptual model to guide future research examining academic, mental health, social/community, and identity outcomes among LGBTQ college students. We encourage researchers to adopt this model or relevant aspects of it to develop knowledge that furthers LGBTQ student inclusion, academic success, and well-being. Although this model has not been empirically tested, it promises to advance LGBTQ campus climate research and provide a foundation for effective policies and programs. We look forward to refining and strengthening it in the future.

Notes

1. Although they are often used (incorrectly) interchangeably, it is important to distinguish sex (male, female, intersex) from gender (man, woman, transgender; see Bilodeau & Renn, 2005). Sex discrimination became a focus in higher education in the 1960s and more sharply in the early 1970s with the passage of Title IX and implementation of Affirmative Action policies.
2. Heterosexist harassment is insensitive verbal and symbolic nonassaultive behaviors that convey animosity toward sexual minorities (Silverschanz et al., 2008); incivility is low-intensity, ambiguous disrespectful behavior.
3. An earlier version of this model was presented to the National Study of LGBTQ Student Success (www.lgbtqsuccess.net) research team. We thank our colleagues for their valuable feedback.

References

Andersen, R., & Fetner, T. (2008). Cohort differences in tolerance of homosexuality attitudinal change in Canada and the United States, 1981–2000. *Public Opinion Quarterly, 72*, 311–330.

Anderson, E. (2008). Inclusive masculinity in a fraternal setting. *Men and Masculinities, 10*(5), 604–620.

Astin, A., W. (1977). *Four critical years*. San Francisco, CA: Jossey-Bass.

Beeman, B., & Eliason, M. (1996). *Queer studies*. New York, NY: University Press.

Beemyn, B., Curtis, B., Davis, M., & Tubbs, N. J. (2005). Transgender issues on college campuses. In R. Sanlo (Ed.), *Gender identity and sexual orientation: Research, policy, and personal perspectives* (pp. 49–60). San Francisco, CA: Jossey-Bass.

Beemyn, B. G., & Rankin, S. (2011). *The lives of transgender people*. New York, NY: Columbia University Press.

Bilodeau, B. L. (2009). *Genderism: Transgender students, binary systems, and higher education*. Saarbrücken, Germany: VDM Verlag.

Bilodeau, B. L., & Renn, K. A. (2005). Analysis of LGBT identity development models and implications for practice. *New Directions for Student Services, 111*, 25–40.

Blount, J. M. (2005). *Fit to teach: Same-sex desire, gender, and school work in the twentieth century.* Albany, NY: SUNY Press.

Bronfenbrenner, U. (1994). Ecological models of human development. In T. Husen & T. N. Postlethwaite (Eds.), *International encyclopedia of education* (2nd ed., Vol. 3, pp. 1643–1647). Oxford, England: Pergamon Press.

Brown, R. D., Clarke, B., Gortmaker, V., & Robinson-Keilig, R. (2004). Assessing the campus climate for gay, lesbian, bisexual, and transgender (GLBT) students using a multiple perspectives approach. *Journal of College Student Development, 45*(1), 8–26.

Chonody, J., Woodford, M. R., Brennan, D. J., Newman, B., & Wang, D. (2014). Attitudes toward gay men and lesbian women among heterosexual social work faculty. *Journal of Social Work Education, 50,* 136–152.

Cole, E. R. (2009). Intersectionality and research in psychology. *American Psychologist, 64*(3), 170–180.

Collins, P. H. (2000). *Black feminist thought: Knowledge, consciousness, and the politics of empowerment.* New York, NY: Routledge.

Currah, P., & Minter, S. (2000). *Transgender equality: A handbook for activists and policymakers.* Washington, DC: National Center for Lesbian Rights and the Policy Institute of the National Gay and Lesbian Task Force.

D'Augelli, A. R., Pilkington, N. W., & Hershberger, S. L. (2002). Incidence and mental health impact of sexual orientation victimization of lesbian, gay, and bisexual youths in high school. *School Psychology Quarterly, 17*(2), 148–167.

D'Emilio, J. (1992). *Making trouble: Essays on gay history, politics, and the university.* New York, NY: Routledge.

Dessel, A. B., Woodford, M. R., & Warren, N. (2011). Intergroup dialogue courses on sexual orientation: Lesbian, gay, and bisexual student experiences and outcomes. *Journal of Homosexuality, 58,* 1132–1150.

Dilley, P. (2002). *Queer man on campus: A history of non-heterosexual college men, 1945–2000.* New York, NY: Routledge-Falmer.

Draughn, T., Elkins, B., & Roy, R. (2002). Allies in the struggle: Eradicating homophobia and heterosexism on campus. *Journal of Lesbian Studies, 6*(3/4), 9–20.

Duggan, L. (2002). The new homonormativity: The sexual politics of neoliberalism. In R. Castronovo & D. D. Nelson (Eds.), *Materializing democracy: Toward a revitalized cultural politics* (pp. 175–194). Chapel Hill, NC: Duke University Press.

Eichstedt, J. L. (1996). Heterosexism and gay/lesbian bisexual experiences: Teaching strategies and exercises. *Teaching Sociology, 24,* 384–388.

Franklin, K. (2000). Antigay behaviors among young adults: Prevalence, patterns, and motivators in a noncriminal population. *Journal of Interpersonal Violence, 15,* 339–362.

Garvey, J. C., & Rankin, S. R. (2015). The influence of campus experiences on the level of outness among trans-spectrum and queer-spectrum students. *Journal of Homosexuality, 62,* 374–393.

Gomez, J. P., & Trierweiler, S. J. (1999). Exploring cross-group discrimination: Measuring the dimensions of inferiorization. *Journal of Applied Social Psychology, 29,* 1900–1926.

Goode-Cross, D. T., & Tager, D. (2011). Negotiating multiple identities: How African-American gay and bisexual men persist at a predominantly White institution. *Journal of Homosexuality, 58*, 1235–1254.

Gurin, P., Dey, E. L., Hurtado, S., & Gurin, G. (2002). Diversity and higher education: Theory and impact on educational outcomes. *Harvard Educational Review, 72*, 330–367.

Hatzenbuehler, M. L. (2011). The social environment and suicide attempts in lesbian, gay, and bisexual youth. *Pediatrics, 127*, 896–903.

Herek, G. M. (1988). Heterosexuals' attitudes toward lesbians and gay men: Correlates and gender differences. *Journal of Sex Research, 25*, 451–477.

Herek, G. M. (1993). Documenting prejudice against lesbians and gay men on campus: The Yale Sexual Orientation Survey. *Journal of Homosexuality, 25*, 15–30.

Holland, L., Matthews, T. L., & Schott, M. R. (2013). "That's so gay!": Exploring college students' attitudes toward the LGBT population. *Journal of Homosexuality, 60*, 575–595.

Hu, S., & Kuh, G. D. (2003). Diversity experiences and college student learning and personal development. *Journal of College Student Development, 44*, 320–334.

Human Rights Campaign. (2014). *Workplace discrimination laws and policies.* Retrieved from www.hrc.org/resources/entry/Workplace-Discrimination-Policies-Laws-and-Legislation

Hurtado, S. (2001). Linking diversity and educational purpose: How diversity affects the classroom environment and student development. In G. E. Orfield, (Ed.), *Diversity challenged: Evidence on the impact of affirmative action* (pp. 187–203). Cambridge, MA: Harvard Education Publishing Group.

Hurtado, S., Alvarez, C., Guillermo-Wann, C., Cuellar, M., & Arellano, L. (2012). A model for diverse learning environments. In J. C. Smart & M. B. Paulsen (Eds.), *Higher education: Handbook of theory and research* (pp. 41–122). New York, NY: Springer.

Hurtado, S., Carter, D. F., & Kardia, D. (1998). The climate for diversity: Key issues for institutional self-study. *New Directions for Institutional Research, 98*, 53–63.

Hurtado, S., Griffin, K. A., Arellano, L., & Cuellar, M (2008). Assessing the value of climate assessments: Progress and future directions. *Journal of Diversity in Higher Education, 1*(4), 204–221.

Hurtado, S., & Ponjuan, L. (2005). Latino educational outcomes and the campus climate. *Journal of Hispanic Higher Education, 4*(3), 235–251.

Jaschik, S. (2014, July 25). The right to expel. *Inside Higher Ed.* Retrieved from www.insidehighered.com/news/2014/07/25/2-christian-colleges-win-title-ix-exemptions-give-them-right-expel-transgender

Jewell, L. M., & Morrison, M. A. (2010). "But there's a million jokes about everybody . . .": Prevalence of, and reasons for, directing negative behaviors toward gay men on a Canadian university campus. *Journal of Interpersonal Violence, 25*, 2094–2112.

King, A. R. (2011). Environmental influences on the development of female college students who identify as multiracial/biracial-bisexual/pansexual. *Journal of College Student Development, 52*, 440–455.

Kosciw, J. G., Greytak, E. A., Palmer, N. A., & Boesen, M. J. (2014). *The 2013 national school climate survey: The experiences of lesbian, gay, bisexual and transgender youth in our nation's schools*. New York, NY: Gay, Lesbian & Straight Education Network.

Linley, J L., Nguyen, D. J., Brazelton, G. B., Becker, B. K., Renn, K. A., & Woodford, M. R. (2016). *National study of LGBTQ student success, 2013*. Manuscript under review.

Marine, S. (2011). Stonewall's legacy: Bisexual, gay, lesbian, and transgender students in higher education. *ASHE Higher Education Report, 37*(4).

Marzullo, M. A., & Libman, A. J. (2009). *Research overview: Hate crimes and violence against lesbian, gay, bisexual and transgendered people*. Retrieved from: www.hrc.org/files/assets/resources/Hatecrimesandviolenceagainstlgbtpeople_2009.pdf

Mayer, K. H., Garofalo, R., & Makadon, H. J. (2014). Promoting the successful development of sexual and gender minority youths. *American Journal of Public Health, 104*, 976–981.

Meyer, I. H. (2003). Prejudice, social stress, and mental health in lesbian, gay, and bisexual populations. *Psychological Bulletin, 129*, 674–697.

Meyer, I. H., Ouellette, S. C., Haile, R., & McFarlane, T. A. (2011). "We'd be free": Narratives of life without homophobia, racism, or sexism. *Sexuality Research and Social Policy, 8*(3), 204–214.

Milem, J. F., Chang, M. J., & Antonio, A. L. (2005). *Making diversity work on campus: A research-based perspective*. Washington, DC: Association of American Colleges and Universities.

Moradi, B., Mohr, J. J., Worthington, R. L., & Fassinger, R. E. (2009). Counseling psychology research on sexual (orientation) minority issues: Conceptual and methodological challenges and opportunities. *Journal of Counseling Psychology, 56*, 5–22.

Morrison, M. A., Morrison, T. G., & Franklin, R. (2009). Modern and old-fashioned homonegativity among samples of Canadian and American university students. *Journal of Cross-Cultural Psychology, 40*, 523–542.

Nadal, K. L., Rivera, D. P., & Corpus, J. H. (2010). Sexual orientation and transgender microaggressions. In D. W. Sue (Ed.), *Microaggressions and marginality: Manifestation, dynamics, and impact* (pp. 217–240). Hoboken, NJ: Wiley.

Nguyen, D., Gonyo, C., Brazelton, G. B., Long, L. D., Secrist, S., Renn, K. A., & Woodford, M. R. (2014, November). *Peers as sources of support to LGBTQ students*. Paper presented at the annual meeting of the Association for the Study of Higher Education, Washington, DC.

O'Loughlin, M. (2103, June 18). Being gay at a Catholic University. *Religion & Politics: Fit for Polite Company*. Retrieved from religionandpolitics.org/2013/06/18/being-gay-at-a-catholic-university

Oswald, R. F., & Holman, E. G. (2013). *Rainbow Illinois: How downstate LGBT communities have changed (2000–2011)*. Urbana: Department of Human and Community Development, University of Illinois at Urbana-Champaign.

Oswalt, S. B., & Wyatt, T. J. (2011). Sexual orientation and differences in mental health, stress, and academic performance in a national sample of US college students. *Journal of Homosexuality, 58*, 1255–1280.

Pascarella, E. T., & Terenzini, P. T. (2005). *How college affects students* (Vol. 2). San Francisco, CA: Jossey-Bass.

Pitcher, E. N., Camacho, T., Renn, K. A., & Woodford, M. R. (2014, November). *Affirming policies, programs, and supportive services: Understanding organizational support for LGBTQ college student success.* Paper presented at the annual meeting of the Association for the Study of Higher Education, Washington, DC.

Rankin, S. R. (2003). *Campus climate for gay, lesbian, bisexual and transgender people: A national perspective.* Retrieved from the Policy Institute of the National Gay and Lesbian Task Force Web site: www.thetaskforce.org/downloads/reports/reports/CampusClimate.pdf

Rankin, S. R. (2005). Campus climates for sexual minorities. *New Directions for Student Services, 111*, 17–23.

Rankin, S. R. (2006). LGBTQA students on campus: Is higher education making the grade? *Journal of Gay and Lesbian Issues in Education, 3*(2/3), 111–117.

Rankin, S., Weber, G., Blumenfeld, W., & Frazer, S. (2010). *2010 state of higher education for lesbian, gay, bisexual & transgender people.* Charlotte, NC: Campus Pride.

Reed, E., Prado, G., Matsumoto, A., & Amaro, H. (2010). Alcohol and drug use and related consequences among gay, lesbian, and bisexual college students: Role of experiencing violence, feeling safe on campus, and perceived stress. *Addictive Behaviors, 35*(2), 168–174.

Renn, K. A. (2007). LGBT student leaders and queer activists: Identities of lesbian, gay, bisexual, transgender, and queer-identified college student leaders and activists. *Journal of College Student Development, 48*(3), 311–330.

Renn, K. A. (2010). LGBT and queer research in higher education: The state and status of the field. *Educational Researcher, 39*(2), 132–141.

Renn, K. A., Woodford, M., R., Nicolazzo, Z., & Brazelton, G. B. (2014, April). *The role of personal resilience and environmental buffers in LGBTQ college student success.* Paper presented at the annual meeting of the American Educational Research Association, Philadelphia, PA.

Russell, S. T. (2005). Beyond risk: Resilience in the lives of sexual minority youth. *Journal of Gay & Lesbian Issues in Education, 2*(3), 5–18.

Saad, L. (2012, May 14). *U.S. acceptance of gay/lesbian relations in the new normal.* Retrieved from www.gallup.com/poll/154634/acceptance-gay-lesbian-relations-new-normal.aspx

Sanford, N. (1966). *Self and society.* New York, NY: Atherton Press.

Sanlo, R. (2004). Lesbian, gay, and bisexual college students: Risk, resiliency, and retention. *Journal of College Students Retention, 61*(1), 97–110.

Silverschanz, P., Cortina, L. M., Konik, J., & Magley, V. J. (2008). Slurs, snubs, and queer jokes: Incidence and impact of heterosexist harassment in academia. *Sex Roles, 58*(3/4), 179–191.

Terenzini, P. T., & Reason, R. D. (2010, June). *Toward a more comprehensive understanding of college effects on student learning.* Paper presented at the 23rd Annual Conference of the Consortium of Higher Education Researchers, Oslo, Norway.

Tinto, V. (1988). Stages of student departure: Reflections on the longitudinal character of student living. *Journal of Higher Education, 59*, 438–455.

Tinto, V. (1993). *Leaving college: Rethinking the causes and cures of student attrition* (2nd ed.). Chicago, IL: University of Chicago Press.

Tinto, V. (2005). Foreword. In A. Seidman (Ed.), *College student retention: Formula for student success* (pp. ix–x). Westport, CT: Praeger.

Waldo, C., Hesson-McInnis, M., & D'Augelli, A. (1998). Antecedents and consequences of victimization of lesbian, gay and bisexual young people: A structural model comparing rural university and urban samples. *American Journal of Community Psychology, 26*(2), 307–334.

Walls, N. E. (2008). Toward a multidimensional understanding of heterosexism: The changing nature of prejudice. *Journal of Homosexuality, 55*, 20–70.

Woodford, M., & Bella, L. (2003). Are we ready to take a stand? Education about heterosexism—fostering anti-oppressive practice. In W. Shera (Ed.), *Emerging perspectives on anti-oppressive practice* (pp. 413–430). Toronto, ON: Canadian Scholars' Press.

Woodford, M. R., Brennan, D. J., Gutiérrez, L., & Luke, K. P. (2013). Factors predicting attitudes toward LGBT people among graduate social work teaching faculty in the United States. *Journal of Social Service Research, 39*(1), 50–62.

Woodford, M. R., Chonody, J., Kulick, A., Brennan, D. J., & Renn, K. A. (in press). Assessing sexual orientation microaggressions on college campuses: An instrument development and validation study. *Journal of Homosexuality*.

Woodford, M. R., Han, Y., Craig, S., Lim, C., & Matney, M. M. (2014). Discrimination and mental health among sexual minority college students: The type and form of discrimination does matter. *Journal of Gay & Lesbian Mental Health, 18*(2), 142–163.

Woodford, M. R., Howell, M. L., Kulick, A., & Silverschanz, P. (2013). Heterosexual male undergraduates and the perpetuation of sexual orientation microaggressions on campus: "That's so gay!" *Journal of Interpersonal Violence, 28*(2), 416-435.

Woodford, M. R., Howell, M. L., Silverschanz, P., & Yu, L. (2012). "That's so gay!" Examining the covariates of hearing this expression among gay, lesbian, and bisexual college students. *Journal of American College Health, 60*, 429–434.

Woodford, M. R., Kolb, C. L., Durocher-Radeka, G., & Javier, G. (2014). Lesbian, gay, bisexual, and transgender ally training programs on campus: Current variations and future directions. *Journal of College Student Development, 55*, 317–322.

Woodford, M. R., Krentzman, A., & Gattis, M. (2012). Alcohol and drug use among sexual minority college students and their heterosexual counterparts: The effects of experiencing and witnessing incivility and hostility on campus. *Substance Abuse and Rehabilitation, 3*(1), 11–23.

Woodford, M. R., & Kulick, A. (2015). Academic and social integration on campus among sexual minority students: The impacts of psychological and experienced campus climate. *American Journal of Community Psychology, 55*(1/2), 13–24.

Woodford, M. R., Kulick, A., & Atteberry, B. (2015). Protective factors, campus climate, and health outcomes among sexual minority college students. *Journal of Diversity in Higher Education, 8*(2), 73–87.

Woodford, M. R., Kulick, A., Sinco, B., & Hong, J. (2014). Contemporary heterosexism on campus and psychological distress among LGBQ students: The mediating role of self-acceptance. *American Journal of Orthopsychiatry, 84*, 519–529.

Woodford, M. R., Silverschanz, P., Swank, E., Scherrer, K. S., & Raiz, L. (2012). Predictors of heterosexual college students' attitudes toward LGBT people. *Journal of LGBT Youth, 9*, 297–320.

Yost, M. R., & Gilmore, S. (2011). Assessing LGBTQ campus climate and creating change. *Journal of Homosexuality, 58*, 1330–1354.

6

AN INTERVIEW WITH MICHAEL R. WOODFORD

Bringing Invisible Communities to Light:
Disciplinary Norms, Collaboration,
and the Quest for Legitimacy

Timothy Hickey-LeClair

Historically, and with a renewed vigor, academic literature paints the experiences of faculty from socially marginalized backgrounds in an overwhelmingly negative light. Such scholars not only are grossly underrepresented in academia but also tend to lack access to insider information about how to navigate the academy. They face increased barriers to tenure and promotion, feel increased pressure to mentor underrepresented students, and experience tokenism and role stereotyping (Jacobson, 2012; Smith, 1989; Sood, Prasad, Schroeder, & Varkey, 2011). With these realities in mind, I interviewed Michael Woodford, an openly gay professor and scholar committed to social justice and to researching the experiences of lesbian, gay, bisexual, transgender, and queer/questioning (LGBTQ) students in higher education, anticipating tales of his struggles in the academy. But he depicts his experience in academia positively and enthusiastically, noting that his research interests are generally well received. I am ashamed to admit that I fell prey to the influences of stereotypes, projecting my preconceptions onto his experience, expecting narratives of inclusion to be an anomaly, although perhaps this is the case.

Almost immediately in the interview Michael reminds me of the loss of power implicit in allowing outsiders to frame the discourse around individual or collective experience.

> I tell people the students I work with are not just college students. I work with LGBTQ students who have *survived* high school. Some do drop out,

but others actively resist this [homophobia and transphobia in schools]. Some of them resist this by dedicating themselves to academic success; some of them become activists.

In the same sense, faculty from marginalized backgrounds have survived years of education in a system that washes from its pages all but the faintest traces of those who look like, act like, or identify with them. They have lived the tragedies and triumphs of careers in institutions not designed for them, at times invisible, where they have been underestimated or dismissed or even forgotten (Lasala, Jenkins, Wheeler, & Fredriksen-Goldsen, 2008; Sears, 2002; Turner & Myers, 2000). Those with hidden LGBTQ identities must function in some capacity as chameleons, negotiating social spaces with an ear for normative expectations and only selectively revealing themselves in an effort to safeguard their emotional, mental, or even physical well-being (Berger, 1990; Faust, 2007; Knoble & Linville, 2012; Vaughan & Waehler, 2010). Those who conceal repress a fundamental piece of themselves, while those who choose to reveal risk exposing themselves to the capricious, painful touch of prejudice.

From personal experience, I know that those who choose the former path may avoid momentary harm or discomfort, but each act of repression feels like a self-betrayal that chips away at esteem, confidence, and self-concept, creating tremors that rumble deep in the psyche. But the shift from the language of victimization to that of survival inherent in Michael's opening remarks is profound. The victim label allows forces outside an individual's control to define his or her experience, while the survivor label still acknowledges the individual's challenges but emphasizes resiliency and achievement in the face of adversity. It is not my intention to minimize the challenges faced by thousands of faculty members throughout the country; for many, subtle and overt discrimination is a regular occurrence (Rankin, Weber, Blumenfeld, & Frazer, 2010). Rather, my intention is to challenge the dominant discourse, to refuse to allow adversity to eclipse the successes and strengths of those who survive.

Michael displays a charismatic resilience and exuberance, speaking comfortably about his identity and his research and their relationship with his academic and professional environments. Operating in social work, a discipline with a strong history of social activism and acknowledgment of alternative perspectives, he thrives. He describes social workers as motivated by a commitment not only to the well-being of their clients but also to a deeper sense of social justice. Social workers navigate the system to yield the best possible outcomes for the vulnerable in society while attempting to reform the system itself. Although his research on LGBTQ communities clearly breaks new ground in the discipline, it fits in this social justice framework by informing efforts to promote the well-being of LGBTQ people and foster social inclusion and empowerment. His work addresses an at-risk, largely invisible population, one that is far too often excluded from the mainstream discourse about diversity.

Michael also acknowledges social work's capacity for critical introspection and its recognition of the value of individual experience. After spending much of his life and his entire career in Canada, he faced a challenging transition in his move to the United States. The sociopolitical context of LGBTQ rights in Michigan proved jarring for him, wearing on his well-being but also driving his commitment to address the marginalization of LGBTQ populations. He notes his success in incorporating this personal experience into the classroom.

> Coming from a place that had same-sex marriage to a place where not only did we not have it, but I actually had officials telling me that I am not entitled—my community is not entitled [to domestic partner health benefits that were being taken away because of the state constitutional prohibition against same-sex marriage]. It really was a feeling of being a second-class citizen. . . . I was teaching a class around the same time as this Michigan ruling happened, and I was teaching about minority stress theory and the significance of policy in people's lives, and I stepped into the personal and talked about this. And people could see and hear my personal struggle in talking about this, and thus how important it was to consider the sociopolitical environment also from a personal well-being standpoint. I think they appreciated that.

This anecdote contrasts sharply with the experience of many others in academia, where true or empirical scholarly work often dismisses the phenomenological as irrelevant or even potentially detrimental (Lather, 2010). Research has been historically marked by an almost obsessive preoccupation with rationality that leaves little room for personal experience, let alone for experience outside society's dominant paradigms. Michael felt comfortable enough to bring his life into the classroom, and students welcomed the way it lent form and substance to the theoretical. As a gay man and current master's student, I find the legitimacy given to his research and pedagogy to be truly inspiring.

However, Michael assured me that other academics did not always embrace his work, as he described some resistance earlier in his academic career.

> When I submitted an early research proposal, the committee asked me why I was doing this—why I had selected such a privileged population [LGBTQ students at the University of Michigan]. . . . Students at a large

research university like Michigan are typically seen as very privileged. Once they get here, there's a tendency to think they're going to be fine. As I'm sure you're aware, that's not always the case.

He suggested that other scholars had constructed a rigid dichotomy of privilege and oppression and that fathoming a clash between the two proved difficult. Further, many members of the LGBTQ community are not immediately identifiable, reducing their visibility on campus and hence their importance in institutional priorities. Yet at the time, Michael noted significant limitations and gaps in the existing literature on LGBTQ students, with such work predominantly examining overt forms of interpersonal LGBTQ prejudice and largely overlooking subtler heterosexism, the often unintentional or unconscious—but nonetheless potent—behaviors such as the use of the phrase "That's so gay" to denote that something is undesirable or unmasculine (Nadal, Rivera, & Corpus, 2010; Woodford, Howell, Silverschanz, & Yu, 2012). The research examining more mundane or subtler forms of discrimination like microaggressions focused heavily on theory development, largely ignoring student outcomes (Buchanan, 2011; Pierce, Carew, Pierce-Gonzalez, & Wills, 1977; Platt & Lenzen, 2013; Sue, 2010).

How does one label a community as privileged when so little is known about it? Michael recognized a need for further research and exploration in an area that aligned closely with his interests in community participation and the health and social inclusion of LGBTQ people. And throughout our conversation, I observed three dominant strategies he employed to counter initial resistance and intimations of illegitimacy. One of the most salient remains his insistence on defining and articulating the practical implications of his research:

> In social work, much like in higher education, we have this confluence of the theoretical and the practical. . . . And maybe it's my background—my undergraduate and graduate degree had a practice focus—but it's not just about advancing theory. We need to focus on practical applications as well, on how the situation can be improved.[1]

While unequivocally advancing the theoretical dimensions of the field, his work also holds the potential to yield tangible benefits that advance social justice and equity. He emphasizes shifting from descriptive analysis of the status quo for LGBTQ students to the assessment of student outcomes to identify areas that need improvement and to inform institutional policy and other interventions.

At the same time, Michael advocates another strategy, coupling research proposals to related events of local or national significance. He observes, "One thing we need to keep in mind is that even when we consider diversity, LGBTQ students are often hidden populations." Since the way in which a proposal is framed determines—at least in part—its success, a researcher must bring such populations and their life issues into the light. By anchoring a proposal to a current event, such as a well-publicized incident of LGBTQ bullying still fresh in the collective consciousness, researchers can provide a brief glimpse into deep-seated or institutional patterns of discrimination, raising the plight of a peripheral group to a national platform. This strategy serves to solidify the importance and legitimacy of the scholarship while amplifying its perceived practical implications. To illustrate his point, he describes being affected deeply by the suicide of Tyler Clementi, a gay Rutgers first-year student, and drawing scholarly inspiration from the tragedy. He notes, "If we don't take these [events] into consideration, what are we doing? And more important, why are we doing it?" This strategy is not intended to be opportunistic or exploitive; rather, the goal is to highlight the relevance of underappreciated or marginalized research, lending it an urgent necessity. This emphasis on practicality is in itself a subtle gesture of defiance. It works to subvert a system characterized by abstract intellectualization, one often criticized for its detachment from society and subjects of inquiry.

The final strategy involves the establishment of cross-disciplinary linkages. Michael's work effectively fuses theoretical frameworks from social work with those from higher education studies, psychology, and other areas. He suggests that this disciplinary integration offers insights and privileges. Shifting between disciplines, he is able to explore subject matter rarely addressed in social work through critical paradigms rarely employed in higher education and allied disciplines.

Interdisciplinarity necessarily entails collaboration and mutual exchange. Research on the margins requires partners and allies, individuals willing to lend support on a variety of levels: administrative, academic, personal, emotional, or even spiritual. And by its very nature, social change necessitates action on a scale that transcends the individual. Michael noted excitedly, "I keep asking myself, why are we doing this work and how do we translate it into practice? I think one of the most effective ways is to develop partnerships." Partnerships provide access to and guidance from wide bodies of knowledge and experiences as well as sounding boards to test the plausibility and relevance of potential research projects. Michael does not limit these partnerships solely to academics; rather, he seeks to draw from practitioners' fonts of experience as well.

My partnerships with academics like Kristen Renn [of Michigan State] have been invaluable, but I gain so much by working with practitioners like Jackie Simpson [director of the University of Michigan Spectrum Center]. I was able to ask, "Does this make sense?" That's extremely valuable.

In my interview with Michael, I expected to hear of a different experience, one marked by heterosexism and attempts to conform with the dominant paradigms of the academy, but instead found inspiration and hope in his excitement and positivity. He strives to bring an invisible community into the light, approaching the subject through the lens of multiple disciplines and in a way that harmonizes theoretical and practical applications. His experience offers valuable insights that help legitimize and prioritize scholarship about communities on the periphery of society. Further, although I am embarrassed by my initial expectations, they reveal something powerful. Scholars focused on social justice often lament a lack of visibility and power in academic circles; however, my preconceptions provide a profound reminder that academic research also reverberates outside the confines of the ivory tower. The tone, content, and spirit of research matter in fact contribute to the processes used to construct social realities. The way we frame the experience of others deeply influences the light in which we see them. And for me, the possibility and responsibility inherent in such a revelation prove simultaneously electrifying and sobering.

Note

1. Michael notes that while his master's of social work focus was on social policy and administration, his professional experience involved clinical, policy, and administrative work.

References

Berger, R. M. (1990). Passing: Impact on the quality of same-sex couple relationships. *Social Work, 35,* 328–332.

Buchanan, N. T. (2011). Microaggressions in everyday life: Race, gender, and sexual orientation. *Psychology of Women Quarterly, 35,* 336–337.

Faust, J. (2007). Moving the academy closer to Utopia: What all professors can do to create LGBT-friendly campuses. *Teaching Philosophy, 30*(2), 201–215.

Jacobson, M. (2012). Breaking silence, building solutions: The role of social justice group work in the retention of faculty of color. *Social Work With Groups, 35*(3), 267–286.

Knoble, N. B., & Linville, D. (2012). Outness and relationship satisfaction in same-gender couples. *Journal of Marital and Family Therapy, 38*, 330–339.

Lasala, M. C., Jenkins, D. A., Wheeler, D. P., & Fredriksen-Goldsen, K. I. (2008). LGBT faculty, research, and researchers: Risks and rewards. *Journal of Gay & Lesbian Social Services, 20*, 253–267.

Lather, P. (2010). *Engaging science policy: From the side of the messy.* New York, NY: Peter Lang.

Nadal, K. L., Rivera, D. P., & Corpus, M. J. H. (2010). Sexual orientation and transgender microaggressions: Implications for mental health and counseling. In D. W. Sue (Ed.), *Microaggressions and marginality: Manifestation, dynamics, and impact* (pp. 217–240). Hoboken, NJ: Wiley.

Pierce, C. M., Carew, J. V., Pierce-Gonzalez, D., & Wills, D. (1977). An experiment in racism: TV commercials. *Education and Urban Society, 10*(1), 61–87.

Platt, L. F., & Lenzen, A. L. (2013). Sexual orientation microaggressions and the experience of sexual minorities. *Journal of Homosexuality, 60*, 1011–1034.

Rankin, S., Weber, G., Blumenfeld, W., & Frazer, S. (2010). *The state of higher education for lesbian, gay, bisexual & transgender people.* Charlotte, NC: Campus Pride.

Sears, J. T. (2002). The institutional climate for lesbian, gay and bisexual education faculty. *Journal of Homosexuality, 43*, 11–37.

Smith, D. G. (1989). *The challenge of diversity: involvement or alienation in the academy?* Washington, DC: School of Education and Human Development, George Washington University.

Sood, A., Prasad, K., Schroeder, D., & Varkey, P. (2011). Stress management and resilience training among department of medicine faculty: A pilot randomized clinical trial. *Journal of General Internal Medicine, 26*, 858–861.

Sue, D. W. (2010). Sexual orientation microaggressions and heterosexism. In D. W. Sue, *Microaggressions in everyday life: Race, gender, and sexual orientation* (pp. 184–206). Hoboken, NJ: Wiley.

Turner, C. S., & Myers, S. L. (2000). *Faculty of color in academe: Bittersweet success.* Boston, MA: Allyn & Bacon.

Vaughan, M. D., & Waehler, C. A. (2010). Coming out growth: Conceptualizing and measuring stress-related growth associated with coming out to others as a sexual minority. *Journal of Adult Development, 17*(2), 94–109.

Woodford, M. R., Howell, M. L., Silverschanz, P., & Yu, L. (2012). "That's so gay!": Examining the covariates of hearing this expression among gay, lesbian, and bisexual college students. *Journal of American College Health, 60*, 429–434.

7

RACIALLY AND SOCIOECONOMICALLY DIVERSE STUDENTS' PATHWAYS TO COLLEGE

An Exploration of Latin@ Students

Angela M. Locks, Dawn Person, Michelle Cuellar, Jeanette Maduena, and Melba Schneider Castro

Important policy conversations are occurring at federal, state, and local levels about how to promote college access, college attendance, and student learning outcomes in postsecondary environments. In a dynamic sociopolitical environment that emphasizes accountability, understanding how students get to college and what they learn in college is a key task for higher education scholars, practitioners, and leaders. Access to resources and college choice is affected by factors such as race, socioeconomic status (SES), and gender (Perez & McDonough, 2008). Other researchers have also found parental involvement in students' aspirations of attending college and actually enrolling is important (Hossler, Braxton, & Coopersmith, 1989; Hossler, Schmit, & Vesper, 1999; Perna, 2000). This chapter presents a praxis-based collaborative program evaluation model that examines these issues, focusing on the work of the Center for Research on Educational Access and Leadership (C-REAL) and its partners' and affiliates' research on a Gaining Early Awareness and Readiness for Undergraduate Programs (GEAR UP) by highlighting the results from two cross-sectional studies. C-REAL and GEAR UP are described later.

Our goal is to add to the discourse on college access programs, including how best to evaluate such programs and create a space where scholars, practitioners, leaders, college access administrators, and various student affairs professionals may engage in thoughtful conversations about the challenges and opportunities facing the higher education community throughout the United States. The conversations we hope to encourage with this chapter hold promise for adding new layers of understanding and complexity that may be gained through theoretically grounded, rigorous, and longitudinal research, and assessment efforts that draw on multiple sources of data about programs designed to promote student access and success.

Seldom do precollege access programs use theory-based approach evaluation models. Despite the plethora of research and literature that exist supporting student success, persistence, and engagement presented throughout this chapter, this information is not often incorporated into research on such programs, whether framed as empirical research, program assessment, or program evaluation. Research using a theory-based approach is increasing in evaluation methods as a result of the rising need to understand how participants respond to programs (Weiss, 1997). In this chapter, we use Hossler, Braxton, and colleagues' (1989) "Understanding Student College Choice" in our broader research effort to frame the examination of the college-going process for a GEAR UP cohort. Through this effort, we are able to assess systematic change for creating a college-going culture in secondary educational settings and identify specific programmatic features that positively affect college-going behaviors and attitudes, and the provision of feedback for program improvement. Specifically, in this chapter we focus on two cross-sectional studies that are part of a 7-year longitudinal study designed to examine the college choice process at each of the stages in Hossler, Braxton, and colleagues.

We begin this chapter with a brief summary of our work, followed by a review of the literature on Latin@s' college-going predispositions, behaviors, and attitudes.[1] Next, we provide a summary of the partnerships that have made the work of evaluating a GEAR UP cohort possible before presenting the findings from two cross-sectional studies. The first study we present examined Latin@ middle school students' current and anticipated school behaviors and attitudes as predictors of the level of algebra they enroll in during the eighth grade, often a predictor of college success. The second study we feature in this chapter examines Latin@ high school students' current and anticipated school behaviors, attitudes, and college degree aspirations in the 10th grade.

Review of the Literature

McDonough's (1997) groundbreaking study on the college choice process for high school students revealed the wide variation of social capital available to adolescents who are dependent on schools', parental, and socioeconomic resources available to them. Access to resources and college choice are affected by factors such as race, SES, and gender (Perez & McDonough, 2008). For example, Perna (2000) conducted a study that found Latin@ students to be less likely to enroll in a 4-year university than White students when gender, costs, benefits, and financial resources were taken into account. However, Latin@ students were as likely as others to enroll in a 4-year institution after taking into account measures of social and cultural capital (Perna, 2000). Parental education, peer encouragement, and financial resources were among the variables that made up social and cultural capital in this specific study.

Additional researchers have also found the importance of parental involvement in students' aspirations of attending college and actually enrolling (Hossler, Braxton, et al., 1989; Hossler, Schmit, et al., 1999; Perna, 2000). In Latin@ families specifically, there is a trend of low levels of parental education (Castillo, Lopez-Arenas, & Saldivar, 2010). Furthermore, several studies have shown that parental and family support is one of the most important factors contributing to a Latin@ student's decision to attend college (Castillo et al., 2010).

Almost 9 out of 10 (89%) Latin@ young adults view a college education as important for success in life (Lopez, 2009). However, according to a national survey of Latin@s by the Pew Hispanic Center, only about half that number (48%) plan to get a college degree (Lopez, 2009). These statistics shed light on the incongruency between Latin@ students' view of the importance of higher education and their level of participation in postsecondary education. When compared to their counterparts, Latin@ students are falling behind not only in college enrollment but also in academic achievement as early as middle school. For example, based on focus groups with Mexican American middle school students Castillo and colleagues (2010) found that family, peers, school personnel, and student responsibility all influenced the participants' decision to attend college. This highlights the importance of understanding the behaviors, attitudes, and recourses available to Latin@ middle school students as they prepare for the transition to high school and develop college-going resources. To grasp what keeps Latin@ students from enrolling in college, we must understand Latin@ students' perceptions to create a college-going culture in the context of programs such as GEAR UP.

GEAR UP

GEAR UP was created as part of the 1998 Amendments to the Higher Education Act of 1965 to increase knowledge and preparation for higher education among low-income students and their families. GEAR UP targets high-poverty schools and provides educational services to their students as well as to parents and teachers. The program begins in seventh grade and runs through students' senior year in college. Intended to cover the whole life of a student, GEAR UP services include tutoring, mentoring, field trips to colleges, career awareness, college-readiness counseling, classes, meetings, parent education about access to higher education, curriculum reform, and teacher training. GEAR UP serves as a means of intervention to the current patterns of low academic achievement and college enrollment affecting Latin@ youth.

In combination with providing college preparation and parent education about higher education, GEAR UP is one example of how to implement a program designed to support low-income college student enrollment. However, in view of the lack of formal research exploring the programmatic effect GEAR UP services have on college enrollment, the research featured in this chapter aims to fill this gap. The cross-sectional studies we describe in this chapter take the first step in identifying factors that may predict student enrollment in more advanced algebra course work that leads to access to higher education as an option beyond high school and examine students' degree aspirations in their 10th grade year.

Evaluation Partners

Creating a strong partnership between the GEAR UP team, the participating school district, and the evaluation team has been essential in creating a fluid path for immediate programmatic feedback. C-REAL at California State University, Fullerton (CSUF), is a data-driven, solution-focused research center that strives to develop strategies in response to the complex challenges of educational access, equity, and achievement gap issues in the P–20 educational system. Additionally, C-REAL conducts program assessments and evaluations for a broad range of educational and community partners with the goals of assessing program effectiveness, making program improvements, and identifying promising practices. The educational partnerships department at CSUF oversees university, school, and community partnerships focused on enhancing access, college matriculation, and student success in higher education. This unit works in partnership with local schools and school districts to provide educational programs that help students attend college. Key initiatives include the Santa Ana Partnership (P–20 Collaborative), Santa Ana Adelante funded by the Lumina foundation, Anaheim Collaborative for Higher Education, Kids to College, and the Parent Institute for Quality Education. In addition, this unit oversees several federally funded TRIO programs, including the two GEAR UP programs featured in this chapter as well as Talent Search, Upward Bound, and the Ronald McNair Scholars Program.

The participating school district area includes 24 elementary schools, 8 middle schools, and 10 high school and serves about 20,000 elementary school students and nearly 40,000 middle and high school students.

Evaluation Model and Design

Our particular efforts on GEAR UP elevate the conversation about college access and success initiatives with strong theoretical foundations and careful attention to exploring notions of educational equity and justice by asking thoughtful questions about how one assesses such programs. Unlike some other program assessment and evaluation initiatives, our evaluation model discusses and employs rigorous methods to determine the effectiveness of interventions that range from college access programs to student learning outcomes in general education courses.

Specifically, C-REAL designed a holistic formative and summative program evaluation plan for the GEAR UP grant that includes longitudinal surveys, intervention surveys, student and parent longitudinal case studies, and a professional development survey that allow continual feedback and a reporting communication loop with project leaders. The model is constructed to answer questions of program effectiveness to modify program components in a timely manner if deemed necessary.

The evaluation team at C-REAL is led by Dawn Person. Although the primary investigators (PIs) of the GEAR UP evaluation featured in this chapter are Dawn Person and Angela M. Locks, experienced scholar practitioners, the day-to-day evaluation work is carried out in collaboration with graduate students, faculty, and student affairs professionals. The team that conducted the evaluation includes scholar practitioners, graduate students, and undergraduate students from California State University at Fullerton and Long Beach.

To achieve a more fluid evaluation process, C-REAL's program director worked closely with the GEAR UP director and the school district to routinely complete and record all required data. We worked in conjunction with the host school sites and the database center for student records (managed by CoBro Consulting), and the types of data collected were based on identified needs, anticipated outcomes, and measurable indicators. Triangulation of data from students, parents, and teachers provided an opportunity to complete analyses that assist us in understanding a variety of issues. Analyses of quantitative and qualitative data are used for project decision making, dissemination, and sustainability initiatives. Analyses and recommendations are customized in final reports based on requests from GEAR UP and school district partners. Reports capture a variety of information, including participant survey results, student performance, assessment of program impact, participant attendance at programs or events, and teacher survey results. This method of ongoing routine data collection and analysis is used to complete reports not only to the U.S. Department of Education but also to community stakeholders to systematically identify outcomes and to use these findings to strategically plan for the following program year.

GEAR UP Cohort Description

The U.S. Department of Education requires that entire cohorts be served; therefore, in any given year, all students in a grade year are considered part of the GEAR UP cohort (i.e., the original group of students in the program begins in seventh grade, and as they make their way to the 12th grade, any new students who join their cohort are added to the overall GEAR UP cohort). In 2009–2010, as part of ongoing program assessment efforts, all eighth graders at the two middle schools participating in the GEAR UP cohort were invited to complete the survey; 426 students responded to the survey with their parents' consent. These two middle schools served just over 1,000 eighth grade students, 70% of whom were eligible for free and reduced-price lunches. In 2011–2012, neither school was on track to meet the No Child Left Behind math proficiency by 2014, and only about 40% of students were meeting or exceeding school standards in math and English, which was below California state averages. In 2009–2010 the GEAR UP cohort arrived in 10th grade and was dispersed across three high schools. About 672 Mexican American/Chicano, Puerto Rican, or other Latin@ students and their parents consented to participate in this study.

A rich portrait of 426 middle school students enrolled in a 6-year college access program is provided through descriptive statistics, factor analyses, and the results of a multiple regression model. Results of an exploratory factor analysis offer conceptualizations of Latin@ students' attitudes toward college going and their behaviors in school settings, adapted from the University of California, Los Angeles Higher Education Research Institute's Cooperative Institutional Research Program's (CIRP) Your First College Year (YFCY; www.heri.ucla.edu). Factors include academic and community engagement, help-seeking orientation, and participation in structured activities. It is important to note that students' gender, age, academic and community engagement, contact with school counselors, and plans to take advanced placement exams are positive predictors of taking more advanced algebra course work in eighth grade. In addition, the usage of math tutoring and anticipation of the need for help in high school are negative predictors of algebra enrollment. Implications for college access programs and the use of a model to assess student needs prior to college enrollment are presented next. Factors that include attendance, pluralistic orientation, orientation toward helping others, and intellectual self-confidence were regressed on to degree aspirations. Implications for GEAR UP and other college access programs are presented as well as recommendations for secondary school counselors and postsecondary outreach professionals.

A Brief Discussion of the Theoretical Framework

Hossler, Braxton, and colleagues' (1989) "Understanding Student College Choice" was used to frame this study. According to their study the college choice process occurs in three stages for students weighing postsecondary educational options: predisposition, search, and choice. Hossler and Gallagher (1987) define the predisposition stage the *predisposition stage* as the earliest stage of development in the college choice process, where students answer the question of college attendance in a dichotomous manner: Do I attend college or not? Other stages are characterized by weighing options through exploring various institutional types and specific campuses (search) and making a decision about which specific institution to attend (choice).

Although the larger examination, a 6-year longitudinal study ending in 2014, used Hossler, Braxton, and colleagues' (1989) model to examine all three stages of the college choice process, exploratory studies featured in this chapter focused on the predisposition stage. Specifically, we sought to determine if survey items adapted from CIRP's YFCY survey would generate stable factors for eighth grade and 10th grade Latin@ middle school students; we wanted to understand which factors might predict middle school enrollment in more advanced algebra course work and which factors might predict degree aspirations in the 10th grade. In the following sections, we present the two cross-sectional studies followed by a discussion of their significance.

Study 1

Objective and Methods

The primary purpose of this cross-sectional study, "Adapting the CIRP to Understand Latin@ Middle School Students' College Going Behaviors, Attitudes, and Algebra Enrollment," was to complete descriptive statistics, exploratory factor analyses, and a regression model that examined Latin@ middle school students' current and anticipated school behaviors and attitudes. In addition, we explored which of these behaviors and attitudes were positive predictors of enrollment in more advanced algebra course work during the eighth grade, which is often a precursor to college success.

Instrument and Sample

In the spring of 2010, 426 GEAR UP students were administered a survey asking about their background characteristics, behaviors, and attitudes at the end of their eighth grade year. Specific items and scales included in these analyses are detailed in Tables 7.1 and 7.2. The sample for this study was drawn from Latin@ students who were part of the GEAR UP cohort during the 2009–10 academic year. All students were enrolled in one of two middle schools during their eighth grade year in the participating school district.

Analyses

Table 7.1 summarizes descriptive statistics for the sample, and a narrative is included in this section. Of these students in the sample, all identified as Mexican American/Chicano, Puerto Rican, or other Latin@. About 42.3% of participants were male and 57.7% of participants were female. Their ages ranged from 13 to 16 years, with 82.1% of students indicating they were 14 years of age. Nearly 68% of students indicated that their first language was not English.

TABLE 7.1
Description of Demographic and Descriptive Survey Items for Eighth Grade Algebra Outcomes

Variables	N	*Mean*	SD	*Scale*
Gender	426	1.52	.500	m=1, f=2
Age	424	14.11	.408	range
Is English your first language?	418	1.32	.465	1=no, 2=yes
Where do you live?	422	1.62	.595	1=private home, 2=apartment or room, 3=group home or foster family
Does your family own or rent?	419	1.33	.470	1=rent, 2=own
Have you had, or do you feel you will need, any special tutoring or extra help in English?	406	1.59	.721	1=no need, 2=will need, 3=have had

(Continues)

TABLE 7.1 *(Continued)*

Variables	N	Mean	SD	Scale
Have you had, or do you feel you will need, any special tutoring or extra help with math?	410	1.89	.739	1=no need, 2=will need, 3=have had
Have you had, or do you feel you will need, any special tutoring or extra help with reading?	404	1.33	.626	1=no need, 2=will need, 3=have had
Have you had, or do you feel you will need, any special tutoring or extra help with writing?	407	1.45	.633	1=no need, 2= will need, 3=have had
How many AP exams are you planning on taking?	391	1.96	.808	1=none, 2=one, 3=two or more
After high school, what is the highest academic degree that you want to earn?	420	3.85	1.15	1=none, 2=vocational certificate or associate, 3=bachelor's, 4=master's, 5=phd or edd, 6=other
How would you describe the racial makeup of the neighborhood where you grew up?	422	3.82	.814	1=completely White, 2=mostly white, 3=roughly half non-White, 4=mostly non-White, 5=completely non-White
How would you describe the racial makeup of your peer groups/friends at school?	419	3.92	.738	1=completely White, 2=mostly White, 3=roughly half non-White, 4=mostly non-White, 5=completely non-White
How would you describe the racial makeup of your peer groups/friends in the neighborhood?	420	4.12	.839	1=completely White, 2=mostly White, 3=roughly half non-White, 4=mostly non-White, 5=completely non-White
If you compared yourself to other people your age, how would you rate yourself on the ability to see the world like someone else does?	414	3.50	.969	1=lowest 10%, 2= below average, 3= average, 4=above average, 5=highest 10%

(Continues)

TABLE 7.1 *(Continued)*

Variables	N	*Mean*	SD	*Scale*
If you compared yourself to other people your age, how would you rate yourself on being open to others with different ideas/beliefs?	417	3.66	.955	1=lowest 10%, 2=below average, 3=average, 4=above average, 5=highest 10%
If you compared yourself to other people your age, how would you rate yourself on being open to someone else questioning what you believe?	417	3.43	1.059	1=lowest 10%, 2=below average, 3= average, 4= above average, 5=highest 10%
If you compared yourself to other people your age, how would you rate yourself on the ability to talk about problems in our society?	413	3.31	1.1335	1=lowest 10%, 2=below average, 3=average, 4=above average, 5=highest 10%
If you compared yourself to other people your age, how would you rate yourself on the ability to work with people who are different from you?	414	4.03	1.013	1=lowest 10%, 2=below average, 3=average, 4=above average, 5=highest 10%
Do you have any concern about paying for your college education?	423	2.36	.607	1=no, 2=maybe, 3=yes
How much total money do you think your parents/guardians earn a year?	385	2.16	.908	1=less than $10,000, 2= $10,000-30,000, 3=$31,000–$50,000, 4=more than $51,000
What is the highest level of school completed by your father?	420	3.55	1.94	1=elementary or less, 2=some high school, 3=high school graduate, 4=vocational, or some college, 5=college degree or some graduate degree, 6=other

(Continues)

TABLE 7.1 *(Continued)*

Variables	N	Mean	SD	Scale
What is the highest level of school completed by your mother?	422	3.46	1.88	1=elementary or less, 2=some high school, 3=high school graduate, 4=vocational, or some college, 5=college degree or some graduate degree, 6=other
Compared to other people your age, rate yourself in your academic ability.	418	3.44	.824	1=lowest 10%, 2=below average, 3=average, 4=above average, 5=highest 10%
Compared to other people your age, rate yourself in your drive to achieve.	420	3.50	1.02	1=lowest 10%, 2=below average, 3=average, 4=above average, 5=highest 10%
Compared to other people your age, rate yourself in your leadership ability.	420	3.39	1.02	1=lowest 10%, 2=below average, 3=average, 4=above average, 5=highest 10%
Compared to other people your age, rate yourself in your public speaking ability.	420	3.00	1.04	1=lowest 10%, 2=below average, 3=average, 4=above average, 5=highest 10%
Compared to other people your age, rate yourself in your self-confidence (learning).	424	3.54	.947	1=lowest 10%, 2=below average, 3= average, 4=above average, 5=highest 10%
Compared to other people your age, rate yourself in your writing ability.	420	3.29	.935	1=lowest 10%, 2=below average, 3=average, 4=above average, 5=highest 10%
In the past year have you broken school rules?	422	1.69	.686	1=not at all, 2=occasionally, 3=frequently
In the past year have you been late to class?	421	1.78	.698	1=not at all, 2=occasionally, 3=frequently
In the past year have you skipped school/class?	419	1.25	.537	1=not at all, 2=occasionally, 3=frequently

(Continues)

TABLE 7.1 *(Continued)*

Variables	N	Mean	SD	Scale
While in high school, what is the chance you will make at least a "B" average?	413	3.57	.609	1=not likely, 2=somewhat likely, 3=very likely, 4=extremely likely
While in high school, what is the chance you will participate in volunteer or community service work?	413	2.62	.959	1=not likely, 2=somewhat likely, 3=very likely, 4=extremely likely
While in high school, what is the chance you will seek personal counseling?	413	2.22	.892	1=not likely, 2=somewhat likely, 3=very likely, 4=extremely likely
While in high school, what is the chance you will communicate regularly with your teachers?	412	2.47	.849	1=not likely, 2=somewhat likely, 3=very likely, 4=extremely likely
While in high school, what is the chance you will communicate regularly with college access program staff?	411	2.63	.877	1=not likely, 2=somewhat likely, 3=very likely, 4=extremely likely
While in high school, what is the chance you will think about schoolwork outside of school?	411	2.89	.875	1=not likely, 2=somewhat likely, 3=very likely, 4=extremely likely
During this school year, how much time did you spend during a typical week socializing with friends?	417	4.20	2.00	1=<1 hr/wk, 2=1–2 hr/wk, 3=3–5 hr/wk, 4=6–10 hr/wk, 5=11–15 hr/wk, 6=16–20 hr/wk, 7=over 20 hr/wk
During this school year, how much time did you spend during a typical week volunteering?	417	1.52	1.07	1=<1 hr/wk, 2=1–2 hr/wk, 3=3–5 hr/wk, 4=6–10 hr/wk, 5=11–15 hr/wk, 6=16–20 hr/wk, 7=over 20 hr/wk

(Continues)

TABLE 7.1 *(Continued)*

Variables	N	*Mean*	SD	*Scale*
During this school year, how much time did you spend during a typical week in student clubs/groups?	413	1.57	1.18	1=<1 hr/wk, 2=1–2 hr/wk, 3=3–5 hr/wk, 4=6–10 hr/wk, 5=11–15 hr/wk, 6=16–20 hr/wk, 7=over 20 hr/wk
During this school year, how much time did you spend during a typical week watching TV?	414	3.25	1.79	1=<1 hr/wk, 2=1–2 hr/wk, 3=3–5 hr/wk, 4=6–10 hr/wk, 5=11–15 hr/wk, 6=16–20 hr/wk, 7=over 20 hr/wk
During this school year, how much time did you spend during a typical week on household/childcare duties?	410	2.50	1.68	1=<1 hr/wk, 2=1–2 hr/wk, 3=3–5 hr/wk, 4=6–10 hr/wk, 5=11–15 hr/wk, 6=16–20 hr/wk, 7=over 20 hr/wk
During this school year, how much time did you spend during a typical week playing video games?	415	2.84	1.84	1=<1 hr/wk, 2=1–2 hr/wk, 3=3–5 hr/wk, 4=6–10 hr/wk, 5=11–15 hr/wk, 6=16–20 hr/wk, 7=over 20 hr/wk
During this school year, how much time did you spend during a typical week on online social networks (MySpace, Facebook, etc.)?	415	2.97	1.94	1=<1 hr/wk, 2=1–2 hr/wk, 3=3–5 hr/wk, 4=6–10 hr/wk, 5=11–15 hr/wk, 6=16–20 hr/wk, 7=over 20 hr/wk
During this school year, how much time did you spend with a school counselor?	426	4.60	1.41	1=0 hours, 2 =.5 hours, 3=1 hour, 4=1+ hours to <2 hours, 5=2+ hours to <3 hours, 6=3+ hours to <4 hours, 7=4+ hours

Note. a. 1 = completely White, 5 = completely non-White; b. 1 = lowest 10%, 5 = highest 10%; c. 0 = not at all, 2 = frequently; d. 0 = not important, 3 = extremely important; e. 1=<1 hr/wk, 2 = 1 -2 hr/wk, 3 = 3 -5 hr/wk, 4 = 6 -10 hr/wk, 5= 11-15 hr/wk, 6 = 16 -20 hr/wk, 7 = over 20 hr/wk

Several survey questions asked about students' residence and family as a way to capture information about students' SES status and familial structures. About 50% of students surveyed resided in private homes, 44% in apartments or rooms, and 6% in foster care or group homes. About two thirds of students' families rented their homes, and the remaining one third owned their homes. Nearly all students (96.7%) lived with their parents.

Nearly two thirds of students reported that their parents earned $30,000 or less of annual income. Given the number of students belonging to families with limited financial resources, it was not surprising that more than 90% of students expressed some level of concern about paying for college. Nearly all students in the sample would be first-generation college students.

Exploratory factor analyses were completed on the 426 cases included in the sample. In the case of each factor displayed in Table 7.2, items were

TABLE 7.2
Means, Standard Deviations, Factor Loadings, and Reliabilities for Eighth Grade Algebra Outcomes

Factors	n	*Mean*	SD	*Loading*
Racial composition precollege environment α = .719[a]				
Racial makeup peers in neighborhood	414	4.12	.836	.970
Racial makeup neighborhood	414	3.82	.849	.612
Racial makeup peers at school	414	3.93	.735	.491
Pluralistic orientation α = .741[b]				
Open to someone else questioning what I believe	405	3.45	1.056	.719
Open to others with different ideas/beliefs	405	3.66	.948	.705
Ability to talk about problems in our society	405	3.33	1.127	.584
Ability to see world like someone else does	405	3.51	.959	.534
Ability to work with people who are different than me	405	4.02	1.019	.469
Attendance patterns α = .661[c]				
Came late to class	416	1.7788	.69707	.721
Broke school rules	416	1.6827	.68039	.656
Skipped school/class	416	1.2524	.53885	.507
Intellectual self-confidence α = .812[b]				
Rate your self-confidence (learning)	403	3.56	.938	.731

(Continues)

TABLE 7.2 *(Continued)*

Factors	n	Mean	SD	Loading
Rate your drive to achieve	403	3.52	1.006	.727
Rate your leadership ability	403	3.41	1.004	.662
Rate your academic ability	403	3.44	.822	.640
Rate your public speaking ability	403	3.02	1.033	.576
Rate your writing ability	403	3.31	.931	.575
Leisure activities α = .716 e				
Time spent playing video games	407	2.8550	1.84528	.660
Time spent online	407	2.9926	1.93807	.656
Time spent socializing	407	4.2285	2.01212	.600
Time spent watching TV	407	3.2531	1.79691	.572
Structured activities α = .594[e]				
Time spent volunteering	405	1.5259	1.08657	.663
Time spent in student clubs	405	1.5630	1.18952	.603
Time spent doing house duties	405	2.5062	1.68514	.520
Anticipated high school activities with adults α = .774[d]				
Teacher communication	408	2.4779	.84673	.718
Using counseling services	408	2.2157	.89636	.691
Volunteering	408	2.6299	.95490	.659
College access program communication	408	2.6348	.87917	.642
Academic and community engagement α = .638[d]				
Doing school work	407	2.8821	.86864	.776
Volunteering	407	2.6241	.95912	.549
Letter B grades	407	3.5725	.60704	.546

Note. a. 1 = completely White, 5 = completely non-White; b. 1 = lowest 10%, 5 = highest 10%; c. 0 = not at all, 2 = frequently; d. 0 = not important, 3 = extremely important; e. 1=<1 hr/wk, 2 = 1 -2 hr/wk, 3 = 3 -5 hr/wk, 4 = 6 -10 hr/wk, 5= 11-15 hr/wk, 6 = 16 -20 hr/wk, 7 = over 20 hr/wk

analyzed using the principal axis factor technique, and a mean substitution was used to replace missing data, which was no more than about 10% for most variables. Cronbach's alphas were calculated to determine reliability for each item displayed.

Factor Analyses Results

Several concepts were explored during the factor analyses. In the higher education literature, several studies discuss the educational benefits of diversity in postsecondary educational environments (Engberg, 2004, 2007; Gurin, Dey, Hurtado & Gurin, 2002). Moreover, students' precollege exposure to diversity has long-term consequences for their capacities to develop skills that facilitate their engagement in a twenty-first-century economy (Engberg, 2007). Thus, we explored the viability of using commonly used items to capture students' precollege racial environment with middle school students. Adequate or good reliabilities and factor loadings exist for the attendance patterns, helping others, intellectual self-confidence, and anticipating involvement in high school (see Table 7.2).

Multiple Regression Results

The dependent variable was the algebra course students were enrolled in during eighth grade in middle school (on a Likert scale of 1 through 4:1 = *remedial algebra*, 4 = *advanced algebra*). Students' gender, age, academic and community engagement, contact with school counselors, artd plans to take advanced placement exams were positive predictors of their taking more advanced algebra course work in eighth grade. Use of math tutoring and anticipating needing help in high school were negative predictors of algebra enrollment in advanced algebra courses.

Study 2

Objectives and Methods

The second cross-sectional study, "Understanding Latin@ High School Students' School Engagement, Academic Self-Perception, and Anticipated High School Extracurricular Engagement and Their Degree Aspirations," provides a rich portrait of 672 high school students. We use descriptive statistics and present results of an exploratory factor analyses and regression in the 10th grade year.

Instrument and Sample

In the spring of 2012, 672 GEAR UP students were administered a survey asking about their background characteristics, behaviors, and attitudes. Specific

TABLE 7.3
Predicting Algebra Course Aspirations for Eighth Graders

	B	SE B	β
Background Variables			
Gender	.136	.067	.092*
Age	-.266	.077	-.147***
Socioeconomic Status			
Current residence	-.016	.057	-.013
Rent or own	.038	.075	.024
Concern paying for college	-.020	.053	-.017
Family income	.034	.039	.040
Father education level	-.003	.023	-.099
Mother education level	-.026	.024	-.066
Language			
English first language	.056	.072	.035
Tutoring			
Tutoring in English	.016	.054	.015
Tutoring in reading	-.098	.060	-.081
Tutoring in writing	-.088	.062	-.074
Tutoring in math	-.130	.045	-.128**
Academic and Community Engagement			
Intellectual self-confidence	.076	.054	.072
Anticipated help-seeking high school behaviors	-.288	.104	-.281**
Leisure activities	.020	.023	.039
Structured activities	-.016	.036	-.020
Anticipated high school activities with adults	.183	.115	.174
Academic and community engagement	.240	.063	.217***

(Continues)

TABLE 7.3 *(Continued)*

	B	SE B	β
Counseling			
Middle school counselor contact hours	.054	.023	.102*
College-Going Knowledge and Attitudes			
Advanced placement exams	.283	.043	.296***
Degree aspirations	.003	.029	.005

Note. *p < .05, **p < .01, ***p < .001.

TABLE 7.4
Description of Demographic and Descriptive Survey Items Aspirations for 10th Grade

Variables	N	Mean	SD	Scale
Gender	672	1.49	.500	m=1, f=2
Where do you live?	668	1.65	.578	1=private home, 2=apartment or room, 3= group home or foster family
Does your family own or rent?	670	1.30	.459	1=rent, 2= own
How much do you think your parents/guardians earn a year?	641	2.16	.912	1=less than $10,000, 2=$10,000-$30,000, 3=$31,000-$50,000, 4=$51,000-$100,000, 5=more than $100,000
What is the highest level of school completed by your father?	651	3.42	1.887	1=elementary or less, 2=some high school, 3=high school graduate, 4= vocational, or some college, 5=college degree or some graduate degree, 6=other
What is the highest level of school completed by your mother?	656	3.26	1.830	1=elementary or less, 2=some high school, 3=high school graduate, 4=vocational, or some college, 5=college degree or some graduate degree, 6=other

(Continues)

TABLE 7.4 *(Continued)*

Variables	N	Mean	SD	Scale
Do you have any concern about paying for your college education?	669	1.51	.618	1=no, 2=maybe, 3=yes
Do you think that you could afford to attend a public 4-year college using financial aid or scholarships?	476	.29	.455	1=no, 2=yes
Has anyone from your school or GEAR UP ever spoken with you about the availability of financial aid?	670	.71	.452	1=no, 2=yes
Have you had, or do you feel you will need, any special tutoring or extra help in English?	641	1.43	.699	1=no need, 2=will need, 3=have had
Have you had, or do you feel you will need, any special tutoring or extra help with math?	614	2.22	.713	1=no need, 2=will need, 3=have had
Have you had, or do you feel you will need, any special tutoring or extra help with reading?	640	1.24	.570	1=no need, 2=will need, 3=have had
Have you had, or do you feel you will need, any special tutoring or extra help with writing?	638	.26	.641	1=no need, 2=will need, 3=have had
How many advanced placement courses will you take in 10th grade?	649	1.16	.413	1=none, 2=one, 3=two or more
How many advanced placement courses will you take in 11th grade?	644	1.62	.748	1=none, 2=one, 3=two or more
How many advanced placement courses will you take in 12th grade?	633	1.80	.817	1=none, 2=one, 3=two or more
How many advanced placement exams will you take in 10th grade?	646	1.19	.452	1=none, 2=one, 3=two or more

(Continues)

TABLE 7.4 *(Continued)*

Variables	N	Mean	SD	Scale
How many advanced placement exams will you take in 11th grade?	643	1.63	.749	1=none, 2=one, 3=two or more
How many advanced placement exams will you take in 12th grade?	633	1.76	.811	1=none, 2=one, 3=two or more
After high school, what is the highest academic degree that you will earn?	649	4.98	2.156	1=none, 2=vocational certificate, 3=associate, 4=bachelor's, 5=master's, 6=PhD or EdD, 7=MD, DL, DDS, OR DVM, 8=JD, 9=BD OR MDIV., 10=other
How would you describe the racial makeup of the neighborhood where you grew up?	669	2.29	.843	1=completely White, 2=mostly White, 3= roughly half non-White, 4=mostly non-White, 5=completely non-White
How would you describe the racial makeup of your peer groups/friends at school?	664	2.15	.638	1=completely white, 2= mostly white, 3=roughly half non-white, 4=mostly non-white, 5=completely non-white
How would you describe the racial makeup of your peer groups/friends in the neighborhood?	665	1.97	.836	1=completely white, 2= mostly white, 3=roughly half non-white, 4=mostly non-white, 5=completely non-white
If you compared yourself to other people your age, how would you rate yourself on the ability to see the world like someone else does?	668	3.54	.828	1=lowest 10%, 2=below average, 3=average, 4= above average, 5=highest 10%
If you compared yourself to other people your age, how would you rate yourself on being open to others with different ideas/beliefs?	668	3.67	.874	1=lowest 10%, 2=below average, 3=average, 4= above average, 5=highest 10%

(Continues)

TABLE 7.4 *(Continued)*

Variables	N	Mean	SD	Scale
If you compared yourself to other people your age, how would you rate yourself on being open to someone else questioning what you believe?	666	3.51	.957	1=lowest 10%, 2=below average, 3=average, 4=above average, 5=highest 10%
If you compared yourself to other people your age, how would you rate yourself on the ability to talk about problems in our society?	662	3.43	1.051	1=lowest 10%, 2=below average, 3= average, 4=above average, 5=highest 10%
If you compared yourself to other people your age, how would you rate yourself on the ability to work with people who are different from you?	667	3.86	.929	1=lowest 10%, 2=below average, 3=average, 4=above average, 5=highest 10%
Compared to other people your age, rate yourself in your academic ability.	671	3.51	.788	1=lowest 10%, 2=below average, 3=average, 4=above average, 5=highest 10%
Compared to other people your age, rate yourself in your drive to achieve.	668	3.47	.953	1=lowest 10%, 2= below average, 3= average, 4=above average, 5=highest 10%
Compared to other people your age, rate yourself in your leadership ability.	670	3.45	.890	1=lowest 10%, 2=below average, 3=average, 4=above average, 5=highest 10%
Compared to other people your age, rate yourself in your public speaking ability.	670	2.89	1.016	1=lowest 10%, 2=below average, 3=average, 4=above average, 5=highest 10%
Compared to other people your age, rate yourself in your self-confidence (learning).	670	3.57	.910	1=lowest 10%, 2=below average, 3=average, 4=above average, 5=highest 10%

(Continues)

TABLE 7.4 *(Continued)*

Variables	N	Mean	SD	Scale
Compared to other people your age, rate yourself in your writing ability.	670	3.24	.883	1=lowest 10%, 2=below average, 3=average, 4=above average, 5=highest 10%
In the past year have you broken school rules?	670	1.56	.641	1=not at all, 2=occasionally, 3=frequently
In the past year have you been late to class?	669	1.95	.699	1=not at all, 2=occasionally, 3=frequently
In the past year have you skipped school/class?	670	1.41	.630	1=not at all, 2=occasionally, 3=frequently
While in high school, what chance do you think you will make at least a B average?	671	3.54	.624	1=not important, 2=somewhat important, 3=very important, 4=extremely important
While in high school, what is the chance you will participate in volunteer or community service work?	672	2.88	.972	1=not important, 2=somewhat important, 3=very important, 4=extremely important
While in high school, what is the chance you will seek personal counseling?	670	2.31	.852	1=not important, 2=somewhat important, 3=very important, 4=extremely important
While in high school, what is the chance you will communicate regularly with your teachers?	671	2.72	.794	1=not important, 2=somewhat important, 3=very important, 4=extremely important
While in high school, what is the chance you will communicate regularly with college access program staff?	670	2.74	.837	1=not important, 2=somewhat important, 3=very important, 4=extremely important
While in high school, what is the chance you will think about school work outside of school?	667	3.13	.860	1=not important, 2=somewhat important, 3=very important, 4=extremely important

(Continues)

TABLE 7.4 *(Continued)*

Variables	N	Mean	SD	Scale
During this school year, how much time did you spend during a typical week socializing with friends?	667	5.20	1.796	1=<1 hr/wk, 2=1–2 hr/wk, 3=3–5 hr/wk, 4= 6–10 hr/wk, 5=11–15 hr/wk, 6=16–20 hr/wk, 7=over 20 hr/wk
During this school year, how much time did you spend during a typical week volunteering?	667	2.03	1.454	1=<1 hr/wk, 2=1–2 hr/wk, 3=3–5 hr/wk, 4=6–10 hr/wk, 5=11–5 hr/wk, 6=16–20 hr/wk, 7=over 20 hr/wk
During this school year, how much time did you spend during a typical week in student clubs/groups?	670	1.84	1.372	1=<1 hr/wk, 2=1–2 hr/wk, 3=3–5 hr/wk, 4=6–10 hr/wk, 5=11–15 hr/wk, 6=16–20 hr/wk, 7=over 20 hr/wk
During this school year, how much time did you spend during a typical week watching TV?	672	3.82	1.737	1=<1 hr/wk, 2=1–2 hr/wk, 3=3-5 hr/wk, 4= 6–10 hr/wk, 5= 11–15 hr/wk, 6=16–20 hr/wk, 7=over 20 hr/wk
During this school year, how much time did you spend during a typical week performing household/childcare duties?	671	3.55	1.774	1=<1 hr/wk, 2=1–2 hr/wk, 3=3–5 hr/wk, 4= 6–10 hr/wk, 5= 11–15 hr/wk, 6=16–20 hr/wk, 7=over 20 hr/wk
During this school year, how much time did you spend during a typical week playing video games?	670	3.08	1.909	1=<1 hr/wk, 2=1–2 hr/wk, 3=3–5 hr/wk, 4= 6–10 hr/wk, 5= 11–15 hr/wk, 6=16–20 hr/wk, 7=over 20 hr/wk
During this school year, how much time did you spend during a typical week online social networks (MySpace, Facebook, etc.)?	670	3.73	1.985	1=<1 hr/wk, 2=1–2 hr/wk, 3=3–5 hr/wk, 4= 6–10 hr/wk, 5= 11–15 hr/wk, 6=16–20 hr/wk, 7=over 20 hr/wk
Has anyone from your school or GEAR UP ever spoken with you about college entrance requirements?	670	.90	.298	1=no, 2=yes

items and scales included in these analyses are detailed in Tables 7.3 and 7.4. The sample for second study was drawn from members of the same GEAR UP cohort, this time focusing on the 2010–11 academic year, when students were enrolled in the 10th grade. All students were enrolled in one of three high schools in the participating school district.

Sample

Of these 672 students, 42.3% were male, and 57.7% were female. Their ages ranged from 13 to 16, with 82.1% of students indicating they were 14 years old. Nearly 68% of students indicated their first language was not English. Several questions concerned students' residence and family as a way to capture information about students' SES and familial structures. Similar to Study 1, about 50% of students surveyed resided in private homes, 44% in apartments or rooms, and 6% in foster care or group homes. About two-thirds of students' families rented their home and the remaining one-third owned their home. Nearly all students (96.7%) lived with their parents. Nearly two thirds of students reported that their parents earned $30,000 or less in annual income. Given the number of students belonging to families with limited financial resources, it was not surprising that more than 90% of students expressed some level of concern about paying for college. Specifically, only 3% of students reported that their father had earned a college degree, and 5% reported their mother had a college degree; these figures include 1% of students who reported that their mother or father had a vocational certificate or degree. Should GEAR UP reach its programmatic goal of supporting its students in pursing pathways to college, nearly all the students in the sample would be first-generation college students.

Factor Analyses

Similar to Study 1, exploratory factor analyses were completed on the 672 10th graders included in the sample. In the case of each factor displayed in Table 7.4, items were analyzed using the principal axis factor technique, and a mean substitution was used to replace missing data of no more than 10% for most variables. Cronbach's alphas were calculated to determine reliability for each item displayed in Table 7.4.

Several concepts were explored during these factor analyses. In the higher education literature, several studies talk about the educational benefits of diversity in postsecondary educational environments (Engberg, 2004, 2007; Gurin et al., 2002). Moreover, students' precollege exposure to diversity has long-term consequences for their capacity to develop skills that facilitate their engagement in a twenty-first century-economy (Engberg, 2007). As with the first study featured in this chapter, we conducted factor analyses collected in 10th grade. The factor racial composition of the precollege environment has a Cronbach's alpha of .662 and acceptable factor loadings so that it could be used in future quantitative analyses. Also, students' pluralistic orientation is related to their ability to participate and function in a diverse democracy; this factor had an acceptable reliability and factor loadings. Adequate or good reliabilities and factor loadings were also present for the attendance patterns, structured activities, intellectual self-confidence, and anticipating involvement in high school (see Table 7.5).

The regression model included background characteristics such as gender and SES as well as students' concerns about their abilities to afford college. Tutoring was also included in the model, as were a number of factors capturing students' engagement in high school as well as college-going behaviors. These results are presented in Table 7.6. Of the items included in the regression model, gender and intellectual self-confidence were positive predictors of degree aspirations in the 10th grade.

TABLE 7.5
Means, Standard Deviations, Factor Loadings, and Reliabilities for Degree Aspirations in 10th Grade

Factors	n	Mean	SD	Loading
Racial composition precollege environment α = .662[a]				
Racial makeup peers in neighborhood	670	1.97	.833	.970
Racial makeup neighborhood	670	2.29	.843	.542
Racial makeup peers at school	670	2.15	.636	.422
Pluralistic orientation α = .800[b]				
Open to someone else questioning what I believe	669	3.51	.954	.734
Open to others with different ideas/beliefs	669	3.67	.874	.809
Ability to talk about problems in our society	669	3.43	1.046	.656
Ability to see world like someone else does	669	3.54	.828	.561
Ability to work with people who are different than me	669	3.86	.928	.584

(Continues)

TABLE 7.5 *(Continued)*

Factors	n	Mean	SD	Loading
Attendance patterns α = .659[c]				
Came late to class	671	1.95	.698	.509
Broke school rules	671	1.56	.641	.646
Skipped school/class	671	1.41	.630	.739
Intellectual self-confidence α = .827[b]				
Rate your self-confidence (learning)	672	3.57	.909	.778
Rate your drive to achieve	672	3.47	.950	.753
Rate your leadership ability	672	3.45	.889	.664
Rate your academic ability	672	3.51	.787	.657
Rate your public speaking ability	672	2.89	1.014	.588
Rate your writing ability	672	3.24	.881	.750
Leisure Activities α = .623[e]				
Time spent playing video games	672	3.08	1.906	.432
Time spent online	672	3.73	1.982	.691
Time spent socializing	672	5.20	1.789	.476
Time spent watching TV	672	3.82	1.737	.575
Structured activities α = .571[e]				
Time spent volunteering	672	2.03	1.448	.571
Time spent in student clubs	672	1.84	1.370	.761
Time spent doing house duties	672	3.55	1.772	.392
Anticipated high school activities with adults α = .711[d]				
Teacher communication	672	2.72	.793	.597
Using counseling services	672	2.31	.851	.626
Volunteering	672	1.84	.753	.455
College access program communication	672	2.74	.835	.798

(Continues)

TABLE 7.5 *(Continued)*

Factors	n	Mean	SD	Loading
Academic and community engagement α = .648[d]				
Doing school work	672	3.13	.857	.660
Volunteering	672	2.88	.972	.711
Letter B grades	672	3.54	.623	.499

Note. [a]1 = completely White; 5 = ompletely non-White. [b]1 = lowest 10%; 5 = highest 10%. [c]0 = not at all. 2 = frequently. [d]0 = not important; 3 = extremely important. [e]1 = <1 hr/wk; 2 = 1–2 hr/wk; 3 = 3–5 hr/wk; 4 = 6–10 hr/wk; 5 = 11–15 hr/wk; 6 = 16–20 hr/wk; 7 = over 20 hr/wk.

TABLE 7.6
Predicting Degree Aspirations for 10th Graders

	B	SE B	β
Background Variables			
Gender	.417	.180	.098*
Socioeconomic Status			
Current residence	.193	.160	.053
Rent or own	-.009	.211	-.002
Family income	.073	.100	.031
Father education level	-.037	.055	-.032
Mother education level	.096	.056	.082
Financial Confidence/Security			
Concern paying for college	-.120	.140	-.035
Affordability	.205	.217	.037
GEAR UP financial aid contact	.082	.188	.018
Tutoring			
Turing in English	-.022	.142	-.007
Tutoring in reading	-.096	.174	-.025
Tutoring in writing	-.058	.156	-.017

(Continues)

TABLE 7.6 *(Continued)*

	B	SE B	β
Tutoring in math	-.114	.124	-.037
Academic and Community Engagement			
Intellectual self-confidence	.394	.149	.123 **
Anticipated help-seeking high school behaviors	.187	.177	.060
Leisure activities	.131	.068	.078
Structured activities	-.109	.088	-.058
Anticipated high school activities with adults	.154	.188	.043
Academic and community engagement	.160	.208	.048
College-Going Knowledge and Attitudes			
Advanced placement courses 10th grade	.298	.314	.057
Advanced placement courses 11th grade	.039	.247`	.014
Advanced placement courses 12th grade	-.026	.224	-.010
Advanced placement exams 10th grade	-.103	.290	-.022
Advanced placement exams 11th grade	.088	.250	.030
Advanced placement exams 12th grade	-.082	.286	-.012
GEAR UP college entrance requirement contact	-.082	.286	-.012

Note. *p<.05, **p<.01, ***p<.001.

The findings from the regression analyses are preliminary and therefore limited, yet they underscore the importance of gender in Latin@ college attendance as well as the importance of encouraging students' intellectual engagement and self-confidence. These findings hold some promise for adding new layers of understanding and complexity that may be gained through the use of longitudinal data that capture students' behaviors, attitudes, resources, and outcomes from high school through college.

Discussion and Scholarly Significance

These two studies are significant in that little to no formal research exists for GEAR UP programs locally or nationally. Moreover, these studies examined the applicability of widely used factors based on the CIRP and Diverse Democracy Surveys to middle school–age children and high school students in assessing their attendance, pluralistic orientation, orientation toward helping others, and intellectual self-confidence. It is our hope that the factors will be used collectively in future quantitative analyses to predict college-going knowledge, behaviors, and attitudes of Latin@ students. Further, the contributions of these studies confirm that some factors used in postsecondary education research may be applied to Latin@ middle and high school students as well as the reverse: that items used in postsecondary educational environments to assess students' intellectual self-confidence may be used in middle school and high school environments.

Multiple regression analysis indicated that increasing students' academic and community engagement through activities such as academic service-learning and volunteerism, contact with school counselors, and early exposure to advanced placement exams may promote Latin@ student enrollment in algebra in the middle school years. This is an important finding as the timing of algebra enrollment remains a key predictor of college access (Choy et al., 2000). To be sure, these positive predictors of advanced algebra enrollment indicate that higher education professionals should consider outreach activities before the middle school years. Such longitudinal data may help improve the nature and structure of programs such as GEAR UP, counselor foci in secondary educational environments, and best practices for higher educational outreach professionals.

Note

1. We use *Latin@* instead of *Latino/a* to avoid according privilege to one gender over another. Some scholars who include transgender Latin@ students also use it as a way to include the Latin@ transgender students on our college campuses.

References

Amendments to the Higher Education Act of 1965, Pub. L. No. 105-244 (1998).
Castillo, L., Lopez-Arenas, A., & Saldivar, I. M. (2010). The influence of acculturation and enculturation on Mexican American high school students' decision to apply to college. *Journal of Multicultural Counseling and Development, 38*(2), 8898.
Choy, S. P., Horn, L. J., Nunez, A., & Chen, S. (2000). Transition to college: what helps at-risk students and students whose parents did not attend college. *New Directions for Institutional Research, 107*, 45–63.

Engberg, M. (2004). Educating the workforce for the 21st century: The impact of diversity on undergraduate students' pluralistic orientation. *Dissertation Abstracts International: Section A, 65*(06), 2111.

Engberg, M. (2007). Educating the workforce for the 21st century: A cross-disciplinary analysis of the impact of the undergraduate experiences on students' development of a pluralistic orientation. *Research in Higher Education, 48,* 283–317.

Gurin, P., Dey, E. L., Hurtado, S., & Gurin, G. (2002). Diversity and higher education: Theory and impact on educational outcomes. *Harvard Educational Review, 72,* 330–366.

Hossler, D., Braxton, J., & Coopersmith, G. (1989). Understanding student college choice. In J. C. Smart (Ed.), *Higher education: Handbook of theory and research* (Vol. 5, pp. 231–288). New York, NY: Agathon Press.

Hossler, D., & Gallagher, K. S. (1987). Studying student college choice: A three-phase model and the implications for policy makers. *College and University, 62*(3), 207–221.

Hossler, D., Schmit, J., & Vesper, N. (1999). *Going to college: How social, economic, and educational factors influence the decisions students make.* Baltimore, MA: Johns Hopkins University Press.

Lopez, M. H. (2009). *Latinos and education: Explaining the attainment gap.* Washington, DC: Pew Hispanic Center.

McDonough, P. (1997). *Choosing colleges: How social class and schools structure opportunity.* Albany, NY: SUNY Press.

Perez, P., & McDonough, P. (2008). Understanding Latina and Latino college choice: A social capital and chain migration analysis. *Journal of Hispanic Higher Education, 7*(3), 249–265.

Perna, L. W. (2000). Differences in the decision to attend college among African Americans, Hispanics, and Whites. *Journal of Higher Education, 71,* 117–141.

Weiss, C. H. (1997). *Evaluation: Studying programs and policies* (2nd ed.). Upper Saddle River, NJ : Prentice Hall.

8

AN INTERVIEW WITH ANGELA M. LOCKS
Understanding the Complexities of the College-Going Process
James M. Ellis

Angela Locks is an assistant professor at California State University, Long Beach (CSULB), and an expert on diversity and college access programs in higher education. Diversity praxis is a key element in Angela's scholarship. Praxis connects theory, research, and practice; components do not operate in silos but rather complement one another. The goal of diversity praxis is to promote educational environment throughout the education pipeline in the United States that serve all students effectively. "Praxis allows research, theory, and practice to become integrated into one's identity to influence engagement in the various responsibilities (research, teaching, and service) of being a faculty member," says Angela. Praxis allows Angela to systematically consider whether higher education practitioners are using her research and if the knowledge gained assists them in developing tools that will promote access and equity for underserved populations throughout the education pipeline.

For Angela, supportive adults who reinforced high educational expectations, helped shape her career aspirations, and retained positive aspects of her racial identity were critical contributors to the positive experiences she has had in school and in her community. She remembers being as young as 4 years old and having conversations with her parents about attending college. These conversations were never about *if* she was going to college but *when* she was going to college. Angela believes this, despite negative stereotypes about educational values among Blacks in the United States, is typical for a lot of African Americans. Her family's church also reinforced the expectation that she would attend college someday. She recalls, "My family went to a Black church, and every Sunday there was always a conversation about people going to college and college students coming back to [the] pulpit Sunday mornings."

Supportive adults also influenced her career aspirations.

> I first started thinking about becoming a professor when I was probably eight, and I would spend some summers in Louisiana with [my] paternal and maternal grandparents. My paternal grandparents were educators, and both had a master's degree. My grandfather's nickname was "Prof," so I always thought he was a professor. I didn't know he "only" had a master's degree. In the small town they were from he was known as Professor; he was a high school principal, he was Professor, so I wanted to be like my grandpa.

Being mindful of her identity as an African American woman is important for Angela. Because of the positive and negative portrayals of African American woman in society, Angela was taught by her parents that she needed to learn how to manage those perceptions when working with people.

> My parents made it very clear to me that "people are going to have a problem with you being a Black woman," and I needed to learn how to manage that. But it wasn't my fault or my responsibility for those perceptions, and they didn't let me off the hook on how to work around people, and that was the message that I got consistently from the fifth grade on.

Angela's participation in her high school's Black Student Union (BSU) provided another venue to inform her racial identity. While attending BSU's annual state conference, she learned about African American history and current issues facing African Americans in communities in California. "The BSU conferences were phenomenal. We had workshops on African and African American history. Everything in the conference was designed [to teach students how to] do well academically and affirm our racial and ethnic identity." Through her interactions and networking with other African Americans at the BSU state conference, Angela further learned how to advocate for herself and others in her school and community.

Angela's childhood experience illustrates the powerful role of parents, family members, and others in shaping the career aspirations of youths. Moreover, having, knowing, and connecting with her family's history and community, along with being a first-generation African American from the South, contributed to her identity and belief in her ability to fulfill her dream of becoming a college professor.

Angela's interest in research related to precollege programs is a function of her childhood experiences and as a program participant. Although she grew up as a middle-class African American, she relied on her participation in a precollege outreach program to help her understand and navigate the racial and gender dynamics at her middle school and high school. Even though Angela received support from her parents and community members, the program provided her with opportunities to build social capital and develop relationships and networks that were instrumental in helping her navigate her school environment and achieve academically. She recalls a meeting with a precollege outreach program staff member in eighth grade:

> Ms. Taylor gave me a pink piece of paper that had all of the classes I was supposed to take and the high school I was going to matriculate into that following academic year if I wanted to go to [a local prestigious 4-year university]. I kept that thing and might still have it. . . . That was my checklist. When my counselor or teachers would not sign off on paperwork to get me into certain classes so that I [could] stay on the college prep and honors track in my high school, that paper along with [the language] . . . Ms. Taylor gave me . . . [helped me] to push back on school personnel not wanting to support my trajectory.

As this recollection illustrates, the advising, encouragement, support, and knowledge Angela received from the early precollege outreach program gave her the necessary tools to advocate for herself regarding her academic progress in high school. Moreover, being economically privileged enabled her parents to share and teach effective strategies for negotiating and navigating behavior in predominantly White and privileged settings. This proved critically important because Angela employed these strategies as she successfully advocated for herself in high school. Her experience illustrates that informal social support (family, friends, and mentors) and formal social support (program activities and staff) are instrumental to positive adolescent development.

Praxis allows Angela to use her life experiences as a way to conduct research that expresses and explains who she is, her educational experiences, and the opportunities she was presented with during her educational journey, a concept she describes as "me-search." She uses me-search principles "to make sure that access is available for people behind me in the pipeline." Angela believes her approach is becoming more crucial in higher education, particularly with the growing diversity among young scholars, and is making significant contributions in advancing research on diversity in higher education.

Me-search influences my current research of middle and high school students' perceptions toward college-going and college choice. My past experiences suggest that what influences participation in pre-college access programs also affects students' cognitive orientations toward pursuing higher education. Students' beliefs about their efficacy to be academically and socially successful as a prospective college student and in their desired occupation affect various college-going decisions. Moreover, the extent to which resources are available that support students' immediate short- and long-term personal and educational needs affects their beliefs and expectations to be successful at the collegiate level. As I reflect on my own scholarship, me-search keeps me grounded and gives me purpose in my work with youth and families, and also provides me an opportunity to share a glimpse of my own personal journey through the lives of the population that I research and serve.

Similarly, Angela's engagement in her research is partly driven by protecting opportunities that promote diversity, equity, and access into higher education, such as GEAR UP and the federal TRIO programs. Some research and policy stakeholders question the veracity of methods used to evaluate the GEAR UP and TRIO programs and use this as a basis to advocate for reforms of such programs. Yet, what seems to go unnoticed are the complex lives of participants, which can ultimately influence their college-going trajectory. Angela says, "Students that are in GEAR UP and TRIO programs come from complex lives and experiences and have complex pathways to college. Thus, our methods [as scholars] have to match the population which we are trying to track or examine." For her, mixed methods are the key to fully observing such complexities. The framing of accountability standards—which may or may not consider the complexity of student experiences—is also a critical methodological issue and may affect future funding for federal college access programs. Moreover, Angela believes that future scholars who are implementing rigorous program assessment and evaluation as part of their research into GEAR UP and TRIO programs will play a critical role in decreasing these programs' vulnerability to funding cuts and ensure that access for low-income students and students of color will continue to increase.

Angela's life story sheds light on the variation in the educational journeys of African American students, and this variation is likely to be reflected in who participates in college access programs such as GEAR UP and TRIO. Capturing the various experiences of students participating in these federal programs will be a challenge for future research because of the difficulty to longitudinally identify which factors explain student developmental and educational outcomes. Additionally, the extent to which research in this area of scholarship captures transition points to identify the particular resources that make a difference for participants will influence how well administrators of college access programs can determine which resources to use.

As I think about my professional and scholarly experience in working with middle school and high school youths, I recognize that they have to manage a variety of academic and nonacademic issues in their daily lives. Many have to contend with increasing academic demands and standards imposed by state, district, and school policies and manage their social life and the expectations of their parents or guardians. Also, life issues posing challenges to academic success are often left out of discussions pertaining to youths in schools. Issues of mental health, child welfare, and foster care are just a few of the challenges many youths face in their homes, schools, and communities that must be considered when trying to fully understand student experiences in educational settings. Scholars examining the effectiveness of precollege programs must be judicious in determining which methods and designs meet scientific standards but also accurately and comprehensively reflect the complexity of programs and the educational experiences of participants. Researchers who do not take this judicious approach may risk misrepresenting the programs and the services provided and the array of students' experiences in the education pipeline.

9

ARCHITECTURE OF DIVERSITY
Using the Lens and Language of Space to Examine Racialized Experiences of Students of Color on College Campuses

Michelle Samura

Examining experiences of college students of color is complicated in the current U.S. racial climate. With the prevalence of postracial ideology that suggests we have moved beyond race, the salience and significance of race in higher education, for students and researchers alike, are put into question. Even as students may desire to move beyond race, they still find racialization inescapable (Fisher & Hartmann, 1995; Jones, Castellanos, & Cole, 2002; Samura, 2011; Solórzano, Ceja, & Yosso, 2000; Solórzano & Villalpando, 1998; Suarez-Balcazar, Orellana-Damacela, Portillo, Rowan, & Andres-Guillen, 2003).[1] Moreover, as we navigate a supposedly color-blind era in which race does not determine people's choices and life chances to the extent it once did, it often is difficult to locate, much less examine, processes of racialization in depth (Bonilla-Silva, 2013; Brown et al., 2003).

Scholars of race suggest that updated approaches are needed to account for continued racial inequality and to make sense of these new circumstances (e.g., Omi, 2001; Winant, 2000, 2004). In making the case for new racial theory, Winant (2000) contends an updated framework "must address the persistence of racial classification and stratification in an era officially committed to racial equality and multiculturalism" (p. 180). In institutions of higher education, then, such a framework also would need to address the disconnect that often exists between the rhetoric and reality of racial diversity—a promotion and celebration of the idea of diversity, on the one hand, and the ways students experience it, on the other. In other words, new approaches are needed to critically examine how students experience, negotiate, contest, and understand processes of racialization.

In this chapter, I argue that an examination of racial diversity in higher education requires serious consideration of space. I propose that a spatial perspective offers a lens for locating and examining processes of racialization. And a spatial approach also provides a language participants and researchers can use to talk about the discreet ways race still operates in everyday interactions, including subtle forms of racism that are overlooked or ignored because race is often understood by students to matter less today. Essentially, a spatial approach sheds light on race relations and racial structures in tangible campus environments.

Drawing on processes of and findings from my research on Asian American college students (Samura, 2011, 2015, 2016), I discuss how a spatial lens locates larger racial meanings in students' lived experiences, concrete environments, and social interactions. I also address how a spatial approach provides an accessible language to discuss experiences of racialization, race making, and racism in higher education. Although the primary focus of this chapter is on the importance of space, I also want to emphasize the importance of more research on Asian American college students' experiences. Including Asian Americans in discussions on racial equity and diversity in higher education is crucial for a nuanced understanding of shifts in racial meanings in the United States (Chang & Kiang, 2002). The complex educational and social realities of students today cannot be fully understood simply through Black-White frameworks (Osajima, 1995). Additionally, Asian American college students are an interesting population to examine because they often are viewed as overrepresented on college campuses. While a number of Asian Americans (of course, not all) are experiencing results of academic success, including socioeconomic mobility and, to a certain extent, social integration, they still experience processes of racialization. In fact, as findings from my research indicate, the dilemmas, tensions, and contradictions experienced by Asian American students reveal the still-tenuous racial landscape of higher education (Samura, 2011, 2015, 2016). Through Asian American students' experiences, we can gain insight into what students of color still must contend with even after inclusion.

In my research, I have found that students tend to not talk about their experiences in explicitly racial terms, and this is especially true for questionable or negative instances such as experiences of racial discrimination. By examining participants' interactions with and views of various college spaces, however, matters of space that also are matters of race become evident. For example, students' tendencies to avoid certain parts of campus can be understood as more than purely a spatial matter. Students may omit or ignore elements of race in favor of more neutral and less tedious explanations for their interactions with and within space. In this way, students' *dilemmas of space* may also be *dilemmas of race*. The aim of this chapter is to examine and demonstrate exactly what I mean about this dilemma.[2]

I begin by discussing the concept of space and offer a working definition of *college space*. I also uniquely situate this work in existing interdisciplinary research on space, space and education, and space and race. Then, I draw upon examples from my research on Asian American college students to highlight three ways a spatial approach to examining racial diversity in higher education is particularly effective.

First, I propose that when students feel uncertain about the significance of race and their racial identities, talking about space is more approachable than talking about race. Second, I focus on how different spaces can be experienced and viewed differently by different people. Third, I discuss how space often involves matters of race combined with other forms of socially constructed difference (e.g., gender, ability, sexuality). Thus, a spatial approach enables us to examine the complex links among categories and identities of difference—that is, intersectionalities (Collins & Andersen, 2013; Crenshaw, 1989, 1991) such as race, class, gender, and sexuality— and illuminate aspects of college spaces that continue to maintain these differences. Finally, I conclude the chapter with thoughts on future directions for spatial approaches in research and practice on diversity in higher education.

Explaining Space

The utility of the concept of space is by no means a new idea. Theoretical and empirical work conducted across a range of disciplines, such as geography, sociology, anthropology, urban planning, and architecture, illustrate how space affects people's interactions and identities (Gieryn, 2000; Gruenewald, 2003; Keith & Pile, 1993; Knowles, 2003; Lipsitz, 2007; Soja, 1989). Critical geographers, in particular, have emphasized a view of space as a social construct and the social as spatially constructed (Harvey, 1993, 1996; Kobayashi & Peake, 2000; Massey, 1993, 1994; Tickamyer, 2000). Space is not neutral, and socially constructed categories of difference often are reflected in material spaces (Massey, 1994; Soja, 1989; Tickamyer, 2000). People shape their surroundings but built environments also affect the types and nature of interactions among people (Gieryn, 2000, 2002; Gruenewald, 2003).

In spite of a sizable body of literature that indicates the great potential of a lens and language of space, research on space in educational settings remains a relatively underdeveloped area (Gulson & Symes, 2007a, 2007b; Taylor, 2009). Definitions and usage of the concept of space in educational research remain unclear and inconsistent. Especially in the field of higher education, there is still little clarity on how space operates and limited work on the relationship between built environments and diverse students' interactions.

Massey (1993) has emphasized the need for researchers to be explicit about their reasons for using terms such as *space* or *spatial* because meanings of space differ from person to person. People often assume that their meaning of space is apparent or uncontested. Therefore, before moving on it is important that I explain how I define and use the concept of space.

My working definition draws on elements of Massey's (1993) and Knowles's (2003) conceptualizations of space. According to Massey, space is embedded with power and symbolism and is composed of "a complex web of relations of domination and subordination, of solidarity and cooperation" (p. 81). Space is constructed out of the "simultaneous coexistence of social interrelations and interactions at all spatial scales, from the most local level to the most global" (Massey, 1993, p. 80). Furthermore, space is "produced by who people are, by what they do, and by the ways in which they connect with other people" (Knowles, 2003, p. 79). It is also important to note that this view of space maintains that it is more than merely a setting, context, or backdrop for where things happen (Tickamyer, 2000).

In my research on college students' experiences (Samura, 2011, 2015, 2016), I use the term *college space* to situate space in the specific context of higher education. *College space*, as I define it, encompasses existing practices, norms, and environments established by institutional policies and student culture. It also involves the connections between past and present meanings of higher education as well as relationships and interactions among people (e.g., students, faculty, staff, alumni) and places (e.g., buildings, landscapes, classrooms). I have further parsed the concept of space into *physical* and *social* to distinguish between tangible, concrete environments (i.e., physical space) and various types and levels of relationships among people or places (i.e., social space). Physical and social spaces often are closely interrelated as social phenomena often have physical manifestations and vice versa.

As I make the case for an updated approach to examining racial diversity in higher education, I focus on space as a concept, location, and experience, and the relationship between college spaces and race making. My reference to the *architecture of diversity*, then, emphasizes the spatiality of diversity and subsequently how students navigate physical and social spaces of higher education.

Studies on Space in Education

In the realm of educational research, space has been given limited attention. Only a handful of educational scholars have engaged in empirical research using an explicitly spatial perspective (e.g., Ferguson & Seddon, 2007; Gulson, 2006; McGregor, 2004; Nespor, 1997). For example, McGregor analyzed classroom spaces to reveal how space is shaped by past practices and is used to maintain and reproduce certain relations of power. McGregor argued that an understanding of the nature of space is important if we are to understand what goes on in institutions of education. Focusing on educational spaces outside of the classroom, Nespor conducted an ethnographic study that situated an urban elementary school within a broader context of the city and revealed the nature of the webs of social relations that connect schools with other social institutions.

In higher education research, it is not that existent literature on college students' experiences has overlooked or ignored the spatial. In fact, a number of studies mention the importance of campus climates, environments, settings, contexts, and institutional conditions, all concepts that are related to space (e.g., Dey & Hurtado, 1994; Hoffman, Richmond, Morrow, & Salomone, 2003; Hurtado, Griffin, Arellano, & Cuellar, 2008; Kuh, 2009; Kuh & Love, 2000; Locks, Hurtado, Bowman, & Oseguera, 2008). Indeed, a rich body of research exists on the need for campus climates and institutional conditions that are conducive to racial diversity and the means by which they may be created (e.g., Hurtado, Milem, Clayton-Pedersen, & Allen, 1998; Pascarella, Edison, Nora, Hagedorn, & Terenzini, 1996; Solórzano et al., 2000; Suarez-Balcazar et al., 2003).

Although this research remains valuable, a number of studies tend to provide only one-time snapshots, via large-scale surveys, of students' attitudes and experiences and are limited in their ability to capture nuances of experiences. Moreover, there remains little clarity and agreement on what exactly constitutes campus climate (Hart & Fellabaum, 2008). Existing conceptualizations of campus climate also tend to primarily focus on structural and institutional aspects of higher education diversity (Hurtado et al., 1998). Even when scholars have sought to examine the ways college transforms students *and* students transform college environments, such as Dey and Hurtado's (1994) use of a social ecological approach, the primary focus is on the ways students help shape the institutions (i.e., through changes in student demography and preferences) rather than on explicit, recursive processes between students and space. In essence, research on college students' experiences has not prioritized space as an explicit dimension of analysis.

One large-scale study of diversity in universities that began to explore college space is worth mentioning. Duster (1991) reported that the research team made a small attempt to map areas of campuses where there were "clear demarcations of racial and ethnic 'spaces,' areas where one or another group dominates in terms of who 'hangs out there' or where other groups 'vote with their feet' regarding spatial domination" (p. 7). In the end, the research team did not pursue this line of inquiry but suggested that it would be very useful to explore where explicitly racial spaces are and how they are created and maintained. Explicitly racial spaces certainly are important to consider when examining racial diversity in higher education. However, the spaces in which race does not seem be a factor also are important, if not more important, to consider because they check and even challenge our assumptions about how racialization and racism operate.

Connecting Race and Space

Scholars from a variety of disciplines are making implicit and explicit connections between space and race (e.g., Delaney, 2002; Gilmore, 2002; Heikkila, 2001; Knowles, 2003; Kobayashi & Peak, 2000; Lipsitz, 2007; Massey, 1994; Neely & Samura, 2011; Pulido, 2000; Woods, 1998). Most applicable to this investigation is the theorization of race-space connections by Lipsitz, Knowles, and Neely and Samura. Specifically, Lipsitz uses the phrases *spatialization of race* and *racialization of space* to underscore the fact that "the lived experience of race has a spatial dimension, and the lived experience of space has a racial dimension" (p. 3). He further suggests that understanding the links between space and race involves an examination of concrete spatial and racial practices. Knowles also connects race and space by suggesting that space be understood as an "active archive of the social processes and social relationships composing racial orders" (p. 80). Space connects the racial past to the racial present, and it interacts with people and their actions in ways that create and recreate race. Furthermore, Knowles contends that race making is a set of spatial practices.

Building on race-space connections being made by Lipsitz (2007), Knowles (2003), and others, Neely and I (2011) suggest that a spatial approach to examining issues of race is particularly useful because the primary characteristics of space (i.e., contested, fluid, interactional, and defined by difference) overlap with primary characteristics of race. We have developed a theoretical framework of racial space that enables researchers to examine race relations and processes of race making in a variety of settings, especially when it seems uncomfortable or unfitting to explicitly include race as a factor. The frameworks I have mentioned here indicate how a spatial perspective can unearth how built environments affect the types and quality of interracial interactions and, in turn, how social relations affect physical space.

So what might we be able to better understand about students' experiences of racial diversity on college campuses through a spatial perspective? In the next section, I present three compelling examples from my research on Asian American college students' experiences to demonstrate the utility of using a spatial approach to examining and understanding racial diversity in higher education (for more details regarding this study, see Samura, 2011, 2015, 2016). All names of people and institutions used in these examples are fictional.

Example A: Belonging, Entitlement, and Contesting Restroom Space

This first example focuses on Beverly's experience in the residence halls. During an interview, I asked Beverly to talk about college space at West University and where she felt comfortable and uncomfortable. As she spoke about various buildings on campus, Beverly mentioned a particular residence hall, named Acacia, that she did not like. What made Beverly's discussion of the residence hall particularly intriguing was the way she spoke about highly racialized experiences and what could be understood as racist experiences in purely spatial terms.

Specifically, I had asked Beverly to tell me about college spaces where she did not feel comfortable. The following is a transcript of part of the conversation that ensued; my initial analysis is included as bracketed, italicized comments.

> Beverly: [pause for several seconds] Probably Acacia (brief strained chuckle). [*Indication of discomfort.*]
> Beverly: [pause] Because it's just so dead. Because I lived in Acacia my freshmen year, I really didn't like it. So I always have a *bad* impression of it.
> Michelle: [softly] Yeah.
> Beverly: And just the whole thing, like I hated Acacia. So I didn't want to go in there. [*There was a notable heighted shift with significant intensification during Beverly's explanations of why she did not feel comfortable in Acacia. First, she commented that the residence hall was "just so dead" and that she had "a bad impression of it." Second, she stated that she "really didn't like it." And then the intensity of and palpable distress in her statements quickly escalated to a point where she declared that she "hated Acacia."*]
> Michelle: So why did you not like Acacia?
> Beverly: Because my floor people were really snobby.
> Michelle: Hmm.
> Beverly: And then they were really mean.
> Michelle: Oh no.
> Beverly: Yeah, so I didn't want to go there. I was never in my room.
> Michelle: Was it a special interest floor? [*I asked this question as a way of trying to get a clearer picture of the types of students who lived on her floor, such*

as racial, ethnic, and gender makeup. However, I did not want to assume that there were racial or ethnic differences between Beverly and the other residents and was waiting to see if she would bring up these topics.]
Beverly: No.
Michelle: It was just a regular floor?
Beverly: Yeah, it was just a regular floor.
Michelle: They were just mean to you? [*At this point, I was still unclear about what was going on but did not want to lead Beverly toward any particular explanation.*]
Beverly: They were just . . . like they were . . . I don't know. [pause] Just like . . . there's a restroom right in front of my room."

And that was when Beverly brought in the restroom as a way of explaining the tenuous relationship with her floormates. Beverly began by describing the spatial arrangement of the floor and the different rooms in the vicinity of the particular restroom. The restroom of interest was located on her floor, directly across from her room. Beverly was adamant about pointing out the proximity of her room to this restroom: "If I open the door, the restroom was *right* there." The fact that she made such an effort to repeatedly and strongly emphasize the close proximity between her room and restroom was meant to validate an assumed entitlement she felt with that restroom. Beverly even commented that all the restrooms on the floor are public restrooms. In her mind, anyone could use any of the restrooms. And given the location of the restroom to her room, logically it would be the one she would use.

Beverly's floormates, however, chose to contest this space—a physical space (i.e., a residence hall floor) that was supposed to be relatively inclusive and a particular place (i.e., a public restroom) that was typically accessible to everyone. For reasons that did not seem clear, at least from Beverly's discussion of the situation, several girls who lived on her floor posted two signs. The first, placed on the restroom door, declared, "This is Jen, Katie, and Ashley's restroom *only*." The second sign, which they placed on the inside of the restroom, stated, "Since we don't poop in your restroom, don't poop in ours. Please clean up your mess. We're not your mom. We don't pick up your shit. Please don't leave your stuff here. This is our restroom."

Throughout her detailed accounts of the situation, there was no explicit discussion of race in her descriptions of the struggle over the restroom space. However, this did not mean that race was a nonfactor in the situation. In fact, Beverly's transition between the discussion of the restroom contestation and the information she then chose to divulge indicated that race, particularly her Asian racial identity, was definitely on her mind. Immediately after describing the bathroom situation, Beverly shifted the discussion to a different but related topic that was explicitly racial. Beverly abruptly ended her discussion of the restroom contestation by stating, "I just was like, okay, you don't have to do that." Without a pause, she continued on into another topic regarding her relationship with her floormates:

> And then, like, my roommate, she's half Japanese, half White. And they didn't know, so they were like always making fun of Asians in front of her and then so she'd be really uncomfortable and then she'd tell me. And I'm like, "Okay, what is this?

It seems that Beverly was, in fact, acutely aware of her floormates' attitudes toward Asians, and subsequently, their attitude toward her. However, this was the first time Beverly mentioned race in the discussion of her experiences in the residence halls; yet even in this discussion, the racial identity she directly commented on was not her own. Rather, she chose to talk about her roommate's biracial identity. And it was only later in the conversation that I learned that Beverly's floormates were White. Even then, I was the one who asked about their racial identities. It was not information Beverly independently chose to share.

The way Beverly elected to bring race into the conversation—that is, following a discussion of the disturbing experiences with the restroom that focused on her roommate and not on herself—illustrates how examining race on college campuses can be complicated. Sometimes the reasons provided by students seem to indicate that race is a factor. Other times, individuals are left to their own devices to make sense of occurrences. Race, then, becomes one of a number of reasons for their experiences. Although students primarily wrestle internally with the role race plays in their experiences, many may wonder whether something happens (or did not) because of their race. In Beverly's case, she was left to decipher questions like, "Did that happen because I'm Asian?"

Conflicts over space often are based on assumed belonging or entitlement (Feagin, Vera, & Imani, 1996; Knowles, 2003; Perrucci et al., 2000). By posting the signs in the bathroom, Beverly's floormates established an *us* versus *them* divide. It was a process of *othering*, and the otherness seemed to be connected to their racial identities. In this way, Beverly's restroom contestation was not only reflective of the campus racial climate or race relations at West University but also a race-making event. Furthermore, we see how racialization is experienced and understood by Beverly. Her retelling of and response to these racialized experiences revealed how uncomfortable and even unwilling she was about talking about her own racial identity in the midst of that difficult experience. The restroom contestations were so traumatic that in the end Beverly and her roommate chose to remove themselves from that space entirely. Had I directly asked Beverly about the role race played in her college experiences or whether her Asian American racial identity seemed to matter at West University, I am uncertain about whether she would have talked about the restroom contestation. In this situation, Beverly was able to talk about space as a way to explore her experiences with race on campus.

Example B: "Sticky Rice" and Changes in College Space

Space is dynamic. It can change in a matter of moments. In my research on Asian American college students' experiences I found that college spaces, particularly physical spaces, are experienced, used, and understood very differently by different people. In fact, because the institutional and public views of the setting (e.g., student demographics, location, accessibility, resources) were significantly different from students' views of the setting (e.g., "White space" and "party space"), I felt it was necessary to write two versions of the study's setting. Doing this enabled me to more thoroughly capture the wide range of perceptions of West University's college space.

In this next example, I illustrate the fluidity of college space by focusing on a recreation center and a phenomenon known as Sticky Rice. I offer the following vignette from my field notes as a way to highlight the intricacies of college spaces, physical (i.e., built environments such as a recreation center) and social (i.e., relationships and interactions among students).

> West University's recreation center is one of the most frequented buildings on campus and was designed to always allow drop-in recreation use. This means that, at any given time, students, faculty, and staff have access to a wide range of exercise equipment and activities. On most days the recreation center is bustling with a diverse group of people, especially the basketball courts. Located in the center of the building, the two courts are often packed as undergraduate and graduate students, faculty, staff, and community members engage in hours of nonstop pickup games.
>
> But not on Saturday nights. On Saturday nights, the basketball courts became a space where a large group of Asian American students congregate to play. They jokingly referred to themselves as "Sticky Rice." While most other students engaged in some other recreational activity on these nights, these students preferred this space to enjoy one another's company. Although they were still able to play on other days among other university patrons, they preferred to play on Saturdays.
>
> Little is known about how this phenomenon came to be. According to Martin, a sixth-year "super senior" who had been around the longest, certain Asian American students somehow flocked to the basketball courts on Saturday nights. No one sent out formal invitations or reminders, but there usually were enough bodies to simultaneously run two full-court games with extra people waiting on the sidelines.

The Sticky Rice phenomenon highlights the complex relationship between college spaces and students and between physical and social spaces. It provides a useful starting point for considering how experiences such as these can help us rethink the ways we view higher education settings and the salience of race for students of color. For example, consider these questions: Why does Sticky Rice exist? How does the recreation center on Saturdays enable and constrain Sticky Rice? And what might we better understand about students' experiences of racial diversity if we examine the range of uses, experiences, and meanings of different spaces in the recreation center and beyond?

Sticky Rice can be viewed as primarily a spatial phenomenon. That is, the same physical space (i.e., the basketball court) is experienced differently by different groups of people at different times. Some people, including academics, third-party observers, and even members of Sticky Rice, would argue that the Saturday night basketball games at the recreation center have little to do with the students' racial identities. Perhaps students came out to play on Saturday nights because their skill level keeps them from being picked up by the constantly morphing teams during the week. Or maybe it was because the students simply preferred to play basketball instead of attending parties. Still others might suggest that students merely choose to *stick* together with people whom they believe are similar.

We know from a rich body of research on racial diversity in higher education that racially diverse student populations do not necessarily result in interracial interactions (e.g., Bowen & Bok, 1998; Chang, Denson, Saenz, & Misa, 2005). In fact, studies have shown how many students in multiracial settings, for a variety of reasons, such as assumed shared experiences and perceived similarities, tend to prefer and develop close associations with same-race peers (Inkelas, 2004; Tatum, 1997; Villalpando, 2003). Same-race living arrangements, campus clubs and organizations, fraternities and sororities, peer groups, and dating patterns are often the norm on campuses with racially diverse student populations.

At the same time, the role of formal, university-sanctioned race- and ethnic-based student organizations in the experiences of students of color also continues to be debated. Scholars have suggested that clubs and organizations that focus on race or ethnicity limit students' interracial interactions and deter from efforts to promote racial diversity (D'Souza, 1991). Other scholars have argued instead that ethnic and racial student organizations are an important factor in the experiences of students of color, helping them to adjust to college life, develop greater awareness of their racial identities, and increase their sense of belonging (Inkelas, 2004; Museus, 2008). In fact, some scholars have suggested that these types of race- or ethnicity-based groups are critical for the retention and success of students of color, that it is more about self-preservation as opposed to self-segregation (Villalpando, 2003).

In this way, Sticky Rice also can be understood as a racial phenomenon, not just a spatial phenomenon. The basketball courts became a type of Asian American space on Saturday nights. That is, the space changes as a result of and resulting in changes in racial composition. It becomes *their space*. Moreover, the space encompasses a specific moment in time and a particular location when Asian American racial identity becomes salient to Sticky Rice, as these students are drawn to the physical and social space. Asian American racial identity also is salient, since observers likely viewed the Saturday night basketball ritual as an Asian or Asian American space.

The examination of Sticky Rice through a lens of space is an example of how a physical space can change in composition and meaning depending on the day and time. This suggests that to fully understand students' experience with racial diversity on college campuses we must consider how, when, and why spaces are used, by whom, and with what outcomes. For example, a number of higher education scholars also would suggest that Sticky Rice illustrates students' efforts to belong. If Sticky Rice is one way a particular group of students works to belong, it would be useful, then, to examine students' belonging as a set of spatial practices (Samura, 2016). As the Sticky Rice phenomenon indicates, there are aspects of student belonging that may be better understood in relationship to space.

Example C: Bodies in Space and Intersectionalities of Difference

The final example is centered on Missy's understanding of her racialized and gendered body in college space. Two points need to be emphasized with this example. First, examining college students' experiences with diversity requires approaches that can account for intersectionalities of difference (e.g., race, gender, sexuality, class). I contend that a spatial approach enables a more nuanced understanding of how these intersectionalities affect students' experiences. Difference is maintained through space. As value (positive or negative) is assigned to particular differences, inequality is produced in and through space. These inequalities are frequently established along the lines of social identities, such as race, gender, class, sexuality, or some combination thereof.

Second, additional methods that unearth how students navigate, experience, and understand college spaces are needed, especially when different identities become salient. I propose that visual methods (e.g., photography, mapping) offer insight into these processes. Surveys are by far the method of choice for research on diversity-related topics, such as campus climate, retention, and belonging. As valuable as surveys are for providing a landscape view, they are limited in their ability to consider the dynamic nature of students' experiences. So in this study, I used an unconventional combination of student-created photo journals, mapping, and interviews in addition to analyzing large-scale survey data. (For more information on methods see Samura, 2016. For more information on visual methodologies, see Collier & Collier, 1986; Harper, 2003; Knowles & Sweetman, 2004; Margolis & Pauwels, 2011; Suchar, 1997.)

One theme that emerged from the photographs taken by the photojournalers was a struggle with being highly aware of one's body on campus and in the neighborhoods surrounding campus. Many students, especially the photojournalers, highlighted various aspects of their physical appearance as a way of talking about how they experienced college space. A number of participants referred to their physical attributes, particularly their weight, to describe their relationship with college space. I should also note that for many of them, college space included university-owned property as well as the surrounding neighborhood or city where the university was located. Two images taken by Missy were prime examples. The first image, "24hr Fitness" (see Figure 9.1), was one of Missy's responses to my request to take photographs in places where she does not feel comfortable.

Missy's photo "24hr Fitness" is visually compelling in that the long walkway and the doors in the distance suggest a metaphorical distance between Missy and this place. One can literally see her perspective of the 24hr Fitness center. Missy also provided written notes to accompany this photograph.

> I'm not comfortable in [this city] at all! Everyone is stick skinny and/or anorexic looking. I have been diagnosed w/bulimia since middle school and this picture represents what I have to do to feel comfortable with myself in order to feel comfortable in other environments.

Missy then added, "I hate the gym. But I go at least four times a week."

Along with "24hr Fitness," Missy provided another image titled "Treadmills" (see Figure 9.2), to comment on salient aspects of her identity. "Treadmills" depicts a row of about 20 treadmills on the right and another long row of elliptical machines on the left side. With this image, Missy noted,

> Weight is a part of the identities that matter at West University. I've never met so many in-shape people. I'm in shape, but not skinny, which Asians are required to be. Every girl seems to worry about it and guys are always trying to bulk up! All my friends have protein powders! I was always self-conscious, but never to this extent. All the girls are scantily clad. . . . I'm not in competition, but I always feel out of place because I'm too self-conscious of my weight.

FIGURE 9.1. Missy: "24hr Fitness"

A number of factors affected how Missy viewed and felt about herself. There were varying meanings of being *in shape*. Also embedded in Missy's understanding of being in shape were expectations of Asians as thin. According to Missy, Asians are "required" to be skinny. Missy's comments highlighted the disconnect she experienced between her own body and expectations of the bodies of Asian women. Her heightened self-consciousness about her body and her weight ("I was always self-conscious but never to this extent") was one reason she gives for always seeming to feel out of place.

The photographs combined with Missy's explanations suggest that racial and gender identification remains closely connected with students' bodies. Racial difference becomes salient when students' Asian American bodies enter what is generally understood to be White space or where Whiteness is the majority, the norm, and the standard. Race tends to become salient when students' physical appearances differ from the norms of the space and even

FIGURE 9.2. Missy: "Treadmills"

the norms of their own racial category. Concomitantly, gender also becomes salient when bodies differ from the expected norms.

By examining how students' views of themselves align (or not) with their understandings of the expectations of different college spaces, we can better understand students' experiences with diversity. Furthermore, we can better understand which intersectionalities of social identities are prevalent for different students and how difference is reproduced and maintained, even in diverse settings.

Closing Thoughts

My hope is that the issues and perspectives I have raised in this chapter will, at the very least, catalyze conversations and inquiries on the utility of spatial approaches in educational research. As the preceding examples have shown, it is difficult to examine the salience of race in students' everyday experiences. Beverly's experiences reveal how tricky and uncomfortable it may be for students to talk about race in questionable interactions. Therefore, students may need to talk about space to talk about race.

Beverly's discussion of the residence hall restroom contestation became a moment when space served as a proxy for race; that is, she talked about space as a way of discussing her belonging (or lack of) in the residence hall. When we are able to examine how students experience interracial interactions, even if race is not explicitly discussed, we can better understand how difference and potentially inequality along the lines of race are maintained and perpetuated. Similarly, the lack of fit revealed through Missy's photographs and comments uncovered the racialized and gendered expectations of West University's college space. Examining expectations of students' bodies in relation to particular spaces may expose processes of racialization (along with other layers of difference) that continue to exist, even in a space that is assumed to promote inclusivity.

There are a number of ways future researchers may want to use and extend spatial approaches. For example, scholars can reexamine concepts related to racial diversity, such as campus climate, belonging, retention, and the like, using a lens of space or the concept of college space. What might we be able to better understand about students' experiences if we examined belonging and retention as a set of spatial practices? Or what aspects of campus climate might be unearthed if we examine how different students use, experience, and understand different college spaces? Researchers also can draw on theoretical frameworks that explicitly connect race and space to examine racial diversity on college campuses. For instance, future research can use the theory of racial space (Neely & Samura, 2011) to examine how college space (and subsequently students' experiences with race) is interactional, fluid, contested, and defined by difference. Insights gained through this research could inform higher education policy, practice, and programming. Further, it is important for scholars to consider critical geography and visual methods (e.g., photography) to provide alternative research approaches that may help us deepen understandings of racism and sexism on college campuses.

Findings from studies that examine college space can help administrators, campus architects, designers, and planners better understand how different spaces are used and experienced by different constituents. This research also can enable key decision makers to make more informed decisions about changes to be made and future projects and programs to facilitate student belonging, inclusion, and success. Scholars, practitioners, and even students would benefit from understanding how changes to campus spaces can in turn change interactions in those spaces and vice versa. Obviously, it may not always be feasible or even necessary to alter built environments. For example, an existing recreation center, such as the one described in the Sticky Rice example, likely will not be significantly altered or transformed into another purpose. However, if research reveals patterns of racially segregated usage of the gym, it would be important for administrators to consider why this may be occurring and whether programmatic changes can or even should be made.

Along with the challenges of examining racial diversity in higher education today come opportunities to reexamine and revise our approaches to address the needs of all students. As we better understand how different college spaces promote or impede meaningful interactions among students, changes can be made to space to more effectively facilitate inclusivity in racially diverse settings. To do this, we need updated frameworks that can capture the complexities of students' experiences. A spatial approach is particularly promising.

Notes

1. Racialization refers to processes by which racial meanings become attached to individuals, groups, and even spaces. Processes of racialization often perpetuate otherness and reinforce a racial hierarchy (Winant, 2004).
2. All names used in this study are pseudonyms. This includes names of individual participants and the university.

References

Bonilla-Silva, E. (2013). *Racism without racists: Color-blind racism and the persistence of racial inequality in America*. Lanham, MD: Rowman & Littlefield.

Bowen, W., & Bok, D. (1998). *The shape of the river: Long-term consequences of considering race in college and university admissions*. Princeton, NJ: Princeton University Press.

Brown, M., Carnoy, M., Currie, E., Duster, T., Oppenheimer, D., Shultz, M., & Wellman, D. (2003). *Whitewashing race: The myth of a color-blind society*. Berkeley: University of California Press.

Chang, M., Denson, N., Saenz, V., & Misa, K. (2005). The educational benefits of sustaining cross-racial interaction among undergraduates. *Journal of Higher Education, 77*(3), 430–455.

Chang, M. J., & Kiang, P. N. (2002). New challenges of representing Asian American students in U.S. higher education. In P. Altbach, K. Lomotey, & W. A. Smith (Eds.), *The racial crisis in American higher education* (pp. 137–158). Albany, NY: SUNY Press.

Collier, J., & Collier, M. (1986). *Visual anthropology: Photography as a research method*. Albuquerque: University of New Mexico Press.

Collins, P. H., & Andersen, M. (2013). *Race, class and gender: An anthology* (8th ed.). Independence, KY: Cengage Learning.

Crenshaw, K. (1989). Demarginalizing the intersection of race and sex: A Black feminist critique of antidiscrimination doctrine, feminist theory and antiracist politics. *University of Chicago Legal Forum, 1,* 139–167.

Crenshaw, K. (1991). Mapping the margins: Intersectionality, identity politics, and violence against women of color. *Stanford Law Review, 43,* 1241–1299.

Delaney, D. (2002). The space that race makes. *Professional Geographer, 54*(1), 6–14.

Dey, E., & Hurtado, S. (1994). College students in changing contexts. In P. G. Altbach, R. O. Berdahl, & P. J. Gumport (Eds.), *Higher education in American society* (3rd ed., pp. 249–268). Amherst, NY: Prometheus.

D'Souza, D. (1991). *Illiberal education: The politics of race and sex on campus.* New York, NY: Free Press.

Duster, T. (Ed.). (1991). *The diversity project: Final report.* Berkeley: Institute for the Study of Social Change, University of California, Berkeley.

Feagin, J., Vera, H., & Imani, N. (1996). *The agony of education: Black students at White colleges and universities.* New York, NY: Routledge.

Ferguson, K., & Seddon, T. (2007). Decentered education: Suggestions for framing a socio-spatial research agenda. *Critical Studies in Education, 48*(1), 111–129.

Fisher, B., & Hartmann, D. (1995). The impact of race on the social experience of college students at a predominantly White university. *Journal of Black Studies, 26*(2), 117–133.

Gieryn, T. (2000). A space for place in sociology. *Annual Review of Sociology, 26,* 463–496.

Gieryn, T. F. (2002). What buildings do. *Theory and Society, 31*(1), 35–74.

Gilmore, R. (2002). Fatal couplings of power and difference: Racism and geography. *Professional Geographer, 54*(1), 15–24.

Gruenewald, D. (2003). The best of both worlds: A critical pedagogy of place. *Educational Researcher, 32*(4), 3–12.

Gulson, K. (2006). A White veneer: Educational policy, space and "race" in the inner city. *Discourse: Studies in the Cultural Politics of Education, 27,* 259–274.

Gulson, K., & Symes, C. (2007a). Knowing one's place: Space, theory, education. *Critical Studies in Education, 48,* 97–110.

Gulson, K. N., & Symes, C. (Eds.). (2007b). *Spatial theories of education: Policy and geography matters.* New York, NY: Routledge.

Harper, D. (2003). Framing photographic ethnography: A case study. *Ethnography, 4,* 241–266.

Hart, J., & Fellabaum, J. (2008). Analyzing campus climate studies: Seeking to define and understand. *Journal of Diversity in Higher Education, 1*(4), 222–234.

Harvey, D. (1993). From space to place and back again: Reflections on the condition of postmodernity. In J. Bird, B. Curtis, T. Putnam, G. Robertson, & L. Tickner (Eds.), *Mapping the futures: Local cultures, global change* (pp. 3–29). London, England: Routledge.

Harvey, D. (1996). *Justice, nature, and the geography of difference.* Oxford, England: Blackwell.

Heikkila, E. J. (2001). Identity and inequality: Race and space in planning. *Planning Theory & Practice, 2,* 261–276.

Hoffman, M., Richmond, J., Morrow, J., & Salomone, K. (2003). Investigating "sense of belonging" in first-year college students. *Journal of College Student Retention, 4*(3), 227–256.

Hurtado, S., Griffin, K., Arellano, L., & Cuellar, M. (2008). Assessing the value of climate assessments: Progress and future directions. *Journal of Diversity in Higher Education, 1*(4), 204–221.

Hurtado, S., Milem, J. F., Clayton-Pedersen, A. R., & Allen, W. R. (1998). Enhancing campus climates for racial/ethnic diversity: Educational policy and practice. *Review of Higher Education, 21*(3), 279–302.

Inkelas, K. (2004). Does participation in ethnic co-curricular activities facilitate a sense of ethnic awareness and understanding? A study of Asian Pacific American undergraduates. *Journal of College Student Development, 45*, 285–302.

Jones, L., Castellanos, J., & Cole, D. (2002). Examining the ethnic minority student experience at predominantly White institutions: A case study. *Journal of Hispanic Higher Education, 1*(1), 19–39.

Keith, M., & Pile, S. (Eds.). (1993). *Place and the politics of identity.* New York, NY: Routledge.

Knowles, C. (2003). *Race and social analysis.* Thousand Oaks, CA: SAGE.

Knowles, C., & Sweetman, P. (Eds.). (2004). *Picturing the social landscape: Visual methods and the sociological imagination.* New York, NY: Routledge.

Kobayashi, A., & Peake, L. (2000). Racism out of place: Thoughts on Whiteness and an antiracist geography in the new millennium. *Annals of the Association of American Geographers, 90*(2), 392–403.

Kuh, G. D. (2009). Understanding campus environments. In G. S. McClellan, J. Stringer, & Associates (Eds.), *The handbook of student affairs administration* (3rd ed., pp. 59–80). San Francisco, CA: Jossey-Bass.

Kuh, G. D., & Love, P. G. (2000). A cultural perspective on student departure. In J. M. Braxton (Ed.), *Reworking the student departure puzzle* (pp. 196–212). Nashville, TN: Vanderbilt University Press.

Lipsitz, G. (2007). The racialization of space and the spatialization of race: Theorizing the hidden architecture of landscape. *Landscape Journal, 26*(1), 1–7.

Locks, A. M., Hurtado, S., Bowman, N. A., & Oseguera, L. (2008). Extending notions of campus climate and diversity to students' transition to college. *Review of Higher Education, 31*(3), 257–285.

Margolis, E., & Pauwels, L. (Eds.). (2011). *The SAGE handbook of visual research methods.* Thousand Oaks, CA: SAGE.

Massey, D. (1993). Politics and space/time. In M. Keith & S. Pile (Eds.), *Place and the politics of identity* (pp. 139–159). New York, NY: Routledge.

Massey, D. (1994). *Space, place, & gender.* Minneapolis: University of Minnesota Press.

McGregor, J. (2004). Space, power, and the classroom. *FORUM, 46*, 13–18.

Museus, S. D. (2008). The role of ethnic student organizations in fostering African American and Asian American students' cultural adjustment and membership at predominantly White institutions. *Journal of College Student Development, 49*, 568–586.

Neely, B., & Samura, M. (2011). Social geographies of race: Connecting race and space. *Ethnic and Racial Studies, 34*, 1933–1952.

Nespor, J. (1997). *Tangled up in school: Politics, space, bodies, and signs in the educational process*. Mahwah, NJ: Erlbaum.

Omi, M. (2001). The changing meaning of race. In N. J. Smelser, W. J. Wilson, & F. Mitchell (Eds.), *America becoming: Racial trends and their consequences* (Vol. 1, pp. 243–263). Washington, DC: National Academies Press.

Osajima, K. (1995). Racial politics and the invisibility of Asian Americans in higher education. *Educational Foundations, 9*(1), 35–53.

Pascarella, E., Edison, M., Nora, A., Hagedorn, L., & Terenzini, P. (1996). Influences on students' openness to diversity and challenge in the first year of college. *Journal of Higher Education, 67*(2), 174–195.

Perrucci, R., Belshaw, R., DeMeritt, A., Frazier, B., Jones, J., Kimbrough, J., & Williams, B. (2000). The two faces of racialized space at a predominantly White university. *International Journal of Contemporary Sociology, 37*, 230–244.

Pulido, L. (2000). Rethinking environmental racism: White privilege and urban development in Southern California. *Annals of the Association of American Geographers, 90*, 12–40.

Samura, M. (2011). Racial transformations in higher education: Emergent meanings of Asian American racial identities. In X. L. Rong & R. Endo (Eds.), *Asian American education: Identities, racial issues, and languages* (pp. 73–100). Charlotte, NC: Information Age.

Samura, M. (2015). Wrestling with expectations: An examination of how Asian American college students negotiate personal, parental, and societal expectations. *Journal of College Student Development, 56*(6), 600–616.

Samura, M. (2016). Remaking selves, repositioning selves, or remaking space: An examination of Asian American college students' processes of "belonging." *Journal of College Student Development, 52*(2), 135–150.

Soja, E. (1989). *Postmodern geographies: The reassertion of space in critical social theory*. New York, NY: Verso.

Solórzano, D., Ceja, M., & Yosso, T. (2000). Critical race theory, racial microaggressions, and campus racial climate: The experiences of African American college students. *Journal of Negro Education, 69*(1/2), 60–73.

Solórzano, D. G., & Villalpando, O. (1998). Critical race theory, marginality, and the experience of students of color in higher education. In C. A. Torres & T. R. Mitchell (Eds.), *Sociology of education: Emerging perspectives* (pp. 211–224). Albany, NY: SUNY Press.

Suarez-Balcazar, Y., Orellana-Damacela, L., Portillo, N., Rowan, J., & Andrews-Guillen, C. (2003). Experiences of differential treatment among college students of color. *Journal of Higher Education, 74*, 428–444.

Suchar, C. (1997). Grounding visual sociology research in shooting scripts. *Qualitative Sociology, 20*(1), 33–55.

Tatum, B. (1997). *"Why are all the Black kids sitting together in the cafeteria?" And other conversations about race*. New York, NY: Basic Books.

Taylor, C. (2009). Towards a geography of education. *Oxford Review of Education, 35*, 651–669.

Tickamyer, A. (2000). Space matters! Spatial inequality in future sociology. *Contemporary Sociology, 29*, 805–813.
Villalpando, O. (2003). Self-segregation or self-preservation? A critical race theory and Latina/o critical theory analysis of a study of Chicana/o college students. *International Journal of Qualitative Studies in Education, 16*, 619–646.
Winant, H. (2000). Race and race theory. *Annual Review of Sociology, 26*, 169–185.
Winant, H. (2004). *The new politics of race: Globalism, difference, justice*. Minneapolis: University of Minnesota Press.
Woods, C. (1998). *Development arrested*. London, England: Verso.

10

AN INTERVIEW WITH MICHELLE SAMURA
How the "Blue Wall" Changes Our Discourses on Race in Higher Education: Stepping Out of the Comfort Zone and Seeing Things in a Different Light

Jimin Kwon

Her mother helped shape how Michelle Samura viewed the world. A lifelong educator, she taught Michelle to approach tasks, problems, and situations with her own perspective, challenging her to think about things in unique ways. For example, when Michelle was observing a situation, her mother would ask, "Who is included here? And who is not included?" With such questions from her mother in mind, she learned to focus on the margins, away from the ways people typically thought about the world. This approach, learned from her mother, was influential in her decision to engage in the study of student diversity in a nontraditional manner by looking at the impact of space on students of color on college campuses.

Michelle's interest in student diversity was also a function of her experience as an Asian American. There were moments when she felt as if she belonged but also moments she felt like an outsider. Growing up, she was aware that her dual identity as insider and outsider was a source of great tension; however, she says she "did not have the language to talk about it and the framework to discuss what was going on." That realization propelled her to pursue graduate education. She felt that graduate school would be a place where she might be able to contextualize her personal experience within larger social, psychological, and political processes.

When she first started thinking about race, she examined her own experience of growing up as an Asian American woman. She also drew from her experience teaching high school students. Michelle observed that her students' racial identification and racialization influenced how they interacted and viewed one another. She realized that such constructs formed a social reality for these students. As she thought about her students, she wanted to learn more about how college students of color experience limits and tensions as they navigate campuses and negotiate their identities. As Michelle began her graduate studies and sought to bring focus to her research agenda, she wondered whether to pursue a comparative analysis of all groups of students of color or to focus on one racial group. It was not an easy choice; she did not want to be labeled as a scholar studying only Asian American students simply because that might be what was expected of her.

The lack of research on Asian American students weighed heavily on Michelle's decision. Michelle felt that in the discourse on diversity in higher education, Asian American students were viewed as an overrepresented minority who had achieved full access to colleges and universities. Yet, she observed that racial identification for Asian American students was still salient, playing out in their daily lives, informing decisions to join social groups, their own expectations, and the studies and careers they chose to pursue. In deciding to focus on Asian American students for her dissertation, she was able to bring their perspective into the conversation about diversity in higher education. Because this group of students was usually seen as being included in higher education, they were a vital addition to discussions about diversity. While she did not necessarily want to focus on the model-minority image, she wanted to know why this stereotypical perception of Asian American students is so persistent and pervasive.

One of the major challenges Michelle faced in developing her research agenda was to find new approaches to complement the exceptional work on race and diversity in higher education. Her interest in notions of space distinguishes her work. She has always been interested in spaces in terms of architecture and design and the social spaces where people interact, so she pondered ideas such as "how painting a wall blue might actually affect what happens when people interact in front of that blue wall."

To expand her interest in space as a method to study race, she started looking at existing scholarship in geography, sociology, architecture, and design and thinking about how geographical and social spaces affect how people think and behave. The interdisciplinary nature of her work challenges her to venture into relatively unfamiliar fields, and Michelle believes it enables her to see issues through different lenses.

While Michelle was working on her master's thesis and as a teaching assistant for an Asian American studies course, she had a conversation with a student at a coffee shop and learned that some of the residential halls on campus had special-interest floors centered on different cultures, including one dedicated to Asian American cultures, colloquially referred to as the "Asian floor."

For a year, Michelle interviewed people on different floors of the residence hall, including the Asian floor, the Black hall, and the Chican@ floor. She invited students from different floors to examine how they understood their racial identities and how they behaved and felt on the different floors and outside them. She found that the students living on a dedicated floor viewed it as a problem when people outside their halls assumed the students on that floor would get along just because they shared racial identities and interests. The students recognized their own diversity of views and the effort needed to maintain their relationships. The students living in the Black hall talked about how people outside their floors made stereotypical assumptions about them, such as when White students would come to their floor to ask to borrow gold chains, baggy jeans, and other props for a campus "ghetto party." Black students who lived in that space expressed discomfort and frustration about these types of racialized experiences, in which racial stereotypes, the racialized space, and their racial identification were all connected in a way that perpetuated otherness.

With these responses from the students of color in mind, Michelle started asking how race and space are connected. Are there racialized spaces on campus? How do changes in space affect how people of different races interact? To explore such issues, Michelle invited students to talk about how they view themselves on campus in the context of a space, using innovative qualitative methods. For example, she asked the students to take pictures of spaces where they spent most of their time or spaces in which they felt they belonged or did not belong. Using a campus map, she asked students to mark places they would go or avoid. She found that some students' spatial experience eventually led to discussions of race.

Michelle is still looking for innovative ways to explore her interest in race, education, and space. Her work has led her to look at areas such as student engagement, community development, and relationship development between universities and surrounding communities. This interdisciplinary journey has invited her to draw on nontraditional and creative approaches to better understand how people experience living in a diverse society today.

Michelle advises students interested in working in diversity scholarship to find mentors. A professor who asked her to participate in an independent research project when she was an undergraduate student was her mentor, giving her help and advice. In her graduate career, she benefited from having friends and colleagues who helped to create an environment that encouraged her to explore and take risks as a scholar. As she works with graduate students today, Michelle encourages them to find similar support networks and to look at things from different angles, just like her mother did for her, asking, "What else do we see? How else can it be viewed? What are other ways that we might be leaving out?"

My conversation with Michelle left me with an exciting challenge: to see things in a different light and escape conventional ways of doing research. Her insights led me to think about how our experience and identity shape our thinking about people. Is our worldview independent of who we are? Is it completely divorced from our experience? How would such racialized experiences influence students on college campuses? How do the spaces where students belong affect their psychology and behavior? As Michelle has said, there is a social reality in higher education and in the world as a whole; racial identification and racialization are still salient for many people of color, especially for students on campus. Unique research approaches, like Michelle's spatial and visual methods, can enhance understanding of how college students of various racial groups manage their identities, relationships, and worldviews.

11

INCLUDING DISABILITY IN THE DISCOURSE

Extending and Advancing the Definition of *Diversity* in Higher Education

Allison Lombardi and Adam Lalor

For centuries, people with disabilities have faced discrimination. Their opportunities in education, employment, recreation, transportation, and other essential areas that contribute to quality of life have been limited. In the early twentieth century the eugenics movement made it acceptable practice to keep people with disabilities from procreating (Wehmeyer, 2013), and laws were passed to keep people with visible disabilities from public view, by outlawing, for example, begging in the street (Schweik, 2010). Later in the twentieth century, the disability rights movement helped reduce the amount of overtly discriminatory and shameful practices toward people with disabilities and eventually influenced policy making (e.g., the Rehabilitation Act of 1973 and the Americans with Disabilities Act of 1990). Thus, over the past 100 years, society has made great strides toward equal treatment of people with disabilities. Yet, we have more work to do.

The stigma of disability is strongly rooted in society. Many people are often unaware how their behavior discriminates against people with disabilities. Historically, our perception of disability has been shaped by medical definitions of *disability*. We are conditioned to diagnose, treat, and cure disability. Diagnoses of disability depend on a statistical measure of normality using standardized test scores. People who score two standard deviations below the mean on a norm-referenced test are defined as *disabled* and eligible to receive support services. Thus, the dominant view of disability is one of deficit, abnormality, and exceptionality. This reinforces the stigma by defining those with disabilities as problematic, abnormal, burdensome, and deserving of pity.

Higher education historically promises opportunity for upward mobility. Yet, equal opportunity to higher education has not always been available to many subgroups, such as women and people of color, and the dominant discourse tends to privilege some subgroups over others. For people with disabilities, success in higher education remains a persistent problem of inclusion in the dominant discourse on diversity and another of integration into the normative practices and policies of the institution. This chapter highlights the experiences of people with disabilities as they have navigated the higher education system for the past 40 years. The chapter concludes with recommendations for integrating disability into the discourse on diversity in higher education.

The Higher Education Climate

College students with disabilities are a diverse group. Disability types span a broad range of categories that are visible and invisible, and the most prevalent are learning disability (LD), attention-deficit/hyperactivity disorder (ADHD), and psychological or mental health diagnoses (Raue & Lewis, 2011). These categories label people with disabilities that are not easily noticeable by the general public in contrast to more visible disabilities. Students with LD, ADHD, or mental illness tend to request and qualify for instructional and exam modifications and accommodations in the postsecondary classroom as opposed to accommodations that concern the nature of the physical space (e.g., wheelchair accessible entrance to the building and classroom). Thus, the majority of college students with disabilities may not be easily recognizable by faculty, staff, and other college students, and they may require instructional modifications and accommodations in college courses.

About 11% of college students have disabilities (Newman et al., 2011). This proportion has steadily increased since the 1980s, reflecting successful policy initiatives, such as the Individuals with Disabilities Education Improvement Act (IDEIA) of 2004. Among rights to access free and appropriate public education, IDEIA mandated that schools incorporate post–high school transition planning into individualized education programs for students with disabilities. With the rise in college- and career-readiness policy initiatives of the past decade, increasing numbers of students from disadvantaged backgrounds and subgroups are attending college. The challenge remains to ensure that these students receive a high-quality postsecondary education and are well equipped for success after college.

More university administrators are making the deliberate decision to include "disability" in the definition of *diversity*. Some may argue this is long overdue. Logically, students with disabilities are marginalized just as those who are marginalized by race, gender, socioeconomic status, and sexual orientation, all markers of diversity and identity. By calling attention to these differences, we perhaps gain a stronger sense of our own belonging. Ability is yet another spectrum of the human condition, another *difference* we classify. As disability is increasingly recognized to fall within the scope of institutional diversity, we now face a pivotal moment. We must capitalize on this recognition by raising awareness of the issues students with disabilities face in higher education to foster a culture more inclusive of a diverse range of abilities and more accepting of all individuals.

The Higher Education Act (HEA) of 1965 was among the earliest policies directed toward decreasing higher education elitism. The seven titles of the original legislation included provisions for financial aid programs as well as scholarships, insured loans, interest subsidies, and work-study programs (Madaus, Kowitt, & Lalor, 2012). In 2008 programs to provide students with disabilities with quality postsecondary education were specified among the general provisions of the HEA reauthorization. This provision led to a funding competition sponsored by the U.S. Department of Education's Office of Postsecondary Education, Demonstration Projects to Ensure Students With Disabilities Receive a High Quality Education Program. In 2008, 23 awards were granted to researchers at institutions nationwide under this program (Madaus et al., 2012). Unfortunately, this program is no longer funded, and many researchers who began or extended their scholarship in disability and higher education were left with little or no resources to continue.

It is important to emphasize that (a) disability is but a single facet of an individual's identity, (b) disability is found in all kinds of groups, (c) disabilities can be visible or invisible, (d) 11% of college students have a disability, and (e) an institution that is compliant with disability law may not necessarily have met its ethical obligations. For the duration of the chapter, we elaborate on these points and discuss the implications.

Research Literature on Disability and Higher Education

Between 2011 and 2015, a research team we were part of engaged in an extensive study of the research literature on disability in higher education that was published through 2012. Using several research databases and targeted searches of higher education journals, we found 1,342 articles on the topic of disability in higher education. After removing articles related to secondary students in transition, non-degree-granting postsecondary programs, and college students without disabilities, 1,025 articles remained.

Our analysis revealed that few articles on the topic were published in academic journals prior to 1970. Since 1970, however, the frequency of such articles has increased steadily, reaching 80 in 2011. Undoubtedly, this increase reflects greater awareness of disability in society, increased public perception that individuals with disabilities can be contributing members of society, changes in disability rights policy and law, and measures taken to improve opportunities in postsecondary education for individuals with disabilities.

Since 1955, the publication date of the earliest article located, research articles focusing on disability in higher education have been published in a wide variety of disciplines, from education, health, law, and social work to computer science, chemistry, and economics. The research team found disability-focused articles in 232 different journals.

Of those 232 journals, 220 (95%) published 10 or fewer articles, and 159 (69%) had only one or two articles. Conversely, 347 articles on disability in higher education (34% of the total found) have been published by two journals: *Journal of Learning Disabilities* (*JLD*) and *Journal of Postsecondary Education and Disability* (*JPED*; formerly the *Bulletin of the Association on Handicapped Student Service Programs in Post-Secondary Education*). *JLD* focuses specifically on learning disabilities and includes research across a number of fields, disciplines, and education levels (e.g., K–12 and higher education). Since 1980 *JLD* has published 64 articles (6% of the total examined) on disability in higher education. The greatest number of articles on disability in higher education has been published in *JPED*, the official journal of the Association on Higher Education and Disability. *JPED* is the only academic journal dedicated solely to publishing research on disability in higher education.

Figure 11.1 shows the distribution of published articles by journal. As of 2012, *JPED* published 283 articles (28% of the total) on disability in higher education. Clearly, published research on disability has been concentrated in a few specialized journals, and logic suggests that as a result, exposure to this research beyond disability specialists has been limited. In fact, of the eight journals that included the most articles published on disability and higher education, only three were higher education research journals other than *JPED*. The remaining journals were intended for special education researchers and practitioners who primarily focus on the K–12 system.

Why has this concentration occurred? Is it because research journals with narrowly defined foci make submission of articles on the topic unlikely?

FIGURE 11.1. Top Eight Journals Publishing the Greatest Frequency of Articles on Higher Education and Disability

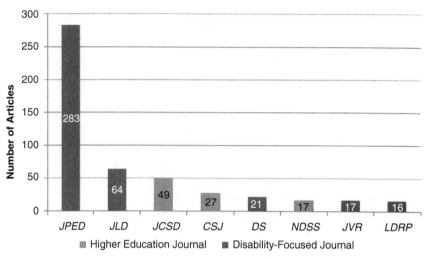

Note. JPED = *Journal of Postsecondary Education and Disability*; JLD = *Journal of Learning Disabilities*; JCSD = *Journal of College Student Development*; CSJ = *College Student Journal*; DS = *Disability and Society*; NDSS = *New Directions for Student Services*; JVR = *Journal of Vocational Rehabilitation*; LDRP = *Learning Disabilities Research and Practice*.

This is doubtful, given the breadth of journals that have published articles on disability in higher education. Could it be because of articles receiving unfavorable reviews in peer review processes? While this is possible, we suggest that this is also unlikely, given multiple reviewers and the breadth of the journals. In our opinion, the likely reason for the concentration of research articles related to disability in higher education is the lack of crossover between K–12 researchers (specifically special education researchers) and higher education researchers.

At present, a limited number of researchers specializing in issues of disability hold faculty positions in higher education and student affairs programs. Scholars who focus their research agenda on disability in higher education are predominantly in academic departments that specialize in disability—namely K–12 special education. Therefore, it is no surprise that articles are submitted to disability-focused journals first and higher education journals second. Further, among the few researchers who focus on disability and higher education, funding sources are dwindling, with the elimination of funding by the Office of Postsecondary Education of the Demonstration Projects being a major reason.

The professionals who read *JPED* are a relevant and appropriate group, but others also serve college students with disabilities. Yet in the many higher education journals that focus on institutional diversity, published articles pertaining to disability are scarce.

In a special issue of the *Journal of Diversity in Higher Education*, Turner (2013) makes the claim that the articles selected for that issue address the overall theme of advancing diversity in higher education by focusing on "race or ethnicity, equity, . . . and topics related to historically underrepresented, underserved, or marginalized populations in higher education" (p. 155). These topics should be at the forefront of higher education reform, but disability is not mentioned. There are no articles in the special issue that address the needs of college students with disabilities, despite the overwhelming evidence that this subgroup is indeed marginalized, underrepresented, and composed of diverse learners. The conversation excludes acknowledgment of this subgroup.

We believe the definition of *diversity* must go beyond race. Race is but one facet of the human condition. It is important to understand intersections of race with other facets of diversity, which might include disability, sexual orientation, and socioeconomic status. Is there a significant interaction between race and disability? If so, do experiences of students of color with disabilities differ from those of White students with disabilities? How so?

Student Perceptions

Student perceptions have been among the most highly researched areas related to disability and higher education (Madaus, Lalor, Gelbar, & Kowitt 2014). Perceptions can lead to the development of long-standing attitudes. Understanding how students with disabilities perceive the college environment and their place within it has implications for psychosocial development (Hadley, 2006; Ryan, Nolan, Keim, & Madsen, 1999). Researchers have studied the place of disability mostly from the perspectives of students with disabilities. Few studies have examined the perspectives of their peers without disabilities.

Students with disabilities have shared their perceptions on a variety of topics, including requesting accommodations (e.g., Hartman-Hall & Haaga, 2002), the impact of their disability on college learning (e.g., Fuller, Bradley, & Healey, 2004), stigma (e.g., Hartmann-Hall & Haaga, 2002; Weiner & Weiner, 1996), social engagement (e.g., Nielsen, 2001; Salzar, 2012), and transition to college (e.g., Heiman & Kariv, 2004). While perceptions vary between and within disability types (Nielsen, 1997), research suggests that many students with disabilities perceive academic (e.g., faculty attitudes, accessing accommodations; Dowrick, Anderson, Heyer, & Acosta, 2005) and social barriers (e.g., stigma, opportunities to connect socially with peers; Murray, Lombardi, Bender, & Gerdes, 2013). Such barriers have been linked to decreased graduation rates (Salzar, 2012), lower self-esteem (Hartmann-Hall & Haaga, 2002), and decreased likelihood of using support services in times of need (Hartmann-Hall & Haaga, 2002). Conversely, research suggests that students with disabilities hold positive perceptions regarding programs (e.g., courses targeting transition-to-college needs of students with disabilities) and pedagogical practices (e.g., universal design for learning and instruction) directed at improving educational access (Chiba & Low, 2007; Schelly, Davies, & Spooner, 2011).

Research on the perceptions of students without disabilities on disability in higher education is less abundant. A cursory review (Madaus et al., 2014) suggests that most articles on the perceptions of students without disabilities toward their peers with disabilities focus on issues of academic accommodations (e.g., Egan & Giuliano, 2009; Upton & Harper, 2002). Essentially, these studies reveal questions of fairness: whether certain accommodations are reasonable and necessary and lead to unfair advantages for students with disabilities. However, other studies suggest that students without disabilities report that their peers with disabilities should not be discriminated against or devalued (Green, 2007).

Despite the small body of research, the perceptions of individuals without disabilities must be understood if the goal is to increase inclusivity of students with disabilities in higher education and improve the disability-related campus climate (Junco & Salter, 2004). Research suggests that negative perceptions and attitudes toward disability held by peers without disabilities have been shown to diminish self-esteem in students with disabilities (Cambra, 1996). Understanding these perceptions is critical and requires greater investigation.

Disability and Identity

Disability identity development has received relatively little attention in the higher education research literature as compared to other aspects of identity development (e.g., race, gender, sexual orientation, socioeconomic status). *Identity* can be considered "the meanings attached to the self by one's self and others" (Michener, DeLamater, & Myers, 2004, p. 85), and *identity development* is "the process of becoming more complex in one's personal and social identity" (McEwen, 2003, p. 205). How do individuals with disabilities make sense of who they are in relation to their strengths and functional limitations in the context of society?

According to Dunn and Burcaw (2013), "much of the available scholarship on disability identity has its origins in the study of disability activism and disability policy studies" (p. 149). At present, few theories exist to help higher education scholars and practitioners understand and intentionally support identity development in college students with disabilities. Lines of disability identity research presently receiving the greatest attention in higher education are those of Olkin (1999) and Gibson (2006). This research, despite limitations and lack of specific focus on college students, has established a foundation for future disability identity research.

Disability identity is but a single facet of a college student's identity (Dunn & Burcaw, 2013; Gibson, 2006). Some findings show that some students with disabilities, particularly African American and first-generation college students, are at a greater disadvantage. Lombardi, Murray, and Gerdes (2012) investigated the intersection between disability and first-generation status. First-generation students with disabilities self-reported greater usage of accommodations and other supports provided by the Office of Disability Services at one university than their peers with disabilities who had at least one parent with a bachelor's degree. They also self-reported significantly higher financial stress and significantly lower family and peer support and earned significantly lower grade point averages (GPAs). Further, first-generation status contributed significantly to a hierarchical regression equation predicting college GPA while controlling for other demographic factors (e.g., race, gender, disability type). These findings suggest that regardless of other background factors and disability type, first-generation students with disabilities are doubly disadvantaged and thus have unique support needs.

Banks (2014) used a case study approach to explore the relationship between secondary transition services and factors contributing to postsecondary success for African American males with disabilities. In this qualitative study, three African American males with disabilities revealed their perceptions of inadequate secondary transition support and competing social and cultural identities. The second theme suggests that all college students, with and without disabilities, struggle with their own identity and relationship to diverse groups. At times, this struggle may include the decision to identify with one group over another (race as opposed to disability), yet identity membership need not be mutually exclusive.

While limited in generalizability, findings from both studies show the importance of the intersections of disability with other facets of identity (Banks, 2014; Lombardi et al., 2012). The findings have implications for student affairs personnel. For one, first-generation students with disabilities may be more dependent on institutional supports than their continuing-generation peers with disabilities (Lombardi et al., 2012) and may need more intensive support from student services personnel. More research is needed to better understand how disability intersects with other facets of identity and how this intersection affects student outcomes.

University Faculty and Staff Perceptions

For years, college faculty have relied on institutional resources (e.g., their school's office for disability services) to provide additional support to students with disabilities. In fact, many faculty may have been unaware they had students with disabilities enrolled in their classes. However, given the steady increase in the population of college students with disabilities and the lack of funding to bolster supports for institutional personnel, faculty now must provide accommodations for and modifications to exams and assignments in their courses. Often, requests for modifications come from students with and without disabilities. Examples of such requests might include (but are not limited to) extended deadlines and alternate exam formats and assignments. Even though more faculty are directly supporting students with disabilities, at most universities there is no professional development or training to ensure faculty are aware of their legal obligations. Further, the majority of faculty receives little to no training in effective teaching practices that will benefit diverse learners, including students with disabilities.

Although scarce, evidence-based faculty development programs exist. Research findings show that faculty who participate in some type of institutional training or workshop report greater awareness of students with disabilities and greater provision of accommodations (Lombardi & Murray, 2011; Lombardi, Murray, & Gerdes, 2011; Murray, Lombardi, Wren, & Keys, 2009). In addition, some research findings further demonstrate the need for disability awareness training to extend beyond faculty to university staff, such as student affairs, counseling centers, and administrative staff (Goad & Robertson, 2000; Murray, Lombardi, & Wren, 2011). These findings are promising and support institutional initiatives to fund and provide such training opportunities to faculty and staff. However, a national survey of 29 public 4-year institutions found that the greatest barrier (reported by 70% of respondents) hindering the implementation of faculty training was limited staff resources and faculty time (Raue & Lewis, 2011). At a time when a growing number of students with disabilities are gaining access to postsecondary settings, federal funds to support training initiatives are declining, and many colleges and universities lack sufficient resources to deliver training opportunities without external support (Newman et al., 2011).

Faculty Teaching Practices

Efforts to promote inclusive teaching practices began with several research groups promoting instructional frameworks based on universal design (Connell et al., 1997), a framework that originated in the field of architecture and was later adapted to fit instruction. Universal design for learning (Rose, Harbour, Johnston, Daley, & Abarbanell, 2006) and universal design for instruction (Scott et al., 2003) are two frameworks that were developed to encourage college faculty to make their teaching more accessible and inclusive. But these broad principles do not necessarily translate into actionable steps. As a result, faculty may not be sure how to go about creating more accessible and inclusive learning environments (Edyburn, 2010; Orr & Hammig, 2009).

Research findings on college faculty using inclusive teaching practices have focused on the development and testing of climate survey instruments and professional development training packages (Murray, Lombardi, Seeley, & Gerdes, 2014; Murray, Wren, Stevens, & Keys, 2009). Disability services personnel and administrators use such instruments to train faculty, one being the inclusive teaching strategies inventory (Lombardi, Murray, & Gerdes, 2011), which measures faculty knowledge of disability and inclusive teaching practices and helps in planning professional development topics. For example, the survey results may show that most faculty understand the process of requesting accommodations, but many do not know how to design an inclusive assessment. With this information, disability services personnel and higher education administrators may prioritize faculty training topics.

Summary

Over the past 40 years, we have learned that college students with disabilities have diverse experiences. Some require unique supports and accommodations, and most, if not all, will benefit from inclusive teaching practices. In fact, all diverse learners could potentially benefit from inclusive classroom environments that demonstrate flexibility with multiple modes of presentation and assessment. We've also seen some promising preliminary results in measuring student and faculty perceptions, teaching practices, and various modes of professional development. Finally, we've seen the small amount of federal funding allocated to these research efforts dwindle.

Given the present context of higher education and disability, we recommend the following to higher education administrators, faculty, and the federal government.

Prioritize disability within higher education research. First and foremost, high-quality research studies on disability must be published in well-known higher education journals. We will know more about students with disabilities if research findings are accessible to a wider audience of student affairs and higher education professionals and researchers. We are more likely to include disability under the diversity umbrella if we are better versed in disability-related topics.

Federal funding sources must be dedicated to higher education and disability. Reviving the Demonstration Projects competition sponsored by the Office of Postsecondary Education is one option. The Institute of Educational Sciences funds a postsecondary education funding competition, but disability is rarely its focus and could be prioritized.

Increase the rigor of disability research. In disability and higher education research studies considered for publication, data-based research should take precedence. In the current research literature on disability and higher education, nearly one-third of studies are not databased and tend to be conceptual or practical articles (Faggella-Luby, Lombardi, Lalor, & Dukes, 2014). In a similar vein, all research studies should report disability as a demographic category, much like race and gender, to improve the overall rigor and quality of the literature.

Hire disability researchers as higher education program faculty. Many higher education scholars study race, gender, socioeconomic status, sexual orientation, and first-generation status. Faculty who study higher education should include disability scholars. The few scholars who now study disability and higher education tend to be housed in special education departments and programs. However, special education is a K–12 institution, and graduate students enrolled in special education programs tend to be preservice teachers preparing for K–12 teaching.

Develop and validate disability identity models. Disability is a facet of identity, not an entire identity, and it intersects with other aspects of identity. But our language suggests it is a conclusive marker of identity (e.g., "the autistic kid" as opposed to "the kid with autism"). Future research should study how disability interacts with other identities, such as race. Past studies on college students with disabilities too often do not collect and report standard demographic categories like race and gender. At a minimum, all disability-related studies should report these demographic data and consider these variables in data analyses.

Prioritize faculty and staff professional development in disability-related topics. We have made progress toward development and validation of assessment tools for faculty, students, and staff (Barnard-Brak, Sulak, Tate, & Lechtenberger, 2010; Lombardi, Murray, & Gerdes, 2011; Murray, Lombardi, & Wren, 2011; Murray, Wren, & Keys, 2008; Vogel, Holt, Sligar, & Leake, 2008). These assessments support a data-driven framework of professional development. Essentially, higher education administrators have the tools they need to assess their campus climate and prioritize professional development topics and opportunities for faculty and staff. Professional development training modules have been developed and packaged with funding from the Office of Postsecondary Education's Demonstration Projects (Murray, Lombardi, Wren, & Keys, 2009; Murray, Lombardi, Seeley, et al., 2014).

We have the tools to raise disability awareness and improve campus climate for all diverse learners, including those with disabilities. It is simply a matter of using them to prioritize disability in higher education and then build from the work we've already completed. Doing so will help us better understand disability identity for college students and increase a positive learning climate for all diverse learners, with and without disabilities. To move forward with this work, we must first include disability in the discourse to extend and advance the definition of *diversity* in higher education. Only then can we properly acknowledge and celebrate this subgroup of college students so they may ultimately experience greater quality of life and equal rights as citizens well into adulthood.

References

Banks, J. (2014). Barriers and supports to postsecondary transition: Case studies of African American students with disabilities. *Remedial and Special Education, 35*(1), 28–39.

Barnard-Brak, L., Sulak, T., Tate, A., & Lechtenberger, D. (2010). Measuring college students' attitudes toward requesting accommodations: A national multi-institutional study. *Assessment for Effective Intervention, 35*(3), 141–147.

Cambra, C. (1996). A comparative study of personality descriptors attributed to the deaf, the blind, and individuals with no sensory disability. *American Annals of the Deaf, 141*(1), 24–28.

Chiba, C., & Low, R. (2007). A course-based model to promote successful transition to college for students with learning disorders. *Journal of Postsecondary Education and Disability, 20*, 40–53.

Connell, B. R., Jones, M., Mace, R., Mueller, J., Mullick, A., & Ostroff, E. (1997). The principles of universal design. Retrieved from www.ncsu.edu/www/ncsu/design/sod5/cud

Dowrick, P. W., Anderson, J., Heyer, K., & Acosta, J. (2005). Post-secondary education across the USA: Experiences of adults with disabilities. *Journal of Vocational Rehabilitation, 22*, 41–47.

Dunn, D. S., & Burcaw, S. (2013). Disability identity: Exploring narrative accounts of disability. *Rehabilitation Psychology, 58*(2), 148–157.

Edyburn, D. L. (2010). Would you recognize universal design for learning if you saw it? Ten propositions for the second decade of UDL. *Learning Disability Quarterly, 33*(1), 1–41.

Egan, P. M., & Giuliano, T. A. (2009). Unaccommodating attitudes: Perceptions of students as a function of academic accommodation use and test performance. *North American Journal of Psychology, 11*, 487–500.

Faggella-Luby, M., Lombardi, A., Lalor, A., & Dukes, L. L. (2014). Methodological trends in disability and higher education research: A historical analysis of the *Journal of Postsecondary Education and Disability*. *Journal of Postsecondary Education and Disability, 27*, 357–368.

Fuller, M., Bradley, A., & Healey, M. (2004). Incorporating disabled students within an inclusive higher education environment. *Disability & Society, 19*, 455–468.

Gibson, J. (2006). Disability and clinical competency: An introduction. *The California Psychologist, 39*, 6–10.

Goad, C. J., & Robertson, J. M. (2000). How university counseling centers serve students with disabilities: A status report. *Journal of College Student Psychotherapy, 14*(3), 13–22.

Green, S. E. (2007). Components of perceived stigma and perceptions of well-being among university students with and without disability experience. *Health Sociology Review, 16*, 328–340. doi:10.5172/hesr.2007.16.3-4.328

Hadley, W. M. (2006). L. D. students' access to higher education: Self-advocacy and support. *Journal of Developmental Education, 30*(2), 10–16.

Hartman-Hall, H. M., & Haaga, D. A. (2002). College students' willingness to seek help for their learning disabilities. *Learning Disability Quarterly, 25*, 263–274.

Heiman, T., & Kariv, D. (2004). Manifestations of learning disabilities in university students: Implications for coping and adjustment. *Education, 125*, 313–324.

Higher Education Act of 1965, 20 U.S.C. § 1001-1155 (2015).

Higher Education Opportunity Act of 2008, 20 U.S.C. § 1001 (2011).

Individuals With Disabilities Education Improvement Act of 2004, 20 U.S.C. § 1400 (2010).

Junco, R., & Salter, D. W. (2004). Improving the campus climate for students with disabilities through the use of online training. *NASPA Journal, 41*, 263–276.

Lombardi, A. R., Gerdes, H., & Murray, C. (2011). Validating an assessment of individual actions, postsecondary, and social supports of college students with disabilities. *Journal of Student Affairs Research and Practice, 49*(1), 107–126.

Lombardi, A. R., & Murray, C. (2011). Measuring university faculty attitudes toward disability: Willingness to accommodate and adopt universal design principles. *Journal of Vocational Rehabilitation, 34*(1), 43–56.

Lombardi, A. R., Murray, C., & Gerdes, H. (2011). College faculty and inclusive instruction: Self-reported attitudes and actions pertaining to universal design. *Journal of Diversity in Higher Education, 4*(4), 250–261.

Lombardi, A. R., Murray, C., & Gerdes, H. (2012). Academic performance of first generation college students with disabilities. *Journal of College Student Development, 53,* 811–826.

Madaus, J. W., Kowitt, J. S., & Lalor, A. R. (2012). The Higher Education Opportunity Act: Impact on students with disabilities. *Rehabilitation Research, Policy, and Education, 26*(1), 33–42.

Madaus, J. W., Lalor, A. R., Gelbar, N., & Kowitt, J. S. (2014). *The Journal of Postsecondary Education and Disability*: From past to present. *Journal of Postsecondary Education and Disability, 27,* 347–356.

McEwen, M. K. (2003). New perspectives on identity development. In S. R. Komives & D. B. Woodard, Jr. (Eds.), *Student services: A handbook for the profession* (4th ed., pp. 203–233). San Francisco, CA: Jossey-Bass.

Michener, H. A., DeLamater, J. D., & Myers, D. J. (2004). *Social psychology* (5th ed.). Belmont, CA: Wadsworth/Thompson Learning.

Murray, C., Lombardi, A. R., Bender, F., & Gerdes, H. (2013). Social support: Main and moderating effects on the relation between financial stress and adjustment among college students with disabilities. *Social Psychology of Education, 16,* 277–295.

Murray, C., Lombardi, A., Seeley, J., & Gerdes, H. (2014). Effects of an intensive disability-focused training experience on university faculty self-efficacy. *Journal of Postsecondary Education and Disability, 27*(2), 179–193.

Murray, C., Lombardi, A., & Wren, C. (2011). The effects of disability-focused training on the attitudes and perceptions of university staff. *Remedial and Special Education, 32*(4), 290–300.

Murray, C., Lombardi, A. R., Wren, C., & Keys, C. (2009). The effects of disability-focused training on attitudes and perceptions of university staff. *Learning Disability Quarterly, 32*(2), 87–102.

Murray, C., Wren, C., & Keys, C. (2008). University faculty perceptions of students with learning disabilities: Correlates and group differences. *Learning Disability Quarterly, 31*(1), 1–19.

Murray, C., Wren, C. T., Stevens, E. B., & Keys, C. (2009). Promoting university faculty and staff awareness of students with learning disabilities: An overview of the Productive Learning u Strategies (PLuS) project. *Journal of Postsecondary Education and Disability, 22,* 117–129.

Newman, L., Wagner, M., Knokey, A., Marder, C., Nagle, K., Shaver, D., & Wei, X. (2011). *The post-high school outcomes of young adults with disabilities up to 8 years after high school: A report from the National Longitudinal Transition Study-2.* Menlo Park, CA: National Center for Special Education Research.

Nielsen, J. A. (1997). Increasing awareness of learning disabilities. *Alberta Journal of Educational Research, 43*(2/3), 169–172.

Nielsen, J. A. (2001). Successful university students with learning disabilities. *Journal of College Student Psychotherapy, 15*(4), 37–48.

Olkin, R. (1999). *What psychotherapists should know about disability*. New York, NY: Guilford Press.

Orr, A. C., & Hammig, S. B. (2009). Inclusive postsecondary strategies for teaching students with learning disabilities: A review of the literature. *Learning Disability Quarterly, 32*(3), 181–196.

Raue, K., & Lewis, L. (2011). *Students with disabilities at degree-granting postsecondary institutions* (NCES 2011018). Washington, DC: National Center for Education Statistics.

Rose, D., Harbour, W., Johnston, S., Daley, S., & Abarbanell, L. (2006). Universal design for learning in postsecondary education: Reflections on principles and their application. *Journal of Postsecondary Education and Disability, 19*(2), 135–151.

Ryan, A. G., Nolan, B. F., Keim, J., & Madsen, W. (1999). Psychosocial adjustment factors of postsecondary students with learning disabilities. *Journal of College Student Psychotherapy, 13*(3), 3–18.

Salzar, M. S. (2012). A comparative study of campus experiences of college students with mental illness versus a general college sample. *Journal of American College Health, 60*(1), 1–7.

Schelly, C. L., Davies, P. L., & Spooner, C. L. (2011). Student perceptions of faculty implementation of universal design for learning. *Journal of Postsecondary Education and Disability, 24*, 19–37.

Schweik, S. M. (2010). *The ugly laws: Disability in public*. New York: New York University Press.

Scott, S. S., McGuire, J. M., & Shaw, S. F. (2003). Universal design of instruction: A new paradigm for adult instruction in postsecondary education. *Remedial and Special Education, 24*, 369–379.

Turner, C. S. (2013). Advancing diversity in higher education. *Journal of Diversity in Higher Education, 6*(3), 155–157.

Upton, T. D., & Harper, D. C. (2002). Multidimensional disability attitudes and equitable evaluation of educational accommodations by college students without disabilities. *Journal of Postsecondary Education and Disability, 15*(2), 1–23.

Vogel, S. A., Holt, J. K., Sligar, S., & Leake, E. (2008). Assessment of campus climate to enhance student success. *Journal of Postsecondary Education and Disability, 21*, 15–31.

Wehmeyer, M. L. (2013). Beyond pathology: Positive psychology and disability. In M. Wehmeyer (Ed.), *The Oxford handbook of positive psychology and disability* (pp. 3–6). New York, NY: Oxford University Press.

Weiner, E., & Weiner, J. (1996). Concerns and needs of university students with psychiatric disabilities. *Journal of Postsecondary Education and Disability, 12*, 2–9.

12

AN INTERVIEW WITH ALLISON LOMBARDI
Including Disability in the Discourse
Lloyd Edward Shelton

Disability in higher education. What does it look like? What should it look like? Should institutions of higher learning empower students with disabilities to explore, value, and embrace their status as a strength? Should they value disability as an aspect of diversity? If so, how can universities and colleges facilitate the personal growth and academic success of students with disabilities?

These are just a few of the questions that have motivated University of Connecticut assistant professor Allison Lombardi for nearly a decade. Allison's research is centered on how students with disabilities perceive themselves in the culture of higher education.

As I prepared for this interview, I was enthusiastic about the opportunity to have an in-depth conversation with an individual who has dedicated her life to the analysis and creation of knowledge about those with disabilities and the ways society can better facilitate their growth and development. After discovering that she was a former National Collegiate Athletic Association Division I-A student athlete, I was also quite curious why she chose disability as her field of study.

As an undergraduate at the University of California, Berkeley, she found professors often adversely judged her for identifying as a student athlete. Allison reached a point where she actually tried to prevent faculty from knowing about her status as a student athlete. She said that this persistent fear she had of being identified as a student athlete led to self-doubt and insecurity, which caused her to feel that she had to constantly prove herself in the classroom. She noted that her "fear of discovery" was similar to the experience of students with hidden disabilities. Berkeley's culture viewed her athleticism as, in essence, a type of disability and a marker of academic inferiority.

I personally found her experience at Berkeley to be absolutely fascinating. It may be an example of a troubling trend at elite institutions whose cultures rigidly restrict how a scholar is supposed to appear or behave. Students in such cultures feel intense pressure to conform to this image of scholarly competence and avoid the appearance of acting or looking different from the norm and therefore unintelligent. At many universities, having a disability may constitute such a cultural abnormality.

In 2000 Allison began the master's program in literacy, society, and culture at Berkeley's School of Education with the goal of becoming an academic adviser for student athletes. While studying for this degree, she worked with student athletes on their academic development, especially those considered academically at risk. As a former student athlete, she thoroughly enjoyed the opportunity to work with student athletes.

Beginning at Berkeley, moving on to the University of Maryland, and eventually ending up at the University of Oregon, Allison spent the next 5 years doing what she referred to as "damage control" as a learning specialist. She assisted student athletes who had come from substandard school systems and were often ill equipped to succeed in top-tier academic institutions. Some of them had diagnosed disabilities, including learning disabilities, attention-deficit/hyperactivity disorder, or emotional behavior disorders. She became more familiar with individualized education plans and other documentation for students with disabilities and interacted with personnel in campus offices for students with disabilities, learning about their procedures for instructional and exam accommodations. This experience was important in influencing her desire to study issues related to students with disabilities. In 2006 she began a PhD program with a focus on special education at the University of Oregon.

As I questioned Allison about the challenges she faced doing this type of research in the academy, she paused for a moment, and then told me a story about her struggles searching for a job after earning a PhD in 2010. She was frequently told that her research specialty—educational transitions for those who learn differently and systemic support mechanisms to increase their success in higher education—was not a good fit. Because her research related to the intersectionality of special education and higher education, she had trouble neatly fitting into special education or higher education circles.

In terms of advice for those who aspire to be faculty members, Allison strongly encourages PhD graduates in search of tenure-track positions to be sure when writing cover letters to explain specifically why they would be a good fit for a particular position, describing the common themes of their work and indicating a clear line of future research. She urges them to publish extensively while completing a PhD, develop credentials, and present their research history cogently.

During her 2-year job hunt, Allison was fortunate to continue to receive funds for her postdoctoral research at the University of Oregon. She published several papers that helped her land a position at the University of Connecticut, which she calls an "uncommonly good fit." The Department of Educational Psychology has a program on transitions (the obstacles students with various learning styles and cognitive disabilities may face) and a specific research focus on secondary and postsecondary education and disability. This aligns with Allison's passion for studying the climate in higher education and its ability to support the development of students with diverse styles of learning and socioeconomic backgrounds that may leave them academically unprepared for success in college.

To say that I found this conversation with Allison enjoyable would be an extreme understatement. It is rare that one is able to interact with someone who not only appreciates the wonderful aspects of a truly diverse environment but also has actually dedicated countless hours and an unquantifiable amount of mental and physical energy assisting those who may fall outside of what the world of academia considers to be normal. Allison is putting her money where her mouth is by making accessibility in higher education and diversity a key component of her life's work.

13

THE IMPACT OF MEDIA IMAGERY ON ACADEMIC IDENTITY DEVELOPMENT FOR BLACK MALE STUDENT ATHLETES

LaVar J. Charleston and Jerlando F. L. Jackson

Past studies have offered evidence of an oppositional relationship between academic and athletic achievement rooted in popular culture and enhanced by media representations (Beamon & Bell, 2006; Harrison, 2009). Overwhelmingly, the influence of media messages and images of African American males is cited as an important contributing factor in this conflict (Beamon & Bell, 2006). Effects of repeated exposure to these portrayals of African American males who participate in intercollegiate athletics is said to cause an overidentification with athletes and sports, an overvaluing of other physical performance activities, and an undervaluing of academic performance and academic identity.

In 2011 the College Board declared that "policymakers must make improving outcomes for young men of color a national priority" (Lee & Ransom, 2011, p. 69). However, there has yet to be a thorough examination of the role that media influences play in shaping the academic identities of Black student athletes who make up the majority of Black males in college (Harper, Williams, & Blackman, 2013). As of 2010, Blacks made up the majority of athletes in National Collegiate Athletic Association (Lapchick, Hoff, & Kaiser, 2010) Division I sports. The persistent disparity in their academic achievement with their White counterparts has implications beyond college (Harper et al., 2013). The existing literature indicates that Blacks are socialized into the athletic world much more powerfully than Whites, often leading them to set unrealistic goals that discount their own professional potential (Beamon, 2010; Morris & Adeyemo, 2012). The media play a particularly influential role in what Harrison (2009) refers to as "athletication,"

(p. 46) or their tendency to downplay Black athletes' intelligence and sensationalize their lifestyles while failing to emphasize their success in the world of professional athletics (Rada & Wulfemeyer, 2005).

Additionally, many studies indicate that sports media tend to emphasize the natural physicality and athleticism of Black male athletes rather than their character, leadership skills, or mental competence, which has major consequences on shaping the identity development of Black viewers (Billings, 2004; Fujioka, 2005). A study by Rada and Wulfemeyer (2010) found that Black athletes were more likely not only to receive negative commentary from sportscasters but also to be described in regard to "their God-given, natural ability," whereas White athletes were portrayed as "hard working and intellectually endowed" (p. 80). Similar conclusions were reached in a study of professional football quarterbacks (Billings, 2004). Such racial stereotypes have been shown to have an impact on the identities of Black athletes. For example, in a study conducted by Martin, Harrison, Stone, and Lawrence (2010), underestimations of the competence of Blacks seen on TV led Black viewers to assess their own intelligence as lower than that of Whites.

Critical analyses of media representations of Blacks in the United States have revealed a complex interplay of ideas and values that undergird the expression, recognition, or assignment of roles to Blacks in film and television (Harper, 2009; McCluskey, 2007). Negative depictions of Black men in media are disproportionately higher than those of any other group in America. While studies have demonstrated that Black males are socialized into sports deliberately and intensively (e.g., Harrison, 2009), what role does media imagery play in the academic development of Black male student athletes?

Methodology and Methods

In an attempt to more fully understand and describe the participants' lived experiences (Creswell, 2002), this study relies on a qualitative approach to investigate the cognitive process of identity formation among Black male student athletes at a large midwestern NCAA Division I institution. A phenomenological design was well suited because our aim was to understand the perspectives and experiences of a group, and it allowed us to use data from participants to develop foundational knowledge (Moustakas, 1994; Shank, 2002). Data were collected using two focus groups (n_1 = 10, n_2 = 12) and 8 one-on-one interviews with freshmen and sophomore Black male athletes who were selected using purposive sampling methods (Bogdan & Biklen, 2007). We, two Black male researchers, conducted the interviews, which lasted 30 to 45 minutes for the individuals and about 80 minutes for the focus groups. The average age of participants was 19 years. Informed consent was obtained orally, and participants were made aware of their right to suspend the session at any time. In the interviews and focus group sessions, a series of closed and open-ended questions were used to gather information relevant to the participants' experiences, paying specific attention to the effects of media messages and images on their student athlete experiences.

Data Analysis

This study primarily employed a grounded theory approach to analyzing the data; it was necessary to use the constant comparative method in an effort to enable us to refocus and shape the study as it progressed (Glesne & Peshkin, 1992). Grounded theory involves collecting and analyzing data concurrently, enabling the development of theoretical explanations for perceived phenomena as they are observed (Glaser & Straus, 1967). Likewise, the use of grounded theory enabled us to seek cases for comparison that illuminated additional aspects of the researched phenomena and to trace the development of our findings. By using the constant comparative method, we were able to continually examine these data in an effort to illuminate patterns of themes and their meanings (Miles & Huberman, 1994).

Validity

To see if the study's results could be generalized, we employed a naturalistic approach. While quantitative empirical research typically considers reliability and the internal and external validity of measures and procedures, naturalistic inquiry considers audibility, credibility, and fittingness (Guba & Lincoln, 1981). Reliability in qualitative research involves the ability to replicate the study given a similar set of circumstances. In naturalistic inquiry, the raw data obtained by the researchers are coded in a way that the themes and theories deduced can be understood by others who can arrive at a similar conclusion by examining these data.

Sample

All 30 participants in the 2 focus groups and one-on-one interviews were classified as Black or African American. The first focus group consisted of 3 freshman and 7 sophomores. The second focus group consisted of 4 freshmen and 8 sophomores. Roughly half of the participants had yet to declare majors, and among the others there were no predominant patterns of fields of study. All participants were scholarship recipients of a Bowl Championship Series football team. They were from geographically dispersed areas in the United States.

Results

Analysis of the interview and focus group data suggests that media sources perpetuate stereotypes. Black male student athletes make a conscious effort to combat these stereotypes (stereotype reactance) by proving themselves academically and socially outside athletics. Participants use proactive tools to help demystify and provide counternarratives regarding being "Black" and "male" and "athletes" in both the social and academic college settings. Although participants sought to combat the impact of negative media portrayals of Black male student athletes by engaging academically as students, many spoke of considerable challenges in doing so.

Student/Academic Engagement

Study participants indicated a desire to combat stereotypes by engaging with other students in a scholarly manner, to let their nonathletic peers know that they "did not think that they were all of that," as one participant recounted. Others perceived that media portrayals perpetuated negative stereotypes that they were "academically lazy" and "just there for the sport." While all participants were Black and male, they indicated that stereotypes about these traits were prevalent for all students who played basketball and football and were often propagated in the sports. One participant stated,

> A lot of people outside your sport think you're uneducated and just here for your respective sport, but the perception is not correct, even though it is generalized for all of us. The media only tends to publish when folks step out of line, when there are actually way more of us actually taking care of business in the classroom than getting into trouble.

Participants also described how impressions of media coverage negatively affect their engagement on college campuses and make it difficult for them to be themselves in their interactions with professors and even with their peers. Participants stated that the media portray football players particularly negatively, and as a result other students think "athletes get everything" and "think we're dumb." Additionally, they felt that while many nonstudent athletes were free to enjoy media—and social media in particular—student athletes were not allowed the same liberties. "We cannot open up on social media," one participant stated. "We have to be super cautious of forming a negative identity of ourselves." Participants felt especially attuned to negatively skewed media coverage of Black male athletes, which they believed resulted from a failure of mass media professionals to get to know student athletes as individuals. As one participant said, "They fail to realize that we're just like everybody else. We are normal people. It's crazy." Participants blamed media for taking many mundane aspects of the sport (e.g., celebration) the wrong way and for being very quick to "bring out negative aspects."

Participants felt that negative stereotypes about Black male student athletes were pervasive among their professors. One participant said he had a professor who seemed to always "look at me all the time, waiting on me to do something wrong, so they can tell the coaches." But participants stated that they "feel more welcomed when professors are understanding." One participant described his internal dilemma about engaging in classroom settings.

> It [negative stereotypes] kind of holds me back. I don't want to be perceived as this athlete who thinks he knows it all or sit back and let everyone do everything. . . . You know the answer but don't answer, because if you get it wrong, it's like "He's an athlete. He doesn't know anything." Or, "He thinks he knows everything." It's a two-edged sword.

Participants also felt that media-propagated stereotypes had an impact on their relationships with female students. Some described judgmental looks from female students who assumed that "all athletes are dogs and just use women." Consequently, participants stated that "women tend to talk about all the athletes and spread it around," and athletes tend to "get blasted on social media." Participants even noted difficulty in discussing their choice of major with nonathletes, fearing that they would be judged no matter what they chose. One participant who plays football and runs track offered similar sentiments.

> This girl asked me what my major was, and I told her sociology, and then she replies, "So you're majoring in track then." It makes you angry because she assumes I'm just worried about football just because my major is sociology, which I am genuinely interested in.

All in all, participants exhibited exasperation related to their efforts to combat negative stereotypes they felt were perpetuated by the media. The media's tendency to bash athletes was attributed to a lack of connection. Participants blamed the ignorance of sports broadcasters or their portrayals of Black male student athletes, noting that many never played sports and therefore lacked understanding of certain sport-related dynamics. "A lot of people like to harp on negative stuff," said one participant. "You can't be yourself around too many people." Participants also dismissed media as "self-serving," with one student-athlete offering that "the biggest problem with all of it" is that people look at TV sports commentators like Skip Bayless and

Steven A. Smith (ESPN sports analysts) "as experts of the sports" when one played neither college nor pro sports and the other played only briefly in college.

In light of the negative images perpetuated in the media and encountered regularly on campus, many Black athletes felt safe only by remaining in their "athletic bubble." One participant described feelings of powerlessness in altering others' perceptions and a need to "block it out" and disengage.

> I feel like we can do what we do, but it ain't gonna change what people do or think. We just have to block it out. We just do what we do. Ignore it and go about my business. At the end of the day, if you get your degree, that's all that matters.

Moreover, participants said they felt more comfortable around other student athletes who understood their shared plight. Participants felt nonathlete peers either wanted to "put them on a pedestal" or "tear them down." One participant dejectedly said,

> A lot of people act like they like us but really don't, because they think we got it made. If we can be around folks we know, we got our brotherhood, our family is right here. We don't need to go outside of that.

Another participant expressed similar sentiments:

> It's only so much you can do. Non-student-athletes don't appreciate what they got, the fact that they can take a nap whenever they want. You try to explain to people what we do, and they say, "I work. I get up at nine o'clock." . . . But we're held to a ridiculously strict schedule. You can't do what you normally could do as a regular student. We feel like we're in this shell, but we can't do what you all can do; we might get kicked off the team for stuff normal students can do.

Ultimately, students felt that attempts to actively engage in nonathlete academic and social circles often resulted in more harm than good and that they were victims of their athletic status. Although previous studies have highlighted the importance of engagement as a predictor of academic success in college, perceptions of persistently negative images and stereotypes in the media present a considerable obstacle to deeper academic engagement for Black male student athletes who endeavor to develop scholarly identities. Many become victims of the very stereotypes they wish to combat by seeking solace in an isolating athletic bubble.

Conclusions

While previous studies have investigated academic achievement in relation to intercollegiate athletes, this study demonstrates that the existing literature may miss important aspects of college athletes' academic identity formation. Through the use of grounded theory and naturalistic inquiry, these data reveal Black male student athletes' perspectives in their own words, demonstrating the considerable ways perceptions of negative stereotypes in the media hinder deeper academic engagement. Data from this study, when coupled with existing related literature, show a systemic bias against Black male athletes in relationship to the media and collegiate athletics—a bias with potentially detrimental effects on Black male student athletes.

Findings in this study are twofold. First, interviews confirmed that Black male college athletes are keenly aware of the unfavorable stereotypes projected onto them, and they consider such stereotypes in their own behavioral choices. This finding is in line with existing research into stereotype threat or anxiety about "being at risk of confirming, as self-characteristic, a negative stereotype about one's group" (Steele & Aronson, 1995, p. 797). Second, this study offers confirmation that Black male student athletes are especially cognizant of the danger of their own behavior perpetuating stereotypes in their academic environments.

As a result of stereotype threat, study participants found it extremely difficult to develop an academic self-identity. Many felt their identities typically were predetermined, unfairly assigned to them by their peers and professors. Common sentiments among participants included being falsely portrayed as lazy, privileged students who lacked the scholarly ambitions of their nonathlete peers. Conversely, respondents also expressed concerns about appearing too confident, especially to their professors. These results indicate the coercive effects of external pressures, originating among peers, professors, and the media, on the development of Black male student athletes' academic identities. Moreover, participants felt helpless to combat incorrect and potentially damaging stigmas as they lacked access to the appropriate media to express themselves as individuals rather than stereotypes.

Respondents attributed the source of these stereotypes to the negative relationships Black male athletes have historically had with the media, which confirmed the findings of previous studies. One factor that respondents felt perpetuated stigma was a scarcity of high-profile sports media personalities who challenged negative depictions of Black male student athletes and who truly understood their lived experiences. Participants blamed the media for portraying Black male athletes in a negative manner not indicative of their true identities. They felt prejudged based on historical stereotypes of Black male athletes, and within society as a whole. Despite being students at an elite university, many described experiences in which they felt their nonathlete peers and professors viewed them unfairly through a prism of negative images of Black males in society. These findings indicate the need for greater efforts to address institutionalized prejudices and biases against Black male student athletes.

In line with other studies, isolation was another common consequence of this stigma, as Black male student athletes reported feeling misunderstood by the nonathletes on campus. Many subjects felt as though their nonathlete peers lacked a proper understanding of their experiences and struggles, which led to feelings of resentment and envy. Participants described numerous examples of academic and social interactions they felt were lacking in empathy. As a result, participants felt discouraged from mingling with peers outside their athletic bubble. Feelings of isolation have been shown to be associated with lower levels of self-efficacy, which in turn can be a further detriment to success. Social isolation also prevents Black male student athletes from fully participating in and benefiting from the full college experience (Comeaux & Harrison, 2011). Existing research has shown that deeper student engagement and involvement and positive relationships with faculty are predictors of collegiate success. Therefore, it is important for college administrators, professors, and policymakers to address the social stigmas experienced by Black male athletes to smooth the path to academic success for all participants in collegiate athletics.

Implications

This study offers a unique source of data regarding the struggles of Black male college athletes and their perceptions of negative media portrayals. When considered in combination with the existing literatures on collegiate success, stereotype threat, and images of Black males in the media, we offer several recommendations to enhance academic potential for Black male student athletes.

Media

Many of the respondents in this study attributed feeling misunderstood by their peers and professors to media stereotypes, particularly in sports. Although negative portrayals of Black male athletes may never be fully eradicated, coverage can be more balanced with a greater focus on the positive attributes and academic successes of Black male student athletes. As previously noted, sports media have been shown to disproportionately note Black athletes' physical prowess and behavioral issues while downplaying their academic successes, intellectual or leadership skills, or other positive academic-related characteristics (Rada & Wulfemeyer, 2005). Additionally, respondents felt the media were too quick to focus on their negative behaviors and overlooked their individual characters. Participants described a disconnect between prominent sportscasters and athletes, which could be remedied by hiring sportscasters with firsthand knowledge of the struggles of Black male student athletes and a willingness to recognize the broader achievements of students outside athletics.

The University Community

Another major theme articulated by respondents was the tendency of media to falsely sensationalize their lifestyles, causing unwarranted resentment from nonathletes on campus. Many athletes believed that the media portrayed them as more entitled and less intelligent, and as a result many felt judged by their nonathlete student peers for receiving so-called special treatment. Some who felt they pushed themselves academically to succeed resented it when athletes were admitted to the same competitive institution without that same kind of effort (Simons, Bosworth, Fujita, & Jensen, 2007). However, student athletes felt that the many hours they dedicated to meetings, practices, study tables, and tutoring sessions too often went unnoticed. To be academically successful, athletes must feel welcome in their educational environments. This requires more substantial and effective engagement between athletes and their peers—as well as between athletes and their professors—which may be accomplished through relationship-building activities and informational sessions between athletes and nonathletes, faculty, and staff. Athletic administrators, student affairs practitioners, residence hall directors, and faculty and staff must play a more active role in providing opportunities for interaction between student athletes and the rest of the university community.

The Plight of Black Males in Higher Education

A recurring theme in this study was the continued ill treatment experienced by Black males in higher education, despite often false perceptions that such students are provided with more advantages in college. Policy modifications are necessary to ensure the academic success of these men, and more care must be taken to adequately prepare them for what may be a hostile living and learning environment. More specifically, Black male athletes should be exposed to methods for navigating the higher education system. The experiences of participants in this study offer evidence of yet another barrier to success that Black men face in their pursuit of postsecondary education. Consequentially, when Black males complete their college careers, they are often underprepared for careers outside athletics, and if they become professional athletes, they are frequently underestimated intellectually by mass media, further perpetuating the cycle for future generations. This study was a rare opportunity to present their perspective in their own words, and more research is needed to develop concrete solutions to counter the negative effects of media images on the academic identity development of Black male student athletes.

References

Beamon, K. (2010). Are sports overemphasized in the socialization process of African American males? A qualitative analysis of former collegiate athletes' perception of sports socialization. *Journal of Black Studies, 41*, 281–300.

Beamon, K., & Bell, P. A. (2006). Academics versus athletics: An examination of the effects of background and socialization on African American male student athletes. *Social Science Journal, 43*, 393–403.

Billings, A. (2004). Depicting the quarterback in Black and White: A content analysis of college and professional football broadcast commentary. *Howard Journal of Communications, 15*(4), 201–210.

Bogdan, R., & Biklen, S. (2007). *Qualitative research for education: An introduction to theories and methods* (5th ed.). Boston, MA: Allyn & Bacon.

Comeaux, E., & Harrison, C. (2011). A conceptual model of academic success for student-athletes. *Educational Researcher, 40*, 235–245.

Creswell, J. W. (2002). *Educational research: Planning, conducting, and evaluating quantitative and qualitative research.* Upper Saddle River, NJ: Merrill Prentice Hall.

Fujioka, Y. (2005). Black media images as a perceived threat to African American ethnic identity: Coping responses, perceived public perception, and attitudes towards Affirmative Action. *Journal of Broadcasting & Electronic Media, 49*, 450–467.

Glaser, B., & Strauss, A. (1967). *The discovery of grounded theory.* Chicago, IL: Aldine.

Glesne, C., & Peshkin, A. (1992). *Becoming qualitative researchers: An introduction.* White Plains, NY: Longman.

Guba, E., & Lincoln, Y. (1981). *Effective evaluation: Improving the usefulness of evaluation results through responsive and naturalistic approaches.* San Francisco, CA: Jossey-Bass.

Harper, S. R. (2009). Niggers no more: A critical race counternarrative on Black male student achievement at predominantly White colleges and universities. *International Journal of Qualitative Studies in Education, 22*, 697–712.

Harper, S. R., Williams, C. D., & Blackman, H. W. (2013). *Black male student-athletes and racial inequities in NCAA Division I college sports.* Philadelphia: University of Pennsylvania, Center for the Study of Race and Equity in Education.

Harrison, K. (2009). "Athleticated" versus educated: A qualitative investigation of campus perceptions, recruiting and African American male student-athletes. *Challenge: The Journal of African American Men, 14*(1), 39–60.

Lapchick, R., Hoff, B., & Kaiser, C. (2010). The 2010 racial and gender report card: College sport. Retrieved from www. tidesport.org/rgrc/2010/2010_college _rgrc_final. pdf

Lee Jr., J., & Ransom, T. (2011). *The educational experience of young men of color: A review of research, pathways and progress*. New York, NY: College Board.

Martin, B., Harrison, C. K., Stone, J., & Lawrence, S. M. (2010). Athletic voices and academic victories: African American male student-athlete experiences in the Pac Ten. *Journal of Sport & Social Issues, 34*, 131–153.

McCluskey, A. T. (2007). *Imaging blackness: Race and racial representation in film poster art*. Bloomington: Indiana University Press.

Miles, M. B., & Huberman, A. M. (1994). *Qualitative data analysis: An expanded sourcebook*. Thousand Oaks, CA: SAGE.

Morris, J., & Adeyemo, A. (2012). Touchdowns and honor societies expanding the focus of Black male excellence. *Phi Delta Kappan, 93*(5), 28–32.

Moustakas, C. (1994). *Phenomenological research methods*. Thousand Oaks, CA: SAGE.

Rada, J., & Wulfemeyer, K. (2005). Color coded: Racial descriptors in television coverage of intercollegiate sports. *Journal of Broadcasting & Electronic Media, 49*, 65–85.

Shank, G. D. (2002). *Qualitative research: A personal skills approach*. Upper Saddle River, NJ: Merrill Prentice Hall.

Simons, H., Bosworth, C., Fujita, S., & Jensen, M. (2007). The athlete stigma in higher education. *College Student Journal, 41*, 251–273.

Steele, C., & Aronson, J. (1995). Stereotype threat and the intellectual test performance of African Americans. *Journal of Personality and Social Psychology, 69*, 797–811.

14

AN INTERVIEW WITH JERLANDO F. L. JACKSON

An Instrumental Diversity Researcher

Carly Wegner

Jerlando F. L. Jackson grew up on Fort Benning in Georgia. Fort Benning is home to the School of the Americas (now known as the Western Hemisphere Institute for Security Cooperation), which provides "professional education and training to eligible military, law enforcement, and civilian personnel of nations of the Western Hemisphere within the context of democratic principles" (Western Hemisphere Institute for Security Cooperation, n.d.). His experience growing up on Fort Benning provided him with a childhood rich in cultural interactions and experiences, which would eventually influence his research agenda in graduate school.[1]

As an undergraduate student at the University of Southern Mississippi (USM), Jerlando was a music major who hoped to play in a professional orchestra, specifically the Boston Philharmonic. A conversation with one of his instructors played an instrumental role in his decision to change directions and study higher education in graduate school.

While earning a master's degree in higher education administration at Auburn University, he set his sights on becoming a vice president for student affairs, but he said,

> One particular event caused me to reconsider. One of the most revered and feared faculty, who did not traditionally give A's in her course, left a note on my final assignment that said, "One day you will make a significant contribution to the study of education." (White, 2014, para. 12)

That note solidified his path, and he continued on to the higher education doctoral program at Iowa State University, eventually landing his first academic job as an assistant professor at the University of Wisconsin–Madison.

Jerlando initially studied the behavior of senior administrators in higher education. His transition to diversity scholarship happened after he became a faculty member. Some early influences drew him to this research, specifically his relationships with administrators of color and African American male student athletes. While in his master's program, he served as the academic study hall monitor for Auburn's football team. During our interaction, he recalls,

> In order to not have to go to study hall five nights a week, you have to achieve a specific GPA. For the most part, the study hall was almost exclusively African American males. These young men worked hard and focused on their coursework, in spite of their GPAs, and that story does not often get told.

His subsequent work has focused on African American student athletes.

Also influential to the development of his research agenda has been his participation in conversations with other men of color researching diversity in higher education. In graduate school Jerlando and four other African American academics—Lamont A. Flowers, Juan E. Gilbert, Chance W. Lewis, and James L. Moore III—formed a collective to discuss life and challenges in the academy. The book *Brothers of the Academy: Up and Coming Black Scholars Earning Our Way in Higher Education* (Jones, 2000) helped the five understand there were other African American males in the academy who had been breaking down similar barriers and gaining notoriety as intellectuals in higher education. Their informal network provided a needed space for collaboration and allowed them to encourage one another in their academic endeavors. Jerlando credits "tea time" conversations in this group for the launch of some major projects. "I carved out a space studying Black male professionals in the academy and through symmetry and 'tea time' talks, we started doing some large scale projects together to advance the knowledge base" (Watson, 2014, para. 32).

Jerlando is the Vilas Distinguished Professor of Higher Education at the University of Wisconsin–Madison, the first African American faculty member hired in the Department of Educational Leadership and Policy Analysis and the first African American in the department to earn tenure, be promoted to full professor, and receive a named professorship. His growing list of accomplishments and the barriers he has broken down during his academic career are impressive. Beyond his departmental responsibilities, he is a faculty affiliate for the Wisconsin Center for the Advancement of Postsecondary Education, and he is the founder and chief research scientist of Wisconsin's Equity and Inclusion Laboratory (Wei LAB, n.d.) where "the goal is to emerge as an international leader and champion for equitable and inclusive educational organizations" (para. 1).

Jerlando has a promising academic career ahead as a full professor with a research agenda focused on organizational science in higher education, with a special interest in hiring practices, career mobility, workforce diversity, and workplace discrimination. As advice for early-career scholars and graduate students, he suggests to me and others that "quality research is driven by insightful research questions, illuminating frameworks, and research methods grounded in the best traditions of empirical practice." As a student of higher education, I would add that it is important to share ideas and be open to criticism. Jerlando shares this advice with graduate students and early-career scholars interested in a tenure-track faculty position, and, notably, it is the same guidance that has aided him in his thriving academic career.

Jerlando's research and academic achievements are a direct result of his hard work and dedication to diversity and the higher education community. He is a strong model for higher education scholars. The higher education community has a great deal to learn from him, and his research contributions will continue to educate and inform scholars for years to come.

Note

1. This chapter includes information from previous interviews with Jerlando (Watson, 2014; White, 2014).

References

Jones, L. (Ed.). (2000). *Brothers of the academy: Up and coming Black scholars earning our way in higher education*. Sterling, VA: Stylus

Watson, J. (2014, February 18). "Brothers" bound by passion for research on Black male experience. *Diverse Issues in Higher Education*. Retrieved from diverseeducation.com/article/60802

Western Hemisphere Institute for Security Cooperation. (n.d.). *WHINSEC mission*. Retrieved from www.benning.army.mil/tenant/whinsec/mission.html

White, C. (2014, March 10). *Changing a culture: UW's Jerlando F. L. Jackson is driven for diversity*. Retrieved from www.education.wisc.edu/soe/news-events/news/2014/03/10/changing-a-culture-uw%27s-jerlando-f.-l.-jackson-is-driven for-diversity

Wisconsin's Equity and Inclusion Laboratory. (n.d.). *About Wei LAB: Mission*. Retrieved from weilab.wceruw.org/about

15

RACIALIZED AND GENDERED EXPERIENCES OF AFRICAN AMERICAN FEMALE FACULTY AT PUBLIC COMMUNITY COLLEGES

Tamara Nichele Stevenson and Eboni M. Zamani-Gallaher

I don't feel safe in the class anymore. I definitely feel like I'm a target in the class. I don't feel like students respect me. Those students were trying to undermine my authority from the get-go and I told the lawyer at the investigatory meeting that, you know, you have basically helped those three White male students succeed in undermining my authority as one of the few remaining Black female professors here. (Shannon Gibney, full-time, tenured African American female faculty member in English at Minneapolis Community and Technical College)

In a November 2013 interview with Minneapolis Community and Technical College's (MCTC) student newspaper *City College News*, Shannon Gibney described her shock at a White male student's interruption of her lecture (Kilkenny, 2013). The student questioned the frequency of structural racism as a topic in her Introduction to Mass Communications course. He stated that he felt personally attacked by the nature and extent of the discussion. After Gibney responded to the student's concerns and explained that the subject matter of structural racism was not a personal attack against the White males in the classroom but instead an examination of racism and race relations in the United States, she advised him to seek legal counsel and file a racial discrimination complaint. Subsequently, three White male students filed a formal complaint and, in response, a letter of reprimand was placed in Gibney's employee file and she was mandated to attend two one-on-one diversity/sensitivity training sessions with the college's chief diversity officer (Flaherty, 2013; Watson, 2013).

This incident, as reported in local and national headlines (e.g., Binkley, 2013; Kilkenny, 2013; Kingcade, 2013; Rupar, 2013), documents the lived experience of an African American female[1] faculty member at a community college. While community colleges have often been on the periphery of higher education scholarship, African American female faculty have been the rare subject of attention in the literature. Gibney's story is not an anomaly as social conditions and racialized issues plaguing society manifest themselves on a micro level in institutions of higher learning (Bennett, 2004; Chang, Witt, Jones, & Hakuta, 2003; Smith, Yosso, & Solórzano, 2006); it is reasonable to consider that sexism and gendered hostilities manifest themselves similarly. African American female faculty members at public community colleges are likely to experience many of the same social conditions external to the academy within this distinct sector of American higher education.[2]

Demographics: Presence of African American Females in the Professoriate

In 2014, 1,313,000 full- and part-time positions, 1% of all jobs in the United States, were at public and private colleges and universities (Bureau of Labor Statistics, 2016). There is a great paradox in the faculty ranks of postsecondary education in the United States. Although academia is becoming increasingly diverse, institutions of higher learning remain overwhelmingly White and male. As of fall 2013, White men and women collectively held 76% of the total number of American college and university faculty posts (39% male and 37% female), a slight decrease from 79% in 2011 (National Center for Education Statistics [NCES], 2013a, 2014a). Among faculty of color, African Americans held 7% of faculty positions[3] (NCES, 2014a). Overall, the upward trend of full-time Black faculty participation has been sluggish, from 4.9% in 1998 (Johnson & Pichon, 2007), to 5.3% in fall 2005, to 5.5% in fall 2007, and stagnating at 5.6% from 2009 to 2013 (NCES, 2008, 2013b, 2014b). African Americans (Black or African American alone) compose 13.2% of the total population (U.S. Census Bureau, 2014). Faculty of color[4] overall (inclusive of African American/Black, Hispanic, Asian, American Indian/Alaskan Native, and or two or more races) held 21.5% of full-time faculty positions collectively in fall 2013, reflecting gradual increases from 16.5% in fall 2005 (not inclusive of the "or two or more races" category), 18.2% in fall 2007, 19.2% in fall 2009, and 20.7% in fall 2011 (NCES, 2008, 2013b, 2014b). Cole and Barber (2003), Hurtado, Milem, Clayton-Pedersen, and Allen (1999), and Milem (2003) are among a number of researchers who discuss the significance of faculty diversity for students' academic involvement and success during and after college, especially for students of color.

Persistent segmentation and low numbers of African American females characterize the faculty ranks across institutional type. As of fall 2013, Black female faculty compose only 3.1% of full-time faculty across academic rank (NCES, 2014a), with most teaching at historically Black colleges and universities or community colleges (Wilder, Jones, & Osborne-Lampkin, 2013). Subsequently, the experiences and perspectives of African American female faculty have not received attention in the extant literature. While there are similarities in the experiences of Black female faculty across institutional contexts (Jain & Turner, 2011), the limited research on Black female faculty is generally concentrated in 4-year, historically White institutions,[5] where their representation is considerably nonexistent in comparison to their representation at public community colleges (see Table 15.1).

Several studies about African American female faculty juxtapose their perspectives with other populations—for example, Black male faculty, male or female faculty of color, White female faculty, and Black administrators (Aurora, Welton, Martinez, & Cortez, 2013; Cobb-Roberts, & Agosto, 2011; Griffin, Bennett, & Harris, 2013; Joseph & Hirshfield, 2011; Menges & Exum, 1983; Patitu & Hinton, 2003; Pittman, 2010; Singh, Robinson, & Williams-Green, 1995; Smith & Johnson-Bailey, 2011; Sulé, 2011; Thomas & Hollenshead, 2001). The topics often addressed in the scholarship of Black female faculty include hiring, recruitment and retention, promotion and tenure, salary, coping/support/survival, mentoring, career development, satisfaction/success, departure, narratives/life experiences, and perspectives by discipline (e.g., English, sociology, engineering, and public relations).

Community Colleges Defined

Community colleges are accredited, open-admission institutions that provide a range of educational options, including vocational/technical training, remedial education, continuing education, and general education courses (e.g., classes that transfer to 4-year institutions and may be applied to baccalaureate degree requirements). Along with awarding certificates in a variety of occupational fields, the associate degree is the highest degree conferred by a community college (Cohen, Brawer, & Kisker, 2014). Publicly controlled community colleges are operated by publicly elected or appointed officials and supported by public (federal, state, and local) funding; privately controlled (nonprofit and proprietary) institutions function with major funding from nonpublic sources (Katsinas, 2003). Community colleges are often described as teaching colleges. Quality instruction is the chief expectation, and teaching excellence is a defining component of the community college mission (Bragg, 2001; Cohen et al., 2014; Hardy & Laanan, 2006; Harvey, 1994; Levin, 2000).

TABLE 15.1
Number and Percentage of Female Faculty in Degree-Granting Public 2-Year Institutions by Race/Ethnicity (Fall 2011)

		Faculty of Color							
		African American/ Black	Hispanic/ Latina	Asian	Native Hawaiian/ Pacific Islander	American Indian/Alaskan Native	Two or More Races	Race/Ethnicity Unknown	Nonresident Alien
Total	61,240	5,063	3,219	2,256	241	393	382	1,101	300
Percentage	100	8.3	5.3	3.7	0.4	0.6	0.6	1.8	0.5

Note. From "IPEDS Human Resources: Full-Time Instruction/Research/Public Service Staff, by Tenure Status, Academic Rank, Race/Ethnicity, and Gender (Degree-Granting Institutions With 15 or More Full-Time Employees)." National Center for Education Statistics. (2012a).

One of the most significant contributions of the community college to the U.S. higher education enterprise is the expansion of access to postsecondary education for students who may not have participated otherwise (Cohen et al., 2014). For example, the community college has been and remains a major postsecondary option for African American students and continues to be a viable and attractive gateway into higher education for Blacks (Bower, 2002; Lewis & Middleton, 2003; Lovell, Alexander, & Kirkpatrick, 2002; Zamani, 2006). Cohen and colleagues reported that African American students constitute nearly 16% of all community college students, noting that their enrollment surpassed the African American proportion of the U.S. population of 13.2% (Black or African American alone; U.S. Census Bureau, 2014). As of fall 2014, 52% of 2-year college undergraduates were African American (American Association of Community Colleges, 2016).

Scholarship on African American Faculty at Community Colleges

In the sixth edition of *The American Community College*, one of the leading publications on the 2-year college, Cohen and colleagues (2014) call attention to the minimal scholarship about community colleges beyond those entities (researchers, professional organizations, etc.) directly involved with this particular institutional context. Additionally, there is a dearth of research on faculty of color at community colleges (Bower, 2002; Brown, 1988; Corbin, 2001; Perna, 2003; Stanley, 2006; Sutherland, 1990; Turner & Myers, 2000). Furthermore, few qualitative inquiries on community college faculty of color, particularly African American faculty, appear in the literature (Bower, 2002; Stanley, 2006; Townsend & Twombly, 2007). The literature concerning faculty of color issues in the community college is almost nonexistent (Isaac & Boyer, 2007) beyond efforts by Johnson and Pichon (2007), and Thompson and Dey (1998). In sum, there is a lack of scholarship exclusive to the experiences of Black female public community college faculty.

Aims of the Study and Conceptual Underpinnings

The overarching aim of this chapter is to problematize the institutional contextuality of Black female public 2-year college faculty. Racial battle fatigue (RBF) provided this study's predominant conceptual underpinning and subject of inquiry: To what extent is RBF experienced by full-time African American female faculty at public community colleges?

Smith (2004) developed and defines *RBF* as the social psychological stress response by an African American (or other person of color) resulting from encountering racism on a constant basis. Symptoms of RBF include (but are not limited to) physiological, psychological, and emotional or behavioral symptoms, ranging from tension headaches, constant anxiety, and ulcers to increased swearing and complaining, insomnia, rapid mood swings, difficulty thinking or speaking, and social withdrawal (Smith, 2004; Smith et al., 2006). RBF, likened to the severe and life-threatening exchange of military combat, manifests itself through three concurrent and distinguishing forms: psychological, physiological, and emotional or behavioral. The few Black female faculty members at public 2-year colleges are among faculty of color who contend with "chilly" campus climates and a "White-male-dominated institutional culture that undervalues the contributions and/or presence of women and people of color" (Turner & Myers, 2000, p. 78).

Methodology and Methods

The noted research questions were explored through a qualitative multiple case study approach to engage in an in-depth form of inquiry with detailed descriptions and significance of meaning that lead to understanding, explanation, and meaning of social phenomena in its natural setting with as little disruption as possible (Bogdan & Bilken, 2007; Merriam, 1998).

Potential participants were identified and sought through telephone calls made or e-mails sent directly to African American faculty at public 2-year colleges, based on information and photographs posted on departmental or faculty Web pages. Individuals, departments, or offices with close associations to faculty, such as faculty union offices, academic unit leaders, and human resource departments, were also contacted and asked to forward requests for participation to African Americans with full-time faculty status. The two criteria for inclusion in the study were holding a full-time faculty role at a public community college and being a native-born U.S. citizen with ancestry from any group of the continent of Africa (self-reported by participants). This second criterion was essential to include in relation to participants' exposure to and interaction with the distinctive complexities of race relations in the United States. Participants were asked to share their experiences as public community college faculty in general and as African American faculty in particular. Thirteen women ranging between 35 and 64 years of age were interviewed in person as part of the larger research study. They came from six public community colleges in various teaching disciplines and fields, such as business, counseling, English, math, sociology, speech, and technology. One female participant withdrew from the study weeks after being interviewed, citing "professional and ethical reasons." She was possibly concerned about expressing criticism about her working conditions that might generate unwanted attention and scrutiny, or she may have wanted to mitigate any (perceived) risk of jeopardizing her employment.

In-depth (semistructured, open-ended) interviews served as the primary means of data collection. Resulting interview transcripts (representing each case) were analyzed via Miles and Huberman's (1994) three-step analytical process of data reduction, data display, and conclusion, drawing within and across the cases to identify patterns of content (themes) using the racial battle fatigue stress responses.

Findings

Several themes emerged through an indicative analysis of the resulting narratives generated from this research inquiry, displaying forms of racialized role strain articulated through the RBF stress responses. The two themes presented here are important and useful to highlight to convey the symbolic and substantive parallels of the (neglected, overlooked, challenged, yet resilient) visibilities, voices, and experiences of Black female faculty at public community colleges with their nominal inclusion in existing research literature. The expressions conveyed in the excerpts have been preserved in their raw form; no grammatical corrections have been made.[6] Pseudonyms are used to protect the identity of the participants.

Veneers of Invisibility and Shattering the Myths

Given the low numbers of Black female faculty in public community colleges, their physical visibility on a public 2-year college campus could be interpreted as that institution's commitment to racial (and gender) diversity, whether intentional or otherwise. Gloria was the first full-time African American female hired in her academic department and the second African American woman hired at the campus location of her multisite historically White public community college system in the late 1980s. Her presence on campus as an African American female teaching mathematics, especially at the time of her hire, could be considered a triple threat in favor of her public community college if challenged about the lack of faculty diversity. In her 30-plus years as a public community college faculty member, Gloria has noticed a pattern, particularly among students in her upper-level courses, of their never having taken a course with a Black instructor. "Then you have an African American teacher that's teaching calculus and sometimes that can be very unsettling to people. Then it's a woman, too, which can be very unsettling." Gloria expounds on the gendered aspects of teaching in a STEM (science, technology, engineering, and mathematics) field, drawing attention to the different impressions and reactions that depend on whether the instructor or colleague is male or female.

> I think that it is difficult for women teaching in math and science because I think students come with certain expectations that they have for a woman that [they] do not have for a male. I think you really encounter some of those difficulties overcoming those expectations. A female really encounters a lot of challenges teaching the subject matter that I'm teaching. I think a lot of people struggle with seeing a woman who is very clear and concise and direct because that kind of goes against their image of what a woman should be. Some of the students struggle with that. Some of the males have a difficult time with a woman that's very direct. Some of the males struggle with that. I've stood back and watched there are certain things my male colleagues can say and there's no question about it. It just feels natural and normal. A woman can say the same thing whether it's me or another woman and there are all kinds of issues with it. So you do get into some interesting gender issues and you have to be very, very self-assured and clear about who you are and what your purpose is so that you don't get caught up in the emotion and the craziness.

Gloria applies her philosophy of confidence and composure while surrounded by antagonistic racialized and gendered situations with colleagues as well as with students. Gloria recalled an incident with a White male student whose learning difficulties affected his interaction with her.

> He just had a problem from the first day of class. We later found out the reason he was having a problem [was] because the guy had a learning disability, pretty severe learning disability but he would not go and enroll . . . to get the support services because he was this proud male. He could not admit that he had a learning disability to tap into the services. So what he thought he would do is put pressure on me and muscle me into giving him a grade or giving him a break. So he went behind my back. He went to the department chair and started raising issues of competence. Then he went to the dean . . . the dean was African American. Oh my god! He went to the campus president and he was African American, too. This guy was so angry and so mad because he just felt this big huge loss of power he had envisioned because each step of the way. But part of it, which he never looked at, was his own fault. A big huge piece of it and that is that he did have a learning disability. He was dyslexic and it came across and he would not go and get the help. He did it to himself because he couldn't get past acknowledging the problem.

With previous work experience in other industries, including K–12 education and the banking industry, Gloria's strategy of focus and self-control has been useful for her survival and longevity in her public community college faculty role, particularly in her observation that "corporate America is not going to change. It's going to be racist, sexist, and all of that."

Remaining focused has been a useful approach for Annette as well, especially in resistance to hostile surroundings. As a faculty member and "quasi administrator" in instructional technology at her historically White public 2-year college, Annette is invigorated by the opportunities to disprove speculations about her competence, especially when she first started her job nearly 15 years ago.

> When people around me think that I can't do it, I dig in. There were nights when I would stay here 'til 12 o'clock at night to make sure it worked. And I didn't really—and I knew I was by myself and I needed to do it to make it work. And to this day, I still am like that. I don't let—just because you don't wanna do it—stop me. So in that respect, it did—that's just the nature of my personality and so the misconception was as I had blockers and obstacles, that is—the assumption in their mind was that they were stopping me. The assumption in my mind is that I can always come up—as an out-of-the-box thinker—I'll come up with a plan to work around you, and it's gonna work.

Annette's visibility drew the attention of one individual because she relocated from another part of the United States and moved from a 4-year to a public 2-year college. The subsequent interrogation clarified the tenor of the assumptions associated with her presence and her ability to fulfill the tasks and responsibilities of her faculty role.

> Now obviously I'm African American and one of the things that happened to me—I think it was my second day here on this campus—is I had a full-time, tenured faculty member see me walk across campus and I had on a business suit and everything, and he stopped me and he asked—and he wasn't African American—and he asked me, he said, "Well, who are you?" And I told him who I was and he said, "Well, clearly because you're wearing a suit, I knew you weren't a student here." And he says, So . . ." and he says, you know, he asked me what my position was and I told him. And he said, "Well, what was my"—and he asked me what my qualification was for the job. And I told him and he said, "Well, it sounds to me like you're overqualified for this job. And that's probably because you're Black. And you would have to be overqualified for this job in order to have it."

Annette's reflection of the exchange verbalizes the unspoken suppositions of her new colleagues and students: "It was clear that when I came that there was an assumption that I did not know my—what I was doing. There was a perception that . . . here's this Black woman. We need to teach her what technology is about."

Silence Is Not Always Golden

Sharon has been a faculty member at her historically White public 2-year college for nearly three decades. As one of the few African American faculty members on her campus (the only speech instructor), her visibility is more pronounced in comparison to that of her White colleagues. Despite her longevity at the institution, she finds her day-to-day existence rather isolating, invoking various forms of silence: little to no social interaction with colleagues and the constant angst to determine the root cause or causes of the segregation.

> It's strange. I don't know how to explain to you but other than it's been strange. My experience at [public community college] has been strange in terms of colleagues and I don't know if it has to do with race. I don't know if it has to do with gender or personality. Let's say that we have a faculty meeting and I'm there and I will come early because I don't want that "CP Time." [*CP Time* refers to an African American colloquialism known as *Colored People's Time,* a label for the stereotypical notion that African Americans are always late or unable to be punctual.] I come early and I'll sit at a table and my first few years there, all the tables around me would fill up before anybody would sit at the table with me. So I thought that was strange. And when there are people sitting at the table with me, occasionally someone from the same department will come and say, "Hello" to them and they will ask them, "Do you want to go to lunch? Do you want to go lunch?" But they never ask me to go to lunch. So I've been used to eating lunch alone. And I'm not sure if it's [pause] I don't know why that is.

Sharon's efforts to arrive early for faculty meetings and situate herself at a lunch table to combat a negative stereotype or to show herself friendly or nonthreatening to her White colleagues have been ineffective. She concludes that she has become accustomed to "eating lunch alone."

Even though Melanie, an English instructor, was angered by a White male colleague's repeated patronizing greeting, she did not directly confront him about the issue. Melanie attributed his behavior to ignorance, unworthy of sacrificing her sanity, composure, or image as an African American professional at her historically White public community college, where she has been a faculty member for 5 years.

> So this White male faculty member would see me in the hallways and he says, "Hello, sunshine" and I'm like, "What the F?" And it was only because another White faculty member heard him say that [and] that made him like "You don't address her as sunshine! What the hell?" and it's stuff like that that I'm like "These people are ignorant." It's just stuff like that that you pull back and don't interact and I don't have the mental fortitude because I think that in any situation, whether you're in business, education, any job, I think a Black professional knows that there are things they're gonna have to deal with and you have to look at the larger goal of learning how to deal with these people and not reacting in such a way where it compromises your role as a Black professional. I don't know. Sometimes I know I don't handle that well. I know I don't handle that well. I don't know. Sometimes I feel like I have to say something now and let them know but it was only because that other faculty member intervened that he never said it again. From now on, he says, "Good morning" and that's it.

Melanie's narrative indicates that silence was not indicative of her permission or assent to be repeatedly exposed to a greeting with sexist undertones. She had the intention to end her silence had the condescending salutation continued, voice her displeasure and disapproval, and instruct the White male colleague to avoid addressing her in that manner. In another incident, a different White male colleague leisurely entered Melanie's classroom during a class meeting without seeking her permission, or at a minimum greeting her, to obtain an item from a storage closet. "Once he found what he was looking for, [he] came out of the storage [room] and walked out of the classroom and didn't say a single word to me." When she confronted him about the matter at a later time, Melanie recalled that she "almost acted like a fool." However, reactions from colleagues who witnessed the exchange prompted a meeting with her associate dean.

> And then the associate dean sat down and talked to me and says, "Well, he's just shy just like you are." I'm like if I had to go into somebody's classroom I would have said, "Excuse me." And I [say], "Why are you making excuses for this person?" I'm like, he's not an idiot. He just walked into my classroom and interrupted it. I said it would have been fine if he had said, "Excuse me, I have to interrupt your classroom" but he actually walked in there as if no one was in that classroom and I wasn't talking. No consideration at all. Now it might have seemed like a small thing but to me, those types of interactions, and that degree of respect matter to me. And you can't tell me that if he had been in the classroom and I had walked in there and not said anything, sometimes it's those double standards like, "Why are you copping an attitude" or she has an attitude. I don't have an attitude. It's just people need to stop acting like a fool.

The option to remain silent was short-lived for Melanie, likely because of the continued pardon of the White male colleague's actions and the mockery made of Melanie's reaction to the incident. The struggle between silence and speaking out to make one's voice heard is contingent on one's endurance to function effectively in the public 2-year college environment without discord as an African American female public community college faculty member.

> I knew that one, I was going to feel bad about it, and I knew it was going to be a frustrating experience trying to deal with that situation. It's always—the initial response in those situations is always just anger. . . . [The situation where] I just went off on that guy, I felt yeah, I could have been a little bit nicer about it and things like that. And then I had to sit in front of the dean [who said], "Well, he is sorry. He just felt—" but he never apologized to me and things like that. But I'm like I have to sit here and listen to the dean make me the bad guy and it seemed like such a small thing. It made me feel like why am I even getting upset over this issue? And that's because you're always aware of having to constantly defend your position as a Black faculty member. That the little things like a White male faculty member walking through your classroom as if you weren't even teaching, that just bothers you. So it was always anger and frustration, I think.

The public community college faculty role is anything but serene for the African American woman. For Melanie, she could no longer remain silent in light of the multiple instances of disrespect and racial antipathy perpetrated by her White colleagues. In time, Melanie found it necessary to confront such incidents, refusing to be ignored or dismissed.

Similarly, Theresa, a sociology instructor for 7 years, identified antagonistic teaching conditions that she characterizes as "strikes": "I look younger than I am so there's an age issue—ageism issue. With me being a woman, again, that's an obstacle, as well as being Black, that is an obstacle." Theresa's teaching discipline of sociology compounds the issues that she faces in her faculty role. Her descriptions about her teaching experiences and encounters with White students in her classes illustrate her rationale for having to make pedagogical adjustments to her course curriculum as a consequence of her race, gender, and age. To illustrate the example of the additional attention to instructional detail that Theresa feels is necessary in the planning and execution of race-based course content, she recalled a confrontation with a White male student who threatened to approach her dean about a portion of her lecture in which he claimed Theresa said she "hated all White people."

And I told him, "You do what you need to do." Gave him [the dean's] number, office number, office hours and I said—I just left it alone. But what I had said in class was I can understand how someone could hate White people because of their experiences, but we have to step away from that and say there's something more—like I was talking about a Ku Klux Klan rally I had gone to and I said at that moment, "I could see myself hating all White people." Then I started thinking, I like my friend, she's White, so okay. I hate all White people but her, you know, go on and on and then finally you realize you don't hate all White people. These people are White. You don't like what they're saying. He of course didn't hear all that part. He just picked the part that was going to help him in his case.

For Theresa, this encounter with the White male student who not only misinterpreted her lecture comments but also declared that he would report her (because he was genuinely offended or he simply wanted to cause trouble) confirms her need for discretion when facilitating discussions on race in her classes. She believes that White faculty members (especially those who are male) are exempt from having to downplay such fundamental aspects of their identity in the classroom for the sake of the teaching and learning process and to maintain student rapport. Theresa added that she positions herself in a place of distance when discussing racialized content, a practice she presumes that "White male instructors would [not] ever think about doing. So we [Black female faculty] have to be very aware of our race, very aware of our gender when talking about certain subjects, absolutely."

Discussion

Along with the traditional responsibilities and demands of the public 2-year college faculty role, African American women faculty perform the duties of their role fraught with racialized and gendered hostilities. The constant weight of combating raced and gendered stereotypes and hostile encounters with students and colleagues while adhering to personal values and principles of self-discipline and professionalism exacerbates the African American female public community college faculty role, especially for the women who work in historically White institutions. These conditions are aggravated by "having to deal with alienation, racism, and sexism. . . . African American women faculty members are continuously confronted with the challenge to prove that they do not have their job because of affirmative action, tokenism, or 'opportunity hire'" (Harley, 2008, p. 26–27). These conditions readily apply to Black women situated at public community colleges.

In addition to the core tasks and responsibilities of the faculty role (inclusive of teaching, advising students, committee participation, service activities, etc.), Black women deal with racialized and gendered slights that usually go unnoticed, unacknowledged, and unresolved. The participants expressed enjoyment for their work as public 2-year college faculty members. Their commitment to the mission of the public community college, to expand access to postsecondary education to those individuals and populations that would not otherwise have access, was described as fulfilling. The alignment of the mission and their educational philosophy mitigated some of the negative experiences of being a female faculty of color.

The narratives depict instances of RBF as a result of racial microaggressions: subtle, conscious or unconscious, intentional or unintentional, layered, cumulative, verbal and nonverbal, behavioral, and environmental insults directed at people of color based on race and other distinguishing characteristics that cause unnecessary stress in people of color while benefiting Whites (Smith, 2004; Smith et al., 2006; Sue, Capodilupo, & Holder, 2008; Sue, Lin, Torino, Capodilupo, & Rivera, 2009). Accumulated over time, racial microaggressions can cause various forms of mental, emotional, and physical strain. The constant threat of racial microaggressions can cause RBF to remain "switched on," and symptoms can occur in anticipation of a racist event: rapid breathing, upset stomach, frequent diarrhea, or urination (Smith, 2004, p. 180). The constant battle with racial stress agitates the lives of people of color, and the subsequent symptoms of RBF can be lethal when gone unnoticed, untreated, misdiagnosed, or dismissed (Smith et al., 2006). The *Diagnostic and Statistical Manual of Mental Disorders, Fifth Edition*, acknowledges that constant exposure to subtle racism (e.g., racial microaggressions) is a form of race-based trauma that generates effects similar to post-traumatic stress disorder, shifting from previous guidelines that such trauma occurred only in association with a specific racially hostile incident (Harris, 2013; Williams, 2013). For African Americans and other populations of color, the ongoing exposure to and accrual of racial microaggressions generate RBF, and as the narratives from the women show, this is the case for African American female faculty who work in public community colleges.

Environmental microaggressions are visible or invisible, conscious or unconscious words and behaviors that convey racially derogatory messages or systemically insult or invalidate people of color (Sue, 2010). Among the circumstances that are systemically embedded in the culture and climate of the public community college campus—and directly affect the existence of African American female public community college faculty—are challenges and inspection of faculty role performance and comparisons to White colleagues that imply inadequacy. Examples of individually enacted microaggressions described by participants in the narratives consisted of challenges to a Black female public 2-year college faculty member's qualifications and teaching, isolation, disregard, and mockery of one's existence. In these cases, the racial microaggressions were perpetuated by White males advancing veiled (and overt) messages that African Americans are deficient and lack competence as faculty in comparison to the standard image of the public community college instructor: White and male (i.e., the ivory tower).

The psychological form of RBF is illustrated in the narratives. Specific psychological stress responses include frustration, shock, anger, anxiety disappointment, hopelessness, helplessness, and fear (Smith, 2004; Smith et al., 2006). In describing their experiences, participants used words or phrases that either articulated or alluded to their distressed mental or emotional state during or after a racially charged exchange or in reaction to the general atmosphere on their historically White 2-year college campuses. For example, Gloria explains her strategy to "be very, very self-assured and clear . . . so that you don't get caught up in the emotion and craziness," which could signal the tactic to mediate anger and frustration. Sharon's observation of peculiarity surrounding the isolation she regularly experiences at her historically White public community college is indicative of disappointment, helplessness, and anxiety, especially as she describes her ambiguity about the causes of the isolation. For Melanie, the two incidents with White male colleagues and the process used to handle both situations provoked anger and frustration, which she explicitly named repeatedly. Theresa described her race, gender, and age as "strikes" and "obstacles" as they are alleged in the racially hostile environment that is the (historically White) public community college campus. These word choices could signify the psychological stress responses of anger and frustration.

These conditions and encounters described by the African American female community college faculty members in this chapter are not only racialized but also gendered in nature. As exhibited in narratives, participants integrated the racialized and gendered dimensions of their experiences. This combined form of expression illustrates intersectionality, one of the three foundational components of Black feminist thought (Collins, 2009). For Collins, Black feminist thought facilitates "women's efforts to come to terms with lived experiences within intersecting oppressions of race, class, gender, sexuality, ethnicity, nation, and religion" (p. 12). She argues that Black women's realities are negated in White feminist studies or ideologies based on race and Black male social and political thought because of gender (Collins, 2009).

Exemplified in two particular narratives are the intertwined aspects of each participant's identity in relation to their existence on the public 2-year college campus. Sharon named three aspects of her identity (race, gender, and/or personality) in her speculation of the cause or causes of the isolation she has experienced on her historically White public community college campus.

Theresa observed the need for Black female faculty to be "very aware" of race and gender when discussing certain course content. As part of the explanation of the interlocking nature of oppression, Collins (1986) specifies the error in separating or dissecting the points of discrimination: This approach "typically prioritizes one form of oppression as being primary, then handles remaining types of oppression as variables within what is seen as the most important system" (p. 20).

The narratives presented in this chapter emphasize the implicit and explicit patterns of racism, sexism, and discrimination for some African American female professors at public 2-year institutions. There is a lack of scholarship that exclusively examines Black female faculty, particularly at community colleges. This is inconsistent with the fact that the majority of female faculty of color in public 2-year colleges are Black women. Given this gap, scholarly opportunities abound in this subject area, including the targeted exploration of gendered racism (Essed, 1991), which describes the tangled components of racism and sexism.

Along with the narratives presented here, Shannon Gibney's story at the beginning of this chapter indicates the compulsion to negotiate her visibility and voice in her faculty role. To update her situation, Gibney filed a grievance through MCTC's faculty union in response to the college's ruling and subsequent reprimand. One week prior to a scheduled union-sponsored arbitration meeting, MCTC president Phillip L. Davis rescinded the reprimand (via a letter dated May 21, 2014). The letter of reprimand was removed from her permanent file; however, MCTC's ruling of the violation against the students' civil rights remains. The following excerpt of an e-mail Gibney sent to the *Twin Cities Daily Planet* (Turck, 2014) conveys her sentiments about the classroom incident in light of the nullification of the reprimand:

> This last-minute removal of the letter of reprimand, especially if it is a full expungement, after all of President Davis' and the Chancellor Rosenstone's public claims that I deserved the letter of reprimand and that the press and everyone else didn't know all the facts, now rings completely hollow. And the harm that this caused my reputation, institutional ethos, and authority in the classroom—as well as the stress it inflicted on me and my family, can never really be repaired. So, anyone who advances the "no harm was done here" narrative is absolutely wrong. The deeper questions of ongoing institutional racism in MCTC and throughout the MnSCU [Minnesota State Colleges and Universities] system—especially for employees and students of color—still demand real and systemic attention and redress, however my case ends or develops. And this whole experience has left me with no faith in the system's ability to correct itself, especially since I was offered a buy-out at one point in the grievance process if I would simply leave MCTC altogether (of course, I declined).

According to the story in the *Twin Cities Daily Planet*, Gibney reportedly was scheduled for an upcoming sabbatical leave (Turck, 2014). Gibney's statement reiterates the most obvious, indisputable steps that public community colleges—indeed, all institutions of higher education in the United States—need to take: Undergird the institution's rhetorical commitment to diversity with deliberate, targeted, tangible, and meaningful resources to increase diversity in the student, faculty, and administrative ranks and to eliminate chilly campus climates for all members of the college or university campus.

Notes

1. The term *female* is used as the primary gender identifier throughout this chapter, although the term *woman* may be noted or cited from referenced sources.
2. The terms *African American* and *Black* are used interchangeably throughout this chapter; the terms *community college* and *2-year college* are used interchangeably throughout this chapter.
3. The percentages noted result from the total count of full-time faculty positions, including nonresident alien and excluding race/ethnicity unknown.
4. The terms *faculty* and *students of color* are used in this chapter to refer to racial or ethnic minority populations in concurrence with Laden and Hagedorn's (2000) statement preferring to avoid a derogatory connotation conveyed through the term *minority*.
5. To parallel the terminology of *historically Black institutions* to refer to those colleges and universities established prior to 1964 to educate Black Americans, the term *historically White institutions* is used instead of *predominantly White institutions* in this chapter to acknowledge "the binarism and exclusion supported by the United States prior to 1964" (Brown & Dancy, 2010, p. 523).
6. The choice to avoid editing participants' statements for grammar was deliberate to invite the reader to hear the voices of the research participants. Although some of the language may appear to typify negative stereotypes about African Americans and so-called proper forms of speech, the fundamental aim of this research study was to amplify the voices of the research participants. In addition, code switching, or the concurrent usage of standard English and African American English vernacular (or Ebonics) is not an unconventional occurrence in particular settings (DeBose, 1992) and is a likely indicator of these college-educated research participants' increased sense of rapport, trust, and confidence in the research inquiry.

References

American Association of Community Colleges. (2016). *2016 Community college fact sheet* [Brochure]. Retrieved from www.aacc.nche.edu/AboutCC/Documents/AACCFactSheetsR2.pdf

American Psychiatric Association. (2013). *Diagnostic and statistical manual of mental disorders* (5th ed.). Arlington, VA: Author.

Aurora, C., Welton, A. D., Martinez, M. A., & Cortez, L. (2013). Becoming academicians: An ethnographic analysis of the figured worlds of racially underrepresented female faculty. *Negro Educational Review, 64*(1/4), 97–118.

Bennett, C. I. (2004). Research on racial issues in American higher education. In J. A. Banks & C. A. Banks (Eds.), *Handbook of research on multicultural education* (2nd ed., pp. 847–868). San Francisco, CA: Jossey-Bass.

Binkley, M. (2013, November 20). *Controversy at MCTC following lesson on structural racism*. Retrieved from minnesota.cbslocal.com/2013/11/20/controversy-at-mctc-following-lesson-on-structural-racism

Bogdan, R. C., & Biklen, S. K. (2007). *Qualitative research for education: An introduction to theory and methods* (5th ed.). Boston, MA: Pearson Education.

Bower, B. (2002). Campus life for faculty of color: Still strangers after all these years. *New Directions for Community Colleges, 118*, 79–87.

Bragg, D. D. (2001). Community college access, mission, and outcomes: Considering intriguing intersections and challenges. *Peabody Journal of Education, 76*(1), 93–116.

Brown, M. C., II, & Dancy, T. E., II. (2010). Predominantly White institutions. In K. Lomotey (Ed.), *Encyclopedia of African American education* (pp. 524–527). Thousand Oaks, CA: SAGE.

Brown, S. (1988). *Increasing minority faculty: An elusive goal*. Princeton, NJ: Educational Testing Service.

Bureau of Labor Statistics. (2016). *Occupational outlook handbook: Postsecondary teachers*. Retrieved from www.bls.gov/ooh/education-training-and-library/postsecondary-teachers.htm

Chang, M. J., Witt, D., Jones, J., & Hakuta, K. (Eds.). (2003). *Compelling interest: Examining the evidence on racial dynamics in colleges and universities*. Stanford, CA: Stanford University Press.

Cobb-Roberts, D., & Agosto, V. (2011). Underrepresented women in higher education: An overview. *Negro Educational Review, 62/63*(1/4), 7–11.

Cohen, A. M., Brawer, F. B., & Kisker, C. B., (2014). *The American community college* (6th ed.). San Francisco, CA: Jossey-Bass.

Cole, S., & Barber, E. (2003). *Increasing faculty diversity: The occupational choices of high-achieving minority students*. Cambridge, MA: Harvard University Press.

Collins, P. (1986). Learning from the outsider within: The sociological significance of Black feminist thought. *Social Problems, 33*(6), 14–32.

Collins, P. H. (2009). *Black feminist thought: Knowledge, consciousness, and the politics of empowerment* (2nd ed.). New York, NY: Routledge.

Corbin, S. (2001). Role perceptions and job satisfaction of community college faculty. *Inquiry, 6*(1). Retrieved from www.vccaedu.org/inquiry/inquiry-spring2001/i-61-corbin.html

DeBose, C. E. (1992). Codeswitching: Black English and standard English in the African-American linguistic repertoire. *Journal of Multilingual and Multicultural Development, 13*(1/2), 157–167.

Essed, P. (1991). *Understanding everyday racism: An interdisciplinary theory* (2nd ed.). Newbury Park, CA: SAGE.

Flaherty, C. (2013). Taboo subject? *Inside Higher Ed*. Retrieved from www.insidehighered.com/news/2013/12/03/black-professors-essay-raises-questions-why-she-was-investigated-after-offending

Griffin, K. A., Bennett, J. C., & Harris, J. (2013). Marginalizing merit?: Gender differences in Black faculty D/discourses on tenure, advancement, and professional success. *Review of Higher Education, 36*(4), 489–512.

Hardy, D. E., & Laanan, F. (2006). Characteristics and perspectives of faculty at public 2-year colleges. *Community College Journal of Research and Practice, 30*, 78–811.

Harley, D. A. (2008). Maids of academe: African American women faculty at predominantly White institutions. *Journal of African American Studies, 12*, 19–36.

Harris, N. (2013, May 23). Changes in *DSM-5*: Racism can cause PTSD similar to that of soldiers after war. *Medical Daily*. Retrieved from www.medicaldaily.com/changes-dsm-5-racism-can-cause-ptsd-similar-soldiers-after-war-246177

Harvey, W. B. (Ed.). (1994). African American faculty in community colleges: Why they aren't there. *New Directions for Community Colleges, 87*, 19–26.

Hurtado, S., Milem, J., Clayton-Pedersen, A., & Allen, W. (1999). Enacting diverse learning environments: Improving the climate for racial/ethnic diversity in higher education. *ASHE-ERIC Higher Education Report, 26*(8).

Isaac, E. P., & Boyer, P. G. (2007). Voices of urban and rural community college minority faculty: Satisfaction and opinions. *Community College Journal of Research and Practice, 31*, 359–369.

Jain, D., & Turner, C. S. (2011). Purple is to lavender: Womanism, resistance, and the politics of naming. *Negro Educational Review, 62/63*(1/4), 67–88.

Johnson, B. J., & Pichon, H. (2007). The status of African American faculty in the academy: Where do we go from here? In J. Jackson (Ed.), *Strengthening the African American educational pipeline: Informing research, policy, and practice* (pp. 97–114). Albany, NY: SUNY Press.

Joseph, T. D., & Hirshfield, L. E. (2011). "Why don't you get somebody new to do it?" Race and cultural taxation in the academy. *Ethnic & Racial Studies, 34*(1), 121–141. doi:10.1080/01419870.2010.496489

Katsinas, S. G. (2003). Two-year college classifications based on institutional control, geography, governance, and size. *New Directions for Community Colleges, 122*, 17–28.

Kilkenny, B. (2013, November 6). *City College Air: On campus discrimination*. Retrieved from citycollegenews.com/2013/11/06/city-college-air-discrimination-on-campus

Kingcade, T. (2013, December 3). *Black college instructor claims she was punished for discussing racism*. Retrieved from www.huffingtonpost.com/2013/12/03/shannon-gibney_n_4378635.html

Levin, J. S. (2000). The revised institution: The community college mission at the end of the twentieth century. *Community College Review, 28*(2), 1–25.

Lewis, C., & Middleton, V. (2003). African American in community colleges: A review of research reported in the *Community College Journal of Research and Practice*: 1990–2000. *Community College Journal of Research and Practice, 27*, 787–798.

Lovell, N. B., Alexander, M. L., & Kirkpatrick, L. A. (2002). Minority faculty at community colleges. *Phi Delta Kappa Fastbacks, 490*, 7–36.

Menges, R. J., & Exum, W. H. (1983). Barriers to the progress of women and minority faculty. *Journal of Higher Education, 54*(2), 123–144.

Merriam, S. B. (1998). *Qualitative research and case study applications in education.* San Francisco, CA: Jossey-Bass.

Milem, J. F. (2003). The educational benefits of diversity: Evidence from multiple sectors. In M. Chang, D. Witt, J. Jones, & K. Hakuta (Eds.), *Compelling interest: Examining the evidence on racial dynamics in higher education* (pp. 126–169). Palo Alto, CA: Stanford University Press.

Miles, M. B., & Huberman, A. (1994). *Qualitative data analysis: An expanded sourcebook* (2nd ed.). Thousand Oaks, CA: SAGE.

National Center for Education Statistics. (2008). *Table 236. Employees in degree-granting institutions, by race/ethnicity and residency status, sex, employment status, control and type of institution, and primary occupation: Fall 2005.* Retrieved from nces.ed.gov/pubs2008/2008022.pdf

National Center for Education Statistics. (2013a). *Table 314.40. Employees in degree-granting postsecondary institutions, by race/ethnicity, sex, employment status, control and level of institution, and primary occupation: Fall 2011.* Retrieved from nces.ed.gov/programs/digest/d13/tables/dt13_314.40.asp?referrer=report

National Center for Education Statistics. (2013b). *Table 315.20. Full-time instructional faculty in degree-granting postsecondary institutions, by race/ethnicity, sex, and academic rank: Fall 2007, fall 2009, and fall 2011.* Retrieved from nces.ed.gov/programs/digest/d13/tables/dt13_315.20.asp

National Center for Education Statistics. (2014a). *Table 314.40. Employees in degree-granting postsecondary institutions, by race/ethnicity, sex, employment status, control and level of institution, and primary occupation: Fall 2013.* Retrieved from nces.ed.gov/programs/digest/d14/tables/dt14_314.40.asp?current=yes

National Center for Education Statistics. (2014b). *Table 315.20. Full-time faculty in degree-granting postsecondary institutions, by race/ethnicity, sex, and academic rank: Fall 2009, fall 2011, and fall 2013.* Retrieved from nces.ed.gov/programs/digest/d14/tables/dt14_315.20.asp

National Center for Education Statistics. (2015). *Table 306.20. Total fall enrollment in degree-granting postsecondary institutions, by level and control of institution and race/ethnicity of student: Selected years, 1976 through 2014.* Retrieved from nces.ed.gov/programs/digest/d15/tables/dt15_306.20.asp?current=yes

Patitu, C., & Hinton, K. G. (2003). The experiences of African American women faculty and administrators in higher education: Has anything changed? *New Directions for Student Services, 104*, 79–93.

Perna, L. (2003). The status of women and minorities among community college faculty. In B. Townsend & D. D. Bragg (Eds.), *ASHE reader on community colleges* (3rd ed., pp. 351–378). Boston, MA: Pearson.

Pittman, C. T. (2010). Race and gender oppression in the classroom: The experiences of women faculty of color with White male students. *Teaching Sociology, 38*(3), 183–196. doi:10.1177/0092055X10370120

Rupar, A. (2013, November 27). *MCTC prof reprimanded for alienating White students during structural racism discussion.* Retrieved from blogs.citypages.com/blotter/2013/11/mctc_prof_reprimanded_for_alienating_white_students_during_structural_racism_discussion.php

Singh, K., Robinson, A., & Williams-Green, J. (1995). Differences in perceptions of African American women and men faculty and administrators. *Journal of Negro Education, 64*(4), 401–408. doi:10.2307/2967263.

Smith, B. P., & Johnson-Bailey, J. (2011). Student ratings of teaching effectiveness: Implications for non-White women in the academy. *Negro Educational Review, 62/63*(1/4), 115–140.

Smith, W. A. (2004). Black faculty coping with racial battle fatigue: The campus racial climate in a post–civil rights era. In D. Cleveland (Ed.), *A long way to go: Conversations about race by African American faculty and graduate students* (pp. 171–190). New York, NY: Peter Lang.

Smith, W. A., Yosso, T. J., & Solórzano, D. G. (2006). Challenging racial battle fatigue on historically White campuses: A critical race examination of race-related stress. In C. A. Stanley (Ed.), *Faculty of color: Teaching in predominantly White colleges and universities* (pp. 299–327). Bolton, MA: Anker.

Stanley, C. A. (2006). Coloring the academic landscape: Faculty of color breaking the silence in predominantly White colleges and universities. *American Educational Research Journal, 43*, 701–736.

Sue, D. W. (2010). Microaggressions, marginality and oppression: An introduction. In D. W. Sue (Ed.), *Microaggressions and marginality: Manifestation, dynamics, and impact.* (pp. 3–22). Hoboken, NJ: Wiley.

Sue, D. W., Capodilupo, C. M., & Holder, A. M. (2008). Racial microaggressions in the life experience of Black Americans. *Professional Psychology, Research and Practice, 39*, 329–336.

Sue, D. W., Lin, A. I., Torino, G. C., Capodilupo, C. M., & Rivera, D. P. (2009). Racial microaggressions and difficult dialogues on race in the classroom. *Cultural Diversity and Ethnic Minority Psychology, 15*(2), 183–190.

Sulé, V. T. (2011). Restructuring the master's tools: Black female and Latina faculty navigating and contributing in classrooms through oppositional positions. *Equity & Excellence in Education, 44*(2), 169–187.

Sutherland, M. E. (1990). Black faculty in White academia: The fit is an uneasy one. *Western Journal of Black Studies, 14*(1), 17–23.

Thomas, G. D., & Hollenshead, C. (2001). Resisting from the margins: The coping strategies of Black women and other women of color faculty members at a research university. *Journal of Negro Education, 70*(3), 166–175.

Thompson, C., & Dey, E. (1998). Pushed to the margins: Sources of stress for African American college and university faculty. *Journal of Higher Education, 69*, 324–345.

Townsend, B. K., & Twombly, S. B. (2007). Community college faculty: Overlooked and undervalued. *ASHE Higher Education Report, 32*(6).

Turck, M. (2014, May 23). News Day: Shannon Gibney—reprimand rescinded. *Twin Cities Daily Planet*. Retrieved from www.tcdailyplanet.net/news/2014/05/23/news-day-shannon-gibney-reprimand-rescinded

Turner, C., & Myers, Jr., S. (2000). *Faculty of color in academe: Bittersweet success*. Needham Heights, MA: Allyn & Bacon.

U.S. Census Bureau. (2014). *Sex by age: Black or African American alone*. Retrieved from www.census.gov/quickfacts/table/PST045215/00

Watson, J. (2013, December 16). Minneapolis community college professor denounced for structural racism teachings. *Diverse Issues in Higher Education*. Retrieved from diverseeducation.com/article/59525/

Wilder, J., Bertrand Jones, T., & Osborne-Lampkin, L. (2013). A profile of Black women in the 21st century academy: Still learning from the "outsider-within." *Journal of Research Initiatives*, *1*(1), 27–38.

Williams, M. T. (2013, May 13). Can racism cause PTSD? Implications for *DSM-5*. *Psychology Today*. Retrieved from www.psychologytoday.com/blog/culturally-speaking/201305/can-racism-cause-ptsd-implications-dsm-5

Zamani, E. M. (2006). African American student affairs professionals in community college settings: A commentary for future research. In B. Townsend & D. Bragg (Eds.), *ASHE reader on community colleges* (3rd ed., pp. 173–180). Boston, MA: Pearson.

16

AN INTERVIEW WITH TAMARA NICHELE STEVENSON
Surviving Racial Battle Fatigue: Cultivating Safe Spaces in Racialized Environments

Tonya Kneff

How does a professor who researches and writes about racial battle fatigue on college campuses not experience it herself? Tamara Stevenson of Westminster College in Salt Lake City, Utah, relies heavily on creating and maintaining safe spaces.[1]

In her work on the experiences of African American faculty, Stevenson employs the concept of racialized space and environments. With a background in corporate communications, she made the switch to education after the communications departments at two different agencies where she worked were eliminated. Her experiences in these corporate settings were instrumental in the development of her research.

> I worked in several corporate entities from automotive, healthcare, print and broadcast journalism, and for the most part I would be one of the few or the only African American in my department. . . . I would have some very distinct experiences, but I couldn't name some of the things I would experience around something as simple as tone, or access to information, or promotions.

She describes how these environments were racialized spaces, yet that fact would seem intangible and often go unnamed, in part because of the inability to articulate microaggressions (Solórzano, Ceja, & Yosso, 2000). Yet, Tamara's experiences with racialized spaces did not begin with her entry into the professional realm; she recalls that even in her undergraduate program, an Affirmative Action journalism program established to racially diversify print and broadcast newsrooms across the country, she encountered similar spaces where race mattered.[2]

Tamara explains that she went from "one of many" in her predominantly Black high school classrooms to "one of few" in her college classrooms. She remembers feeling underprepared for college; for example, she had not been exposed to formal citation formatting, and she was not aware of certain opportunities, such as study abroad experiences. She had good grades and a supportive home life, but those were not enough to make her ready for college. "Thankfully," she says, "the journalism program I was in bridged a lot of the gaps for me. It was a specialized program with a safe small space for me to ask questions and gain information."

Tamara followed the conventional wisdom of dissertation writing—study yourself—by examining the Black experience in higher education. More specifically, she wanted to study the experiences of Black faculty. Although her personal experiences had been in 4-year universities (Eastern Michigan and Wayne State), she focused her research on community colleges, where there is a higher number of Black faculty. She set out to find how racialized conditions limit or prevent African Americans from being represented as a critical mass in these institutions of higher education.

Tamara is now a faculty member at a predominantly White institution in a state with only a 1.3% African American population (U.S. Census Bureau, 2014). According to Tamara, Westminster College strives to create a learning environment that is inclusive and accessible to students. As a scholar of the African American faculty experience, however, she is aware of literature that explores the dynamic between White students and faculty of color, including the inability or unwillingness to recognize the legitimacy and credibility of the professor in that situation. "For many of the White faculty, they walk in with legitimacy, and for me, sometimes I have to rebuild it every time I walk in," she said. "And it can be a 14-week semester, and at week 14 sometimes I still have to demonstrate my credibility." This observation resonates with me as an instructor who asks her students to consider to whom they accord legitimacy and, conversely, to whom they may deny legitimacy or question an individual's credibility. Despite these challenges, Tamara has cultivated systems of support and safe spaces to help manage the impact of microaggressions. She recognized early that

> there is a need for safe spaces—a place where you can release those things and develop and practice strategies to combat those conditions. I make sure that I have that, I cultivate that, and I try to be a safe space for others.

Tamara also seems to be highlighting the fact that these spaces do not exist naturally; work must be done to develop and sustain safe spaces. Moreover, the work becomes the responsibility of those who already have to exert a great deal of energy to deal with microaggressions and the effects of racialized spaces.

Tamara defines a *safe space* as one where she feels encouraged and strengthened and can freely discuss her experiences and "not feel like I'm going crazy." Her mentors and advisers play an important role in cultivating these spaces. Her research shows that strategies employed to cope with hostile environments are rooted in identity and ideology. She has found that "there's such a range of how their racial identity was formed and how it impacted their life choices and life decisions, and their world view." For her, she decides what to address or not to address and has found a balance between how she "can be collegial and also command respect."

Being in Utah brings an entirely new layer to her work and experiences. She is the only self-identified African American faculty member on her campus. In spaces where nearly everyone is White, you cannot find others who have lived a similar racialized experience but only potential allies among others. "I had to say to myself, all White people aren't bad. There are some well-enlightened White folks who get it, and they have presented themselves. . . . I've come to recognize and see that, and ultimately, trust it." Several faculty members made a concerted effort to make sure she was welcomed. "People know who I am because visually I stand out." But she describes how there are others who make her feel invisible: "I have to remind myself that I am no shrinking violet. You can't miss me . . . And again, I have those safe spaces."

As Tamara reflects on her work with diversity, she is reminded of a Bible verse she paraphrases: "One plants, one waters, but God gives the increase." The increase in this case seems to refer to change, which may not feel equivalent to the work put into making the change. She continues: "I've recognized two things: One, that things are still happening, even if I can't see it and [two] not to be impatient, but still diligent in doing the work." Tamara's commitment to the work and to engaging others around it is critical to the process of change, even if it is slow or not immediately obvious.

There is much to be done as Tamara still encounters students who have never had a Black teacher. She recognizes that she can do her part and make her impact, even if it may not resonate at first. But she is hopeful that these students may think back on their experience in her class and see "some connections and have some enlightenment which would translate to action." Of course, there are still many challenges.

> Some of the challenges are when there is little to no institutional support. . . . It's important to be diligent in allowing the institution the opportunity to make some headway and being able to address those deficits in terms of racial diversity, so giving people time and space. That can be challenging, it can be disheartening, but when you see some progress it restores the hope to go on further with this work.

While hope is so important, at what point can we say enough is enough? Tamara expresses appreciation for people in her life who tell her to never give up. Yet she wonders, instead of viewing it as giving up, why not reframe it as a matter of readiness? Specifically, "[Diversity] work is a process. We want tangible outcomes, without question. And we shouldn't discount the small outcomes, because maybe the small outcomes can grow collectively into this big influential life-changing outcome." Working with allies is critical in this process as sometimes certain people can enter spaces where others cannot. Tamara's communications training taught her to be strategic and to "put the right face in front of the right audience to get the message across."

Tamara will continue studying racial battle fatigue and the experiences of Black faculty. She also plans to research campus climate issues, exploring the exchanges between students and faculty and how the learning process is affected as a result. Further, she wants to explore individual and collective racialized spaces and what institutions can do to change negative learning environments. "Diversity is for everybody—not just students of color. And that message gets lost. White students can benefit from diverse environments too. I will be more intentional about this message and accompany it with data." Because everyone benefits from diversity, creating inclusive spaces should be a collective effort. Yet, Tamara's own research and experience remind us that this effort can lead to stress, strain, and fatigue. While faculty and students of color may cultivate safe spaces to manage the challenges of their lived experiences, the burden of recognizing racialized spaces and transforming them into diverse, inclusive, and safe spaces belongs to all of us.

Notes

1. *Racial battle fatigue* is defined by Tamara as "a person of color's reaction to the troubling conditions that occur from dealing with racism on a daily basis." For further information, see Smith (2004).
2. It should be noted that because of the 2006 state constitutional amendment that blocked Affirmative Action programs in Michigan, the Journalism Institute for Minorities was reconfigured and renamed the Journalism Institute for Media Diversity.

References

Smith, W. A. (2004). Black faculty coping with racial battle fatigue: The campus racial climate in a post–civil rights era. In D. Cleveland (Ed.), *A long way to go: Conversations about race by African American faculty and graduate students* (pp. 171–190). New York, NY: Peter Lang.

Solórzano, M., Ceja, M., & Yosso, T. (2000). Critical race theory, racial microaggressions, and campus racial climate: The experiences of African American college students. *Journal of Negro Education, 69*(2), 60–73.

Stevenson, T. N. (2012). *Racial battle fatigue, role strain, and African-American faculty at public community colleges* (Doctoral dissertation). Available from ProQuest Dissertations and Theses database. (UMI No. 3540464)

U.S. Census Bureau. (2010). *Quickfacts: Utah.* Retrieved from www.census.gov/quickfacts/table/PST045215/49

17

UNPACKING THE MANDATE RHETORIC OF HISTORICALLY BLACK COLLEGES AND UNIVERSITIES' DIVERSITY DISCOURSES

Courtney Carter

Over the past several decades, U.S. colleges and universities have come to rely on diversity initiatives to ensure racial heterogeneity on campuses (Berrey, 2008; Kirkland & Hansen, 2011; Stevens, 2007). Such efforts are not unique to postsecondary institutions, as diversity is one of the primary frameworks Americans use to deal with race in organizational life (Berrey, 2008; Edelman, Fuller, & Mara-Drita, 2001; Goode, 2001; Kalev, Dobbin, & Kelly, 2006; MacLean, 2008). Following the passage of civil rights legislation in the mid-twentieth century, public sector institutions were required to use Affirmative Action in hiring and admissions policies to compensate for historical exclusion and prevent further discrimination (Collins, 1997; Jackson & Nunn, 2003).

By the 1980s, however, business and higher education organizations began to abandon the original justification for Affirmative Action, largely in response to declining legal and cultural support for compensatory and antidiscrimination measures (MacLean, 2008). In substitution, personnel specialists, Equal Employment Opportunity managers, and academics made the case that race-conscious practices in pursuit of diversity are in organizations' best interests. In making the case for diversity, specialists claim that differences among individuals and between groups translate into valuable assets as workers and students draw from their backgrounds to produce unique insights and skills (Page, 2007). While critical analyses have increasingly drawn attention to the shift in focus from racial justice to institutional advantage (Beckman, 2006; Collins, 2011; Edelman et al., 2001; Embrick, 2011; Green, 2004; MacLean, 2008), the argument that diversity is complementary to organizational priorities has helped race-based policies withstand a challenging climate (Berrey, 2008; Green, 2004).

Historically Black Colleges and Universities and Diversity

Much of the current interest in, and discourse around, diversity in higher education concerns predominantly White institutions (PWIs). However, a look at the broader field reveals that the diversity norm has spread beyond PWIs and into minority schools, such as historically Black colleges and universities (HBCU). The HBCU designation refers to the group of institutions established to educate African Americans during higher education's period of de jure segregation (Allen & Jewell, 2002). The Higher Education Act of 1965 officially defined *HBCUs* as "any . . . college or university that was established prior to 1964, whose principle mission was, and is, the education of black Americans" (Section 321, pp. 138–139).

HBCUs' Racialized Mission

Despite shared origins, there is a great deal of variety among the nation's 105 Black schools, including public and private institutions, single-gender and co-ed schools, religious and secular schools, and junior colleges and universities (Brown, 2003). Still, scholars often cite racial uplift as the common focus uniting HBCUs across institutional type.

In pursuing an agenda of racial uplift, HBCUs emphasize social responsibility by producing a Black population equipped to meet African American communities' cultural, social, and political needs (Allen & Jewell, 2002; Brown, Ricard, Donahoo, Brown, & Freeman, 2004; Gasman, Baez, & Turner, 2008; Jackson & Nunn, 2003; Strayhorn & Hirt, 2008; Thompson, 1973). Also, in an effort to cultivate students' Black racial identity, HBCUs disseminate Black cultures, scholarship, and politics (Brown et al., 2004; Cole, 2010; Jackson & Nunn, 2003). It is worth noting, however, that in pursuing a racial uplift agenda, HBCUs have not engaged in racial discrimination (Brown & Ricard, 2007; Ware, 1994) but have long admitted students of different nationalities, races, and ethnicities (Jewell, 2002).

Currently, about 19% of HBCU students are not African American (National Center for Education Statistics [NCES], 2011). Most of these students are White, but non-White Hispanic and Asian American student enrollment has been increasing for several years (Gasman, 2013). Yet despite HBCUs' tradition of inclusion, the emergence of racial diversity as a taken-for-granted value in higher education has presented these institutions with the challenge of responding to this new norm.[1]

The Diversity Challenge

Conversations about the extent to which HBCUs should—and do—prioritize student racial diversity frame Black schools as being behind the trend. For instance, in the early 1990s Sims (1994) described student body diversity at HBCUs as a "controversial higher education paradigm" (p. 1) for HBCUs, and she compares these schools to the developments made at PWIs. Although Willie, Reddick, and Brown (2005) acknowledge Black schools' existing religious and socioeconomic variation, they maintain that HBCUs "have some distance to go to achieve an acceptable level of racial diversity in student enrollment" (p. 34). A prominent theme of this discussion concerns exactly what groups constitute diversity at predominantly non-White schools.

In his book on higher education Affirmative Action policies, Beckman (2006) states, "Arguably, affirmative action even applies to white male students at HBCUs" (p. 3). Allen and Jewell (2002) encourage Black school officials to be more mindful of the "complicated landscape of 'difference'" (p. 255) by working to attract a greater variety of non-Black students and students from different classes and religious backgrounds as well as sexual orientations. Furthermore, several policy suggestions have already been made that call for the kinds of initiatives used in White schools (Roebuck & Murty, 1993). For instance, Willie and colleagues (2005) advise HBCUs to seek help from philanthropic foundations.

> Given that foundation-sponsored scholarship assistance helped to integrate Black students into White colleges in the 1960s . . . there is no reason not to believe that foundation-sponsored scholarship will help integrate White students into predominantly Black colleges and universities in the early decades of the twenty-first century. (p. 45)

Clearly, HBCUs are engaged in conversations about racial diversity. Still, Black colleges and universities have largely been excluded from empirical diversity scholarship. The research that does address HBCUs focuses on demographic trends or examines Whites' subjective experiences as minority students. The former takes note of non-Black students' enrollment patterns and includes research on the transition of Bluefield State University from a demographically Black school to a predominantly White HBCU (Brown, 2002; Brown, 2004). Studies of White HBCU students indicate their overall satisfaction, citing positive interactions with faculty, few encounters with racial hostilities, but persistent negative attitudes about African Americans (Hall & Closson 2005; Peterson & Hamrick, 2009; Roebuck & Murty, 1993).

Beyond these two areas little attention has been given to the content of diversity messages geared toward HBCUs, to what exactly those who advocate for greater racial diversity in these spaces say it means for Black colleges and universities. In this chapter I address some of these messages by examining the diversity rhetoric within the HBCU community. To do so I draw from a sample of media resources, including newspaper opinion pages, organizational documents, and interviews with HBCU experts, consultants, and school officials.

The Diversity Mandate

In the rest of the chapter I describe the arguments made by HBCU insiders—current and past presidents, academics specializing in research on HBCUs, professionals who consult with Black schools on a number of issues, and school officials—in favor of racial diversity. I refer to them as *diversity advocates*, a term that is not meant to imply that they are actively engaged in implementing diversity initiatives but rather captures the tone of their statements that promote racial diversity. I characterize the arguments promoting racial diversification among HBCUs as a *mandate rhetoric* because advocates describe racial diversity as a necessary response to the two related challenges of institutional viability and institutional legitimacy. Additionally, advocates imply or explicitly state that a failure to use racial diversity for institutional gain may have dire consequences for the future of Black schools.

Institutional Viability

African American student enrollment at HBCUs has been declining since the 1960s. Before then, nearly 90% of Black college students attended HBCUs, but today 11% of Black students choose these institutions (Gasman, 2007; NCES, 2011). Although this is not an issue for every HBCU, particularly the more elite public and private institutions, such steep enrollment drops have affected Black colleges as a whole. Recently, several schools have had very public struggles with low enrollment, leading in certain cases to school closures. Therefore much of the diversity mandate rhetoric frames racial diversity as a practical response to enrollment challenges. One interviewee, a Black school expert, remarked, "The smart presidents, they realize that there's no way they can sustain their enrollment if they don't diversify." Charles Nelms (2012), a former HBCU president, made the same point in an opinion piece:

> I am convinced that the *failure* to diversify the enrollment of HBCUs will, in all probability, *lead to the demise of a selected number of these universities* [emphasis in original]. It is a demographic reality that as the white population declines, and the minority population increases, there will be increased competition for students.

The tone of this statement reflects many advocates' view that HBCU leaders have not been willing to recognize racial diversity as a mechanism to reverse enrollment trends. For example, I interviewed an HBCU consultant and Black college graduate who remarked, "Enrollment has gone down at a lot of HBCUs, and I blame that on not thinking of new ways and new groups to recruit." Diversifying the population, therefore, is characterized as a creative response to changed circumstances.

Institutional Legitimacy

While the question of institutional viability is connected to whether the schools can survive, diversity advocates also link the matter to institutional HBCUs' legitimacy, to the extent to which these schools are considered valuable and effective organizations in the field of higher education. Legitimacy is tied to compliance to legal mandates to desegregate but also to those nonlegal pressures that result from the changing racial norms in higher education.

Legal compliance with desegregation. The desegregation era dramatically changed the landscape of HBCUs, not only through declining Black enrollment but also, in the case of public schools in several states, through externally imposed policies aimed at attracting non–African American students in the decades that followed the landmark *Brown v. Board of Education* (1954) decision shone a spotlight on the slow accomplishment of desegregation in public southern colleges and universities. In Alabama, Tennessee, Mississippi, and Louisiana, legal proceedings introduced measures to integrate White and Black schools (Brown, 1999). For example, as part of the 2002 settlement of *United States v. Fordice*, Mississippi's Black public schools were required to increase their non-Black enrollment to 10% for at least three consecutive years (Jackson & Nunn, 2003). These schools, like other public HBCUs, introduced a variety of diversity structures to attract and retain non-Black students, including scholarships, multicultural affairs offices, diversity officers, cultural month programming, ethnic identity clubs, and so on.

At times the content of the diversity mandate reflects an awareness that the trajectory of diversity at many schools is shaped by their status as public institutions subject to state and federal regulations. As one HBCU expert said in an interview, "Some of the public institutions are under pressure to diversify." Other advocates suggested that the public school status itself attracts non-Black students, inevitably resulting in greater racial diversity. According to one HBCU expert "public institutions have a public mission, and also if something is affiliated with the state, I think that whites in particular are more likely to go to it." An HBCU consultant expressed a similar observation, saying, "Those public ones [HBCUs] come under that umbrella, and it became just another regional campus somewhere, so they automatically become diverse."

Compliance with normative values. Matters of legitimacy, however, extend beyond formal legal compliance. HBCUs, as other colleges and universities, have had to remain relevant by being responsive to higher education's changing values and practices. Therefore, even private HBCUs, although technically exempt from the mandates given to state-assisted institutions, have taken steps to diversify the student population. For instance, private schools such as Paul Quinn College and Fisk University have received attention for their greater efforts at attracting and securing Hispanic students (Gasman, 2012; Mbajekwe, 2006; Shellenbarger, 2011).

This aspect of the mandate rhetoric relies on claims of institutional advantage and moral imperatives. Proponents argue that diversity improves HBCUs' competitiveness in the higher education marketplace. For instance, a set of guidelines from the National Leadership Institute on Multiculturalism at HBCUs explains that racial diversity allows Black colleges and universities to sustain their foremost position in diversity and continue to lead in preparing students to work and live in an interdependent and global world (Bristow, 2004)

Among PWIs, diversity rhetoric often contains moral claims that the institution ensures access for underrepresented groups and is thus an issue of fairness, and that it prepares students to participate in a multicultural, democratic society (Berrey, 2011; Iverson, 2007). The HBCU diversity mandate rhetoric also invokes a moral stance, often by appealing to Black schools' history challenging racial and ethnic exclusion. The following statement from a Black university financial officer illustrates this approach.

> I would say as a Black person I would not want to become what I was created for, meaning, the reason that HBCUs were created was because the whites didn't want us at their schools. So if I turn around and talk about other types of people at my school, I'm no better than they were. And I think, me personally, most HBCUs feel like we're better than that. We're not gonna discriminate against you because of your color.

Relevance. The rhetoric of the diversity mandate not only seeks to position HBCUs in line with normative values but also establishes their continued relevance in the face of accusations that Black schools are at best outdated and at worst promote racial segregation. Therefore, one strategy involves assertions that HBCUs remain relevant because they model racial diversity for the rest of higher education. This leadership potential stems from HBCUs' well-established reputation as antiracist organizational spaces.

According to the National Leadership Institute on Multiculturalism at HBCUs (2004),

> Today's challenges present an *opportunity for HBCUs to exemplify* [emphasis added] the ways in which colleges and universities can successfully and seamlessly implement the principles of multiculturalism and diversity while advancing their primary missions and serving their historical base.

In a 2013 opinion piece, Jarrett Carter, an editor with *HBCU Digest*, explains that compared to PWIs, HBCUs have the capacity to create a diversity agenda that deeply engages the complex issues of race and inclusion.

> But most PWIs have only narrowly embraced diversity as an economic and political asset, and black students have suffered because of the PWI commitment to the concept of diversity instead of the humanity of it. HBCUs now have a chance *to model for America the ideal execution of diversity and inclusion* [emphasis in original]; the abandoning of racial harmony in favor of racial appreciation taught within the context and through the perspective of America's racial minorities. (Carter, 2013)

Other arguments that tie diversity to HBCUs' relevance involve claims about the nature of Black colleges' mission and constituents. Some advocates claim that HBCUs' core constituents are underrepresented students rather than Black students specifically. Student body racial diversity is therefore compatible with the mission. An HBCU consultant makes this point in describing how Black schools' commitment to marginalized students attracts non-Blacks.

> People who are not African American are beginning to seriously consider HBCUs and attending and graduating. It's a place that provides a different level of support than your typical mainstream undergraduate school. It takes people where they are—and we still have those [who are] struggling—and helps to elevate them to levels that enter them into the middle class. *I don't think the mission ever changes.* . . . HBCUs to me still serve the same purpose—*to provide educational access, higher educational access, and opportunities for African Americans and other groups who are interested.*

However, other diversity advocates have claimed that although HBCUs do in fact have a special focus on African Americans, this is not irreconcilable with racial diversity. This position deals with structural diversity, whereby minority students' presence does not alter core organizational values. The implication is that HBCUs' missions have a certain amount of elasticity to accommodate other races while continuing to prioritize African American students. The following statement from one HBCU expert illustrates the claim that a racially specific mission and racial diversity can coexist.

> I think that every HBCU is committed to racial uplift of African Americans, and I don't have a problem with that at all. I think that that should be their mission. Historically that was the mission. . . . I actually am in favor of institutions being more diverse. I just think that's good for everybody, *and I don't think institutions are gonna lose that historic mission.*

Conclusion

Historically Black colleges and universities are dynamic institutions that have been able to play a significant role in American higher education because of their ability to adapt to their circumstances. Diversity, a project shaped in PWIs to address their specific past of racist discrimination and exclusion, has spread to organizations that have long challenged that very same exclusion. In these institutions, racial diversity is offered as a solution to crises of viability and legitimacy. Through diversification, HBCUs are able to increase enrollments, signal compliance with legal and cultural mandates, and establish their relevance among institutions of higher education. What remains to be seen, however, is whether these outcomes come at the expense of Black colleges' commitment to their traditional agendas. What is largely missing from HCBUs' diversity mandate rhetoric is an in-depth discussion of how these schools can continue to promote Black students' social and intellectual welfare while creating campuses palatable to students who may not feel invested in this agenda. The mandate rhetoric needs to include an intentional reckoning with this tension to clearly illustrate a way for HBCUs to succeed with diversity in the future.

Note

1. Conversations about race and student composition are by no means new to HBCUs, but the emphasis on diversity rather than segregation or desegregation has changed.

References

Allen, W. R., & Jewell, J. O. (2002). A backward glance forward: Past, present and future perspectives on historically Black colleges and universities. *Review of Higher Education, 25,* 241–261.

Beckman, J. A. (2006). *Affirmative Action now: A guide for students, families, and counselors.* Westport, CT: Greenwood.

Berrey, E. C. (2008). *A post civil rights vision of racial equality: Diversity rhetorics and initiatives in three organizational cases.* Unpublished manuscript, Department of Sociology, Northwestern University, Evanston IL.

Berrey, E. C. (2011). Why diversity became orthodox in higher education, and how it changed the meaning of race on campus. *Critical Sociology, 37,* 573–596.

Bristow, C. (2004). *Principles and standards of good practice to achieve diversity and multiculturalism at HBCUs.* Retrieved from www.educationupdate.com/archives/2004/may/html/col-multicul.htm

Brown v. Board of Educ., 347 U.S. 483 (1954).

Brown, M. C. (1999). *The quest to define collegiate desegregation: Black colleges, Title VI compliance, and post-Adams litigation.* Westport, CT: Greenwood.

Brown, M. C. (2002). Good intentions: Collegiate desegregation and transdemographic enrollments. *Review of Higher Education, 25,* 263–280.

Brown, M. C. (2003). Emics and etics of researching Black colleges: Applying facts and avoiding fallacies. *New Directions for Institutional Research, 118,* 27–40.

Brown, M. C., & Freeman, K. (2004). *Black colleges: New perspectives on policy and practice.* Westport, CT: Praeger.

Brown, M. C., Ricard, R. B., Donahoo, S., Brown, M., & Freeman, K. (2004). The changing role of historically black colleges and universities: Vistas on dual missions, desegregation, and diversity. In C. B. (Ed.) & K. F. (Ed.), *Black colleges: New perspectives on policy and practice* (pp. 3–28). Westport, CT: Praeger.

Brown, M. C., II, & Ricard, R. B. (2007, Fall). The honorable past and uncertain future of the nation's HBCUs. *Thought & Action,* 117–130.

Brown, R. P. (2004). *The transition of a historically Black college to a predominantly White institution* (Doctoral dissertation, University of Maryland). Retrieved from www.lib.umd.edu/drum/bitstream/1903/2174/1/umi-umd-2162.pdf

Carter, J. (2013, January 30). HBCUs will benefit from America's post-racial pushback. *Huffington Post.* Retrieved from www.huffingtonpost.com/jarrett-l-carter/hbcus-will-benefit-from a_b_2578383.html

Cole, W. M. (2010). Mandated multiculturalism: An analysis of core curricula at tribal and historically Black colleges. *Poetics, 38,* 481–503.

Collins, S. M. (1997). *Black corporate executives: The making and breaking of a Black middle class.* Philadelphia, PA: Temple University Press.

Collins, S. M. (2011). From affirmative action to diversity: Erasing inequality from organizational responsibility. *Critical Sociology, 37,* 517–520.

Edelman, L. B., Fuller, S. R., & Mara-Drita, I. (2001). Diversity rhetoric and the managerialization of law. *American Journal of Sociology, 106,* 1589–1641.

Embrick, D. G. (2011). The diversity ideology in the business world: A new oppression for a new age. *Critical Sociology, 37,* 541–556.

Gasman, M. (2007). *Envisioning Black colleges: A history of the United Negro College Fund.* Baltimore, MD: Johns Hopkins University Press.

Gasman, M. (2012, November 8). Historically Black colleges and universities must embrace diversity. *Chronicle of Higher Education*. Retrieved from chronicle.com/blogs/conversation/2012/11/08/historically-black-colleges-and-universities-must-embrace-diversity

Gasman. M. (2013). *The changing face of historically Black colleges and universities*. Philadelphia: Center for Minority Serving Institutions, University of Pennsylvania.

Gasman, M., Baez. B., & Turner, C. S. V. (2008). On minority serving institutions. In M. Gasman, B. Baez, & C. S. V. Turner (Eds.), *Understanding minority serving institutions* (pp. 3–17). New York, NY: SUNY Press.

Goode, J. (2001). Let's get our act together: How racial discourses disrupt neighborhood activism. In J. Goode & J. Maskovsky (Eds.), *The new poverty studies: The ethnography of power, politics, and impoverished people in the United States* (pp. 364–398). New York: New York University Press.

Green, D. O. N. (2004). Justice and diversity: Michigan's response to Gratz, Grutter, and the Affirmative Action debate. *Urban Education, 39*, 374–393.

Hall, B., & Closson, R. B. (2005). When the majority is the minority: White graduate students' social adjustment at a historically Black university. *Journal of College Student Development, 46*(1), 28–42.

Higher Education Act, Pub. L. No. 89-329 (1965).

Iverson, S. V. (2007). Camouflaging power and privilege: A critical race analysis of university diversity policies. *Educational Administration Quarterly, 43*, 586–611.

Jackson, C. L., & Nunn, E. F. (2003). *Historically Black colleges and universities: A reference handbook*. Santa Barbara, CA: ABC-CLIO.

Jewell, J. O. (2002). To set an example: The tradition of diversity at historically Black colleges and universities. *Urban Education, 37*(1), 7–21.

Kalev, A., Dobbin, F., & Kelly, E. (2006). Best practices or best guesses? Assessing the efficacy of corporate affirmative action and diversity policies. *American Sociological Review, 71*, 589–617.

Kirkland, A., & Hansen, B. B. (2011). "How do I bring diversity?" Race and class in the college admissions essay. *Law & Society Review, 45*, 103–138.

MacLean, N. (2008). *Freedom is not enough: The opening of the American workplace*. Boston, MA: Harvard University Press.

Mbajekwe, C. O. W. (Ed.). (2006). *The future of historically Black colleges and universities: Ten presidents speak out*. Jefferson, NC: McFarland.

National Center for Education Statistics. (2011). *Fall enrollment, degrees, conferred, and expenditures in degree-granting historically Black colleges and universities, by institution: 2010, 2011, and 2010–11*. Retrieved from nces.ed.gov/programs/digest/d12/tables/dt12_281.asp

Nelms, C. (2012, November 26). Beyond the rhetoric: diversity matters. *Huffington Post*. Retrieved from http://www.huffingtonpost.com/charlie-nelms-edd/historically-black-colleges-universities_b_2162682.html

Page, S. E. (2007). *The difference: How the power of diversity creates better groups, firms, schools and societies.* Princeton, NJ: Princeton University Press.

Peterson, R. D., & Hamrick, F. A. (2009). White, male, and "minority": Racial consciousness among White male undergraduates attending a historically Black university. *Journal of Higher Education, 80*, 34–58.

Roebuck, J. B., & Murty, K. S. (1993). *Historically Black colleges and universities: Their place in American higher education.* Westport, CT: Praeger.

Shellenbarger, S. (2011, August 17). Recruiters at Black colleges break from tradition. *Wall Street Journal.* Retrieved from www.wsj.com/articles/SB10001424053 111903480904576512372651069468

Sims, S. J. (1994). *Diversifying historically Black colleges and universities: A new higher education paradigm.* Westport, CT: Greenwood.

Stevens, M. L. (2009). *Creating a class: College admissions and the education of elites.* Boston, MA: Harvard University Press.

Strayhorn, T. L., & Hirt, J. (2008). Social justice at historically Black and Hispanic-serving institutions: Mission statements and administrative voices. In M. Gasman, B. Baez, & C. S. V. Turner (Eds.), *Understanding minority serving institutions,* (pp. 203–216). New York, NY: SUNY Press.

Thompson, D. C. (1973). *Private Black colleges at the crossroads.* Westport, CT: Greenwood.

Ware, L. (1994). Issues in education law and policy: The most visible vestige: Black colleges after Fordice. *Boston College Law Review, 35*, 633–1203.

Willie, C. V., Reddick, R. J., & Brown, R. (2005). *The Black college mystique.* Lanham, MD: Rowman & Littlefield.

18

AN INTERVIEW WITH COURTNEY CARTER
Unpacking the Mandate Rhetoric of Historically Black Colleges and Universities' Diversity Discourses

Demar F. Lewis IV

When people think of historically Black colleges and universities (HBCU), they may have one of a myriad of initial responses. Some see them solely as Black-only spaces that promote Black history, identity, culture, and unique racial politics. Others might see HBCUs as a derivative form of predominantly White institutions (PWI) that provide a second-rate education to students who are unprepared for the rigor of elite institutions. Courtney Carter asserts that HBCUs have a higher, greater purpose. In the twenty-first century, she believes that HBCUs can provide important insights into creating fair and just organizational spaces.

While many conversations on issues of diversity have taken place at PWIs, administrators of HBCUs are now also thinking about issues of diversity as they explore ways to expand educational access to new student populations. Yet, Courtney realizes it is important to clarify that the perspective of PWIs and HBCUs in understanding diversity is distinctly different.

> We know that in White organizations [diversity] is the newest articulation of a project to manage racial minorities: how much do we integrate them and how much are we really trying to change our institutions to make these places where they're not just present but fully integrated and able to do well? HBCUs are institutions that don't have a history of discrimination and racial discrimination—they do not practice this, they do not ban people of other races from participating.

Courtney fully recognizes there are variations in the ability of organizations to pursue different diversity measures, and the factors that inhibit or propel organizational success can vary greatly. Nonetheless, she has keenly observed that despite holding different perspectives on diversity, HBCU officials are asking themselves a question quite similar to that of PWIs: To successfully desegregate, integrate, and racially diversify, to what extent do you compromise your identity as a (Black) organizational space? However, she finds that HBCUs are often understood as better suited to make this transition because their missions are more amenable to the inclusion of marginalized populations as HBCUs were created for populations that were considered Black in American society. Thus, HBCU university leaders who participated in one of her latest studies almost unanimously agreed that their schools were capable of expanding the inclusivity of their institutional missions because they have done so since their inception.

Courtney's path to becoming a sociologist of education began at an early age. As a young teen in a public high school, she began observing a tension between her White peers wanting to experience and engage with people different from themselves without having to talk about racial equality. When asked about the influences that contributed to her development, she reflected on her experiences as a youth in the public school system that exposed her to the perplexing existence of inequality in integrated spaces. Courtney's family also played a major role in keeping her focused on advancing her education because both of her parents were college-educated.

> College was a given but I had not given any thought to graduate school until I met the director of the McNair Program at my undergraduate institution and was recruited to participate. They told me that "we need more Black PhDs" and I was like "I'll be a Black PhD."

Although she was a strong student in her sociology courses as an undergraduate, few of her professors in her department took the time to let her know that she had the capacity to complete work as a graduate student. Thus, the Ronald E. McNair Postbaccalaureate Achievement Program, a pipeline program designed to prepare underrepresented undergraduate students for graduate education or a career in the professoriate, played a vital role in giving Courtney the opportunity to explore her interests and cultivate necessary skills to navigate in the academy.

> It was really [the McNair] program that put me on this path and has kept me on the path because I feel indebted and obligated to finish. I think that these kinds of programs were very important in giving me a sense of what I would expect in graduate school and letting me know that the kinds of skills required to succeed in grad school were not foreign to me.

Courtney's cohort and peer network and faculty mentors played a key role in her academic success and were also an integral part of her being able to overcome the various obstacles she faced along the road to defending her dissertation.

When Courtney began graduate school, she was primarily focused on exploring racial ideology, racial discourse, and how that discourse was an expression of ideology. More explicitly, she wanted to understand the way that color blindness influenced individual conceptions of race. She found that people who claimed to be color-blind also frequently celebrated diversity, which seemed to contradict the basic tenets of the color-blind racial ideology. Courtney was then inspired to explore the relationship between color blindness and diversity in the context of organizations, and she later expanded this question to examine racial ideologies in organizational spaces. Reflecting on this evolution, she believes that her decision to move away from analyzing organizations to understanding how race and power play out in organizational spaces was one of the most significant developments in her research trajectory. Overall, Courtney sees this evolution as her current focus situated within a larger question about the reconstruction of race in contemporary society. Her unique contribution to the field is to look at HBCUs in education because HBCUs are understudied in sociology. Courtney's scholarship is a genuine attempt to bring minority institutions into the conversation and advance the theoretical conversations about race in organizations. While her work does not conform to the normative discourse of diversity in education, Courtney has found few obstacles in pursuing her research interests in the academy. In fact, many of her mentors, colleagues, and research subjects have been extremely receptive to engaging in conversations on diversity at HBCUs.

> I haven't faced any challenges because diversity is a popular topic, particularly if you are going to be talking to administrators. It is the way to talk about race—it is the legitimate way to do it. In colleges we're not really talking color blindness, we're talking about how having these multiethnic, multicultural, international populations is a sign of prestige and that you're doing it "right." So I say I'm studying diversity at HBCUs and people say, "Finally, someone interested in bringing us to the conversation."

Courtney's work illustrates that administrators of HBCUs have begun to consider various ways to define *diversity* at their institutions, including looking at class and socioeconomic status, ethnicity, culture, and sexual identity. Furthermore, her research suggests that HBCUs are capable of modeling how institutions can provide educational access and institutional support to students with intersectional identities.

Courtney is a role model for other aspiring McNair Scholars, women, and people of color. When prompted on advice she would give to young scholars interested in doing work around diversity in education, she stated that there is a great need in the field to evaluate diversity initiatives in colleges, minority-serving institutions, and other schools that are currently underresearched. Additionally, she also encourages early-career scholars to pursue interdisciplinary work when seeking to address their research questions. She has benefited tremendously from working collaboratively with scholars in education to answer her questions about diversity because it has allowed her to clarify her questions as a sociologist. Courtney advises graduate students who are interested in pursuing tenure-track careers at research institutions to start submitting papers for publication and presenting at conferences so that students can get constructive feedback on their work to help them move to the next stage. Thinking about her discipline, Courtney encourages aspiring sociologists of education to "try to understand why certain initiatives work at one institution versus another, and then unpack the policies, processes, [and so on], that legitimize these initiatives at different institutions." Although there is no shortage of work for those aspiring to make the academy their future home, Courtney has proven that the dream is possible for those of us coming behind her.

I thoroughly enjoyed the opportunity to speak with Courtney and learn about her journey to earning her PhD. In many ways, our journeys are similar. Both of my parents were college-educated and instilled in me a strong desire to excel academically and pursue a college degree. When I was a teenager at Regis Jesuit High School, I had a revelatory moment when I learned the Emancipation Proclamation was a lever of racial politics that prevented the French from joining ranks with the Confederate Army in the South during the Civil War—its primary intent was not to abolish the institution of slavery or rectify the unjust treatment of Black people in the United States, as is often celebrated in public discourse. These influences prompted me to learn more about American society and the behavior of bureaucratic organizations. Subsequently, I pursued focused studies in international business administration and American culture and difference studies at the University of St. Thomas in Minnesota.

As a former McNair Scholar, I would not be in a professional school at the University of Michigan (or have dreamed of graduate education) had it not been for the instrumental guidance of my program directors, professors, and mentors. Their investment in my development as a young adult and scholar not only inspires me to pursue a career in the professoriate as a researcher but also motivates me to serve as an instructor and mentor to forthcoming generations of students. Following in my directors', professors', and mentors' footsteps, I aspire to prepare a new generation of young adults to be scholar activists, leaders, and idealists who are strongly motivated to change the world and fight to preserve the welfare of humanity.

A major theme that resonates with me after interviewing Courtney is that race (under the guise of diversity) is still on the minds of decision makers in higher education institutions despite the limitations of Proposal 2, a 2006 ballot initiative adopted by voters in the state of Michigan to eliminate equal opportunity programs in Michigan's public sector (Berrey, 2015; Hollowell, 2008). It was later appealed and upheld as constitutional by the Supreme Court in 2014 (University of Michigan, 2016). It is true that genuine efforts are being made to enhance socioeconomic, regional, experiential, and other forms of diversity on campuses, but race-conscious decisions are still being made in the absence of Affirmative Action: We must not pretend that higher education is operating in a postracial world. Additionally, one of the implicit messages I took away from our conversation is that if institutions are *truly* aspiring to change, they must be transparent about their willingness and ability to expand their organizational missions. It is not an accident that HBCUs were created at a time when PWIs refused to support the social and cultural mobility of racial minorities. Yet, institutions often fail to explicitly identify the constructions within their organizational habitus that hinder the success of minorities or others of marginalized identities when discussing diversity initiatives (McDonough, 1998; Museus, Ravello, & Vega, 2011).

Considering this issue, and others, I hope to contribute toward ensuring the success and mobility of men and women of color or marginalized groups in higher education, organizations, and civic life across the United States. It is for these reasons that I strive to become a Black PhD.

References

Berrey, E. (2015). *The enigma of diversity: The language of race and the limits of racial justice*. Chicago, IL: University of Chicago Press.

Hollowell, M. (2008). In the wake of Proposal 2: The challenge to equality of opportunity in Michigan. *Thurgood Marshall Law Review, 34*, 203–256.

McDonough, P. (1998). Structuring college opportunities: A cross-case analysis of organizational cultures, climates, & habiti. In C. A. Torres & T. R. Mitchell (Eds.), *Sociology of education: Emerging perspectives* (pp. 181–210). Albany, NY: SUNY Press.

Museus, S. D., Ravello, J. N., & Vega, B. E. (2011). The campus racial culture: A critical race counterstory. In S. D. Museus & U. M. Jayakumar (Eds.), *Creating campus cultures: Fostering success among racially diverse student populations* (pp. 28–45). New York, NY: Routledge.

University of Michigan. (2016). Diversity, equity & inclusion: Proposal 2 FAQs. Retrieved from diversity.umich.edu/our-commitment/legal-issues/2006-proposal-2/proposal-2-faqs

19

TRANSFORMING DEMOGRAPHY, DEMOCRACY, AND DISCOURSE THROUGH DIVERSITY IN EDUCATION AND SOCIETY

John C. Burkhardt and Marie P. Ting

This book examines how the concept of diversity is understood and shaped by the work of scholars who have entered their professional careers after the twentieth-century framings of race, ethnicity, gender, class, sexual orientation, nationality, and ability have lost their authority. In encouraging each contributor to take up the challenge of explaining this crucially important concept in an original way, the book provides a unique insight into how different individuals, using the tools of different disciplines, wrestle with complicated and disputed topics, in this case one that has contributed to shaping them as individuals and as scholars.

The manner in which a complex matter is framed, studied, and discussed has obvious implications for how it is understood and eventually for how it is made real in personal and public behavior. Conceptualizations of diversity have been rapidly shifting in recent years. This is especially true in the United States, where demographic changes; attitude shifts related to gender, race, ethnicity, sexual orientation, and immigration; and even perhaps the election of an African American president seem to have prompted both a new examination and an increasing polarization of views related to equity, inclusion, and diversity in higher education and society.

As described in our opening chapter, the history of the term *diversity* in American higher education covers contexts and circumstances in which the word itself was rarely or never used in the way it is used today. Diversity viewed as an objective to be achieved by colleges and universities is a rather recent occurrence. For most of the nineteenth and twentieth centuries, *diversity* was used as it is more popularly understood, as a descriptive term suggesting alternatives, opportunities, and vitality. During that time frame, it entered educational discourse only as a *term of art*, one that derives a legal meaning under a set of conditions that are considered inseparable from its use. In a more recent context, established by the Supreme Court decision in *Regents of the University of California v. Bakke* (1978), the term *diversity* has been applied almost exclusively to racial representation in an institution. In the opinion of Justice Lewis J. Powell, that decision may have been the last point of general agreement on what diversity means for higher education. Even then it was unclear how *diversity*, transmuted as a term and legitimized as a goal, might be enacted in practice.

From that point to now, the concept of *diversity* has become increasingly difficult to define either in scholarship or in educational practice. In succeeding and widening reinterpretations, issues of gender, ability, and sexual orientation have been encompassed in the meaning of the term. Influenced in part by the interpretations given to decisions in recent court cases, there is an increasing concern for disparities by socioeconomic class in colleges and universities. This too has become a diversity issue, and controlling for these differences has been proposed as a way of increasing racial inequalities within the parameters of the law (Kahlenberg, 2014).

As Milem, Chang, and Antonio (2005) argue, higher education should now adopt a more explicit, more carefully defined *diversity agenda* in higher education. Their argument is compelling, especially in light of current challenges to professional practice that result from the multiple meanings and the diffusion of efforts related to diversity in colleges and universities. This challenge affects the field as a whole as well as administrators of institutions working to clarify and meet commitments to diversity on their own campuses.

Research at the National Center for Institutional Diversity (NCID, 2014, 2015) is showing us just what a problem the confusion about diversity and its implications has become. In 2014 we invited representatives from about 30 colleges and universities to the University of Michigan campus to discuss issues related to campus climate and its associated implications for student success. When issuing the invitations, we anticipated that six to eight institutions would send teams at their own expense to join us in the discussion. Instead, we had requests from nearly all the schools invited to participate. Faced with logistical limitations and a concern that a larger gathering would endanger the opportunity for meaningful exchange, we had to cut off the number at 19 teams of 4 to 5 individuals from each participating campus. Attendees were asked to complete a pre-event survey explaining why they wanted to participate and to answer several questions about climate-related concerns on their campuses. When we shared responses with participants, the reaction was a mix of surprise and, in some cases, disbelief.

At an aggregated level, the majority of participants who volunteered thought issues related to sexual orientation and social class were as important and concerning to them as racial tensions on campus; these perspectives challenged our own preconceptions about why campus leaders were so eager to be included in the discussion. This finding came as a surprise to many participants as well who had assumed that a conversation about improving campus climates would focus primarily on issues of race and the tensions surrounding interracial relationships. Instead, when responses were compared, there was consensus across all campuses that campus discussions about race and gender had declined in frequency and intensity over the past several years. The majority of respondents felt that *diversity* (by whatever definition) was no longer a strong concern for institutional leaders, governing boards, or even many student groups.

Examined at a between-group level (comparing answers across institutions) there were somewhat more predictable differences based on institutional size, location, and political jurisdiction. Institutions located in states where anti–Affirmative Action legislation had been passed reported very specific barriers to diversifying student enrollment. Institutions in states where demographic composition had already shifted to include larger representations of racial minorities described their challenges as more often related to on-campus climate than to enrollments.

However, the real surprises came when within-group differences were examined. Individuals representing the same campus often saw problems they faced quite differently. In some cases one or more individuals in the group reported that the institution had a definite plan to address climate issues, and others said that planning on the issues had not even taken place. Some individuals felt their faculty members were actively engaged in diversity efforts, and others walking the same halls strongly disagreed with this assessment. It became clear that at almost every level—across the system, between institutions, and on each campus—there was a critical need for a more exacting, more focused discussion on diversity and inclusion as a precursor to understanding and dealing with issues related to campus climates (NCID, 2014).

We conducted a study of strategic plans that had been adopted to address diversity goals by large research (so-called flagship) institutions in the Midwest. The definitions associated with the term *diversity* differed substantially from one institution to another and occasionally even within a single institutional plan. Sometimes an infinitely additive approach was attempted: *Diversity* was defined in a way that was so inclusive of so many groups that the term seemed to mean everything and therefore nothing specific. Quite often no definition of the term was offered at all.

We followed our analysis of diversity-related institutional planning documents with visits to four institutions that are members of the Big Ten Conference. During these visits, we conducted extensive interviews with campus diversity officers, faculty, students, and administrators. One of the first questions we asked each group was, What definition of *diversity* have you employed in guiding your institutional planning? Responses indicated that this consideration was frequently overlooked and sometimes purposely avoided. When discussions during countless interview sessions bordered on this topic, and especially when we pressed forward on the question, the parameters associated with diversity enlarged to include many or all constituencies regardless of their differences in identity or in circumstance (NCID, 2015).

Prompted by findings from our own research and coupled with our ongoing review of what has been written to guide the work of scholars and practitioners, we are working to construct a more meaningful and actionable conception of diversity as it is being used in current research, practice, and policy across the system of higher education. In approaching this task, we begin with the observation that the idea of diversity takes in an understanding of demography not merely as the study of groups and their distribution but as a way of thinking about the interplay and socialization of individual differences in an informed collective view of a future society. Demography enjoys a privilege among the social sciences: It is remarkably logical and offers a high reliability in its predictions. The importance of that fact will be made clear in the relationship of demography, democracy, and discourse.

Demography and democracy are closely related and not just because the words share a Greek root. Democracy is premised on an acknowledgment of who we are as a fundamental precursor to determining and then respecting what we want for ourselves. This is why one of the original articles of the U.S. Constitution called for a regular census. It also explains why we have fought so frequently about who is or who is not counted in our society. Democracy is about the arrangement and distribution of power. It is because of the essential relatedness of these two foundational ideas, demography and democracy, that we make issues of diversity, inclusion, and representation central to our public and political discourse.

In pursuing the goal of understanding and better defining contemporary meanings of *diversity*, NCID has taken a number of important steps, beginning with our systematic monitoring of how scholars and the general public speak and write about diversity in our society. Over 5 years, we have constructed a network of more than 300 diversity scholars whose early work has explored one or another aspect of diversity as they have constructed it in their research. Their submissions are often received in the form of books, chapters, and journal articles and have been peer reviewed by faculty from a wide range of disciplines at the University of Michigan. These scholars who were selected through a competitive process were invited into the network as a reflection of the quality and the promise of their first professional contributions. It is encouraging that many of these young scholars have established themselves as assistant, associate, or full professors at institutions across the country. In this book we have benefited from the scholarship that several of them have pursued as members of our Diversity Scholars Network.[1]

As we continue to pursue greater clarity in our understanding of terms, we are asking for a continued engagement with these scholars, encouraging them to submit new work that has the potential to push the edges of our latest conceptualizations of diversity with particular reference to one or more of our identified themes (demography, democracy, and discourse). We will be hosting gatherings of this network on the University of Michigan campus, not with the intention of creating some sort of new professional association or interest group but to allow scholars to learn directly from one another, to challenge each other, and to have greater influence in their disciplines and across the field of higher education.

Beginning this year, we will be offering year-long residencies to relatively established senior scholars whose previous work in areas of diversity deserves greater visibility. It is our intention to create a circulating community of such scholars in Ann Arbor where frequent interaction and combined insights may contribute to a new transdisciplinary understanding of diversity in higher education and American society. We will pair these senior scholars with a team of doctoral students and provide them with the time and means to advance their scholarship to new levels.

We have started a process of applying diversity research from a number of fields to challenges facing leaders and policymakers in higher education. In the past 2 years we have developed partnerships with the American Council on Education, the American Association of Hispanics in Higher Education, and other national groups with the shared intention of revising the curricula that prepare future provosts and presidents for their roles. An extensive infrastructure of leadership development activities exists across higher education. We have no need to compete with the excellent, well-established programs that are in place. It is our goal, however, to change expectations of leaders, of leadership, and about leadership development programs throughout higher education. Central to this ambition is a commitment to ensure that diversity research is better reflected in the ways we prepare future leaders for our colleges and universities.

While we approach our work as a series of long-term investments, we are also quite aware that time is not charitable, particularly in regard to the consequences of higher education's diversity-related challenges. The demographic changes in American society that are so frequently described in ominous and portentous tones are becoming less a set of predictions than emerging facts. While the phrase *majority minority* that is used in referring to our nation is ridden with subjective problems (and is syntactical nonsense) the passing of White plurality has already occurred in several of our states, and yet it will probably not occur for at least a century if at all in many others. Understood in that way, the incessant foretelling of a radical demographic event is statistically meaningless, albeit in different ways, to almost everyone in our country.

Yet, the social and psychological impact of a changing population is nonetheless real in the imagination and in our culture. That aspect of demography's potential impact demands to be taken seriously. With respect to that possibility, democracy and trends in public discourse combine to offer as strong a guarantee of predictability as any science we have. The college students enrolled today will live their adult lives in a very real perceptual state of disequilibrium.

Depending on place, time, and circumstance, this experience of upheaval in identities may or may not affect them in the same ways or at the same time. It will play out dramatically, however, in democratic struggles and in the discourse that envelops them.

This dystopian future can be dispelled only if we make use of the available opportunities we have to prepare future citizens and residents of our country with a clear idea of what will probably be the central challenge of their political future: how to deal with dynamics related to the distribution of power, opportunity, and control in society. Quite different from suggesting the inevitability of conflict, disruption, or a paradise lost, the prospect of greater equity, greater inclusion, and greater opportunity in our society is inspiring. If this hope is secured, it will mean that leaders of our colleges and universities and our system of higher education in the United States recognized the importance of our roles in shaping the way we respond to the social, cultural, and economic changes in our future. This more promising prospect is quite clearly possible, but it is not inevitable. It would require a transformation in our institutions that goes beyond the accommodation of difference that is the best we have so far accomplished.

Having spent well over a year in planning, organizing, and shaping this book, we have reviewed scholarship on the topic of diversity originating from many academic disciplines and considered research premised on a myriad of different assumptions. In the preceding chapters, we have represented the work of very promising scholars as they accepted our invitation to provide their best original ideas on a topic that is, by their own testimonies, something of a life's occupation, and in many cases, could be described as a calling. We believe that their scholarly work, coupled with the interviews conducted by younger scholars still completing their graduate study, offers important contributions to our understanding of the concept that unites and fascinates us all: diversity. This work is only further enhanced by the fact that it originates with individuals who are early in their professional careers and who have the opportunity; the capacity; and, we hope, the longevity to influence thinking in and outside the academy for many pivotal decades.

As the title of this book attempts to make clear, the term *increasing diversity* is simply not a cause quite big enough nor is it an accurate description of what is actually going on or what needs to occur in education or society. As argued several times and in many ways throughout this book, diversity is not something that is suddenly appearing nor is it really changing.

It is our understanding of diversity that must be transformed. Diversity and differences have always been a reality in our lives, just as they dominate and sustain the natural world. Science makes clear that the only environments that are seriously threatened are those that actually lack diversity. Diversity is the natural state. Communities, institutions, nations, and ecologies that suppress it are immediately and seriously vulnerable. In transforming that sense of diversity we can move ahead with the important process of transforming ourselves; our institutions; and, ultimately, our society.

Note

1. Patricia Gurin and Phillip Bowman, the two founding directors of NCID, deserve enormous credit for their vision and energy in constructing the Diversity Scholars Network and in leading NCID in the adoption of its earliest programs and priorities.

References

Kahlenberg, R. D. (Ed.). (2014). *The future of Affirmative Action: New paths to higher education diversity after Fisher v. University of Texas*. New York, NY: Century Foundation.

Milem, J. F., Chang, M. J., & Antonio, A. L. (2005). *Making diversity work on campus: A research-based perspective*. Washington, DC: Association of American Colleges and Universities.

National Center for Institutional Diversity. (2014). *Transforming campus climates for greater student engagement and success*. Ann Arbor, MI: Author.

National Center for Institutional Diversity. (2015). *Strategic diversity plans among selected peer institutions*. Ann Arbor, MI: Author.

Regents of the University of California v. Bakke, 438 U.S. 265, 272–275 (1978).

CONTRIBUTORS

Annie S. Adamian has taught at the middle school level for 15 years in Chico, California. In addition to being a classroom teacher, in 2016 she joined the School of Education at California State University, Chico, as an assistant professor of curriculum and pedagogy. Her research interests include antioppressive education, race and educational equity, teacher and student agency, critical pedagogy, and teacher and student participatory action research.

Diane M. Back received her MSW in community organizing from the University of Michigan in 2014. As a graduate student, Diane worked at the National Center for Institutional Diversity; participated in the School of Social Work Curriculum Committee; cofounded the Social Justice Education Group along with a coalition of students, faculty, and alumni; and was named the 2014 University of Michigan National Association of Social Workers student of the year. Diane currently holds positions with the University of Michigan Community Organizing Learning Community as a post-MSW fellow and Summer Youth Dialogues coordinator, and serves as a restorative practices specialist with the Novi Community School District. Her passions include increasing social justice curriculum offerings, promoting youth voice and dialogue, and advocating for youths and access to education.

Phillip J. Bowman is a professor in the Center for the Study of Higher and Postsecondary Education at the University of Michigan and the founding director of the National Center for Institutional Diversity. Prior to joining the university, Bowman served as director of the Institute for Research on Race and Public Policy at the University of Illinois at Chicago. He has held leadership roles at Northwestern University, including faculty fellow at the Institute for Policy Research, faculty affiliate at the Joint Center for Poverty Research, coordinator of the Spencer Training Grant in Education and Social Policy, coordinator of the Graduate Program in Counseling Psychology, director of the Summer Academic Workshop, and director of the Social and Behavioral Science Scholars Program. Phillip's scholarship focuses on diversity issues in research methodology, higher education, and public policy, social psychological issues in racial/ethnic disparities, and African American studies.

John C. Burkhardt has directed the National Center for Institutional Diversity since 2013. He also is a professor of clinical practice in the Center for the Study of Higher and Postsecondary Education at the University of Michigan and serves as special assistant to the provost for university engagement. He was the founding director of the National Forum on Higher Education for the Public Good, which he led from 2000 to 2013. From 1993 to 2000 he was program director for leadership and higher education at the W. K. Kellogg Foundation, where he led several major initiatives focused on transformation and change in higher education and participated in a comprehensive effort to encourage leadership development among college students. John's research focuses on leadership and transformation, organizational culture, and the role of philanthropy in U.S. society. He has written several books and articles on leadership and on higher education.

Courtney Carter is a native of Chicago and a graduate of Chicago public schools. Courtney earned her BA in sociology and anthropology from Truman State University and her PhD in sociology from the University of Illinois at Chicago. She is currently assistant professor of sociology and African American studies at Mississippi State University. Courtney's research examines race in organizations, focusing on the ways organizations are structured by race and produce racial outcomes. Her current work looks at the institutionalization of diversity at historically Black colleges and universities and the implication for these schools' traditional focus.

LaVar J. Charleston is assistant director and senior research associate at Wisconsin's Equity and Inclusion Laboratory at the University of Wisconsin–Madison (UW). In addition, he teaches courses in the Department of Educational Leadership and Policy Analysis in the School of Education at UW. LaVar's research focuses on graduate school preparation and success, with particular expertise in underrepresented student groups and students interested in science fields. LaVar is currently an editorial board member of the *Journal of African American Males in Education*, where he was previously on the review board; a reviewer for the *American Educational Research Journal (Social and Institutional Analysis)*; and a reviewer for the *Journal of Science Education and Technology*. LaVar's prior appointments include assistant director for development and marketing at the Center for African American Research and Policy, as well as associate editor of *Annuals of the Next Generation*.

Michelle Cuellar is program coordinator at the Center for Research on Educational Access and Leadership at California State University, Fullerton

(CSUF), where she oversees and advises a staff of undergraduate and graduate student researchers. As part of her role in the center, Michelle has led program evaluations for major projects, assisted in writing proposals for external funding, and codeveloped curriculum for various research institutes. She also travels on behalf of the center to many professional conferences to present current educational research and best practices. Michelle is currently an active committee member of the American Association of Colleges for Teacher Education's Networked Improvement Community, which aims to increase enrollment of males from communities of color in the teaching field. Michelle received her master's degree in higher education from CSUF and is currently pursuing a doctorate in education in community college leadership.

James M. Ellis is a PhD candidate in the Center for the Study of Higher and Postsecondary Education at the University of Michigan. James's research focuses on college access and the education pipeline experiences of underrepresented minority and low-income students.

Jarrett T. Gupton is assistant professor in the Department of Organizational Leadership, Policy and Development at the University of Minnesota. His areas of scholarly interest are opportunity and equity with two foci: How might we increase educational opportunities for those most at-risk in society and how might we increase equitable outcomes for marginalized students? Much of his work focuses on low-income students and issues of access and equity in higher and postsecondary education. Jarrett's scholarship highlights the ways social, cultural, and political structures constrain and enable educational equity and opportunity. His work serves as a methodological example of how to employ innovative qualitative research techniques to improve social policy

Timothy Hickey-LeClair earned a dual BA in biology and philosophy from Williams College in 2011. During his time there, his exposure to educational economics and work as a volunteer college adviser stoked his deep interest in higher education. Immediately after graduation, he began work at the Williams College Admission Office, specializing in international admission and recruitment, diversity outreach, and veteran affairs. In 2014 he completed his MA in higher education from the Center for the Study of Higher and Postsecondary Education at the University of Michigan. Timothy is fascinated by organizational behavior and, specifically, the relationship between third-party mediators such as college ranking and accrediting bodies and institutional and social stratification. He currently works as assistant director of admissions at Brandeis University in Massachusetts.

Jerlando F. L. Jackson is the Vilas Distinguished Professor of Higher Education and director and chief research scientist at Wisconsin's Equity and Inclusion Laboratory (Wei LAB) at the University of Wisconsin–Madison. As director of the Wei LAB, he is responsible for managing the Innovation Incubator, National Study of Intercollegiate Athletics, and the International Colloquium on Black Males in Education. His central research interest is organizational science in higher education, with a special interest in hiring practices, career mobility, workforce diversity, and workplace discrimination. He also has a portfolio of research focused on interventions designed to broaden participation for underrepresented groups in the scientific workforce. He is credited with more than 100 publications in high-impact journals, including *Research in Higher Education*, *IEEE Computer*, *American Behavioral Scientist*, *Teachers College Record*, *Review of Higher Education*, and *West's Educational Law Reporter*.

Uma M. Jayakumar is an associate professor of higher education and policy at the University of California, Riverside. After receiving her doctorate from the University of California, Los Angeles, she was an inaugural postdoctoral fellow under Phillip J. Bowman at the National Center for Institutional Diversity. Uma's scholarship examines race, equity, and resistance in higher education, with a focus on how organizational environments and practices shape access, experiences, race relations, and educational outcomes. These themes informed her curricular vision for the higher education and student affairs master's program she cofounded at the University of San Francisco. Uma's research has been generously supported by the Spencer and Ford Foundations.

Jessica Joslin is a PhD candidate in the Center for the Study of Higher and Postsecondary Education at the University of Michigan. Her research interests include the role of religion in higher education; lesbian, gay, bisexual, transgender, and queer or questioning student experiences and success; and critical and feminist pedagogies, theories, and methodologies. She holds a BA in history and social policy from Northwestern University and an MDiv from Harvard University.

Tonya Kneff is a PhD student and graduate instructor in the School of Education at the University of Michigan. Her research interests lie in the intersection of social policy, urban space, and education, and specifically the relationship among race, inequality, segregation, and dispossession in education and housing policies. Tonya is working on a historiography of school closures in the United States. She holds an MA in educational leadership and policy from the University of Michigan and a BA in peace and conflict studies from the University of California, Berkeley. Tonya is the former coordinator of the Postdoctoral Fellowship Program at the National Center for Institutional Diversity, and prior to her graduate work she spent several years in Japan working for the Nagano Prefectural Board of Education.

Jimin Kwon earned her MA in higher education from the Center for the Study of Higher and Postsecondary Education at the University of Michigan with a concentration in diversity and social justice in 2014. She earned a BA in applied psychology from New York University (NYU) in 2013. Before attending NYU, she went to a private high school in Minnesota, where she began to think about diversity, racial climate, social identity, and attitudes. Jimin is interested in taking a social psychological lens into understanding the campus experiences of students of color, which influenced her decision to work at the National Center for Institutional Diversity as a graduate intern during her time at Michigan. Jimin is now looking forward to moving to Chicago, where she will be studying and working as a prospective researcher in the field of social science.

Adam Lalor is a PhD in educational psychology in the University of Connecticut's (UConn) Neag School of Education. His research focuses on postsecondary transition of students with disabilities and the preparation of professionals to support this student population. At UConn Adam serves as a teaching assistant in the special education and higher education and student affairs programs. Adam received his bachelor's degree in psychology from Hamilton College and his MA in educational policy, planning, and leadership with a concentration in higher education administration from the College of William and Mary. Prior to his doctoral study at UConn, he worked as an administrator in higher education in the areas of admission, athletics, and residential life. He also served as executive director of One in Four, a nonprofit organization that provides rape prevention education and training to colleges, universities, and military bases.

Demar F. Lewis IV is a graduate student in the Ford School of Public Policy at the University of Michigan. He has been involved with the Center for Social Impact in the 2014–2015 Board Fellows Program and serves as assistant editor for the *Michigan Journal of Public Affairs*. Demar is a graduate research assistant at the National Center for Institutional Diversity, where he works on a variety of projects. Prior to attending the University of Michigan, he spent some time working in corporate finance, consulting, and community health advocacy. Demar is a proud McNair Scholar and member of Kappa Alpha Psi Fraternity.

Sheela Linstrum received her MA in higher education from the University of Michigan in August 2014. While a graduate student, Sheela worked at the National Center for Institutional Diversity, where she studied the challenges to diversity efforts across higher education and worked to advance this discourse. Prior to her graduate work in higher education, Sheela earned a BA in accounting from the University of Connecticut and an MA in French language and culture from King's College London, United Kingdom. Sheela's professional background is eclectic, including time spent in public accounting, K–12 education, and financial planning. She currently works as a global information and programs manager for the Darden School of Business at the University of Virginia. In this role, Sheela works to support international academic programs and encourage global engagement throughout the school.

Angela M. Locks is an associate professor in the educational leadership department in the College of Education at California State University, Long Beach. She was a member of the University of Michigan community for 17 years, first as an undergraduate, then a social science peer adviser, and assistant director of the Undergraduate Research Opportunity Program (UROP). She left UROP to complete her PhD in the Center for the Study of Higher and Postsecondary Education at the University of Michigan. She has been at California State University, Long Beach, since 2008 and has developed a strong research agenda that explores institutional diversity praxis and the recruitment, retention, and experiences of students of color in colleges and universities. Angela's current research projects include an examination of college attendance from 7th grade through 12th grade and a longitudinal qualitative exploration of low-income students and the college experiences of diverse college students.

Allison Lombardi is an assistant professor in the Department of Educational Psychology at the University of Connecticut. She is also a research associate in the Center on Postsecondary Education and Disability and a research scientist in the Center for Behavioral Education and Research. She teaches undergraduate and graduate courses in the Special Education Program. Lombardi studies college and career readiness and higher education experiences of underrepresented groups, particularly students with disabilities, aspiring first-generation college students, and student athletes. She focuses on survey design methods and has experience in development, field testing, and initial validation of several measures intended for secondary and postsecondary students and college faculty.

Jeanette Maduena is a PhD candidate at California State University, Long Beach, in the Educational Leadership in Community College Higher Education program. She holds an MS in counseling and currently works as a community college counselor. Jeanette's research interests revolve around the experiences of underrepresented students in higher education. Her current research work focuses on the identity development of Latina and Latino undocumented students enrolled in California community colleges.

Karen Miksch is an associate professor in the Department of Organizational Leadership, Policy and Development at the University of Minnesota. Her overarching research question focuses on the key issues related to higher education access and how education scholars can affect policy decisions. Her current case study project attempts to understand how decisions are made to halt (or retain) race-conscious and diversity initiatives in states such as Michigan that have banned racial preferences in university admissions. Karen serves as legal counsel and a member of the Board of the Association for the Study of Higher Education.

Christina Morton is a PhD student in the Center for the Study of Higher and Postsecondary Education at the University of Michigan. She has prior experience in academic and student affairs, serving as an academic success coach in the College of Science, Technology, Engineering, and Mathematics (STEM) at Johnson C. Smith University and a residence director at North Carolina State University. She currently serves as a research assistant at the National Center for Institutional Diversity (NCID), where she engages in curriculum development for NCID leadership institutes and research regarding strategic diversity planning in postsecondary institutions. Her research interests lie in the persistence of students of color in STEM disciplines.

Noe Ortega is assistant director and senior research associate at the National Center for Institutional Diversity at the University of Michigan. Previously, he served as a research associate for the National Forum on Higher Education for the Public Good, where he led several national studies examining access and inclusion for immigrant and Latino students. His latest publications focus on the restructuring of higher education, with particular emphasis on how fiscal constraints shape decision making at public colleges and universities. Noe spent nearly a decade working in the area of enrollment management and served as a P–16 specialist for the Texas Higher Education

Coordinating Board. His work in education stems beyond the United States, having spent 8 years as director of a language institute in Japan, where he trained teachers in early childhood language acquisition. Noe is a PhD candidate in the Center for the Study of Higher and Postsecondary Education at the University of Michigan.

Penny A. Pasque is the Brian E. & Sandra O'Brien Presidential Professor and program area coordinator of adult and higher education in the Department of Educational Leadership and Policy Studies at the University of Oklahoma. She is also an affiliate faculty with women's and gender studies and the Center for Social Justice. Currently, Penny serves as the associate editor for the *Journal of Higher Education*. Her research addresses in/equities in higher education, dis/connections between higher education and society, and complexities in critical qualitative inquiry. She teaches diversity in higher education and qualitative research and has served as a keynote speaker and facilitator on diversity and social justice issues across the country. Her research has appeared in the *Journal of Higher Education, Qualitative Inquiry, Diversity in Higher Education,* and *Review of Higher Education,* among others. She is author of *American Higher Education Leadership and Policy: Critical Issues and the Public Good* (New York, NY: Palgrave Macmillan, 2010), and coeditor of *Empowering Women in Higher Education and Student Affairs* (Sterling, VA: Stylus, 2011), *Qualitative Inquiry for Equity in Higher Education: Methodological Innovations, Implications, and Interventions* (San Francisco, CA: Jossey-Bass, 2012), *Critical Qualitative Inquiry: Foundations and Futures* (Walnut Creek, CA: Left Coast Press, 2015), and *Qualitative Inquiry in Higher Education Organization and Policy Research* (New York, NY: Routledge, 2016).

Dawn Person is a professor of educational leadership at California State University, Fullerton. She serves as coordinator of the Community College Leadership Specialization for the Educational Doctorate. She also serves as director of the Center for Research on Educational Access and Leadership, where she oversees more than 25 evaluation projects and grants with the support of student researchers and faculty colleagues. Her latest work involves laying the foundation for a national study on African American and Latino men in community college settings. Dawn was part of a team who wrote about the undergraduate experience of students of color attending predominantly White colleges, and she is coeditor of a book on the first-year experience and students of color. She has written numerous articles and book chapters on student retention, student cultures in higher education, and success factors influencing the retention of students of color in higher education.

Kristen A. Renn is a professor of higher, adult, and lifelong education, associate dean of undergraduate studies, and director for Student Success Initiatives at Michigan State University. She graduated from Mount Holyoke College and received her PhD in higher education at Boston College. Prior to coming to Michigan State University she was a dean in the Office of Student Life at Brown University. Kris teaches courses on college students and student development, history of higher education, and diversity and equity in postsecondary education. Her research focuses on the intersection of student success with issues of identity in higher education, including studies of mixed race identities; lesbian, gay, bisexual, transgender, and queer or questioning (LGBTQ) students; and leaders of identity-based student organizations. She recently completed a landmark study of women's colleges and universities worldwide. Kris is also coprincipal investigator of the National Study of LGBTQ Student Success.

Michelle Samura is an assistant professor and coordinator of student and community engagement in the College of Educational Studies and founding codirector of the Collaborate Initiative at Chapman University. Michelle's research focuses on the intersections of space, race, and education. She is particularly interested in how a spatial approach offers a unique lens to more effectively examine varying levels of power and a more accessible language to talk about the related dilemmas with which people wrestle. Drawing on theories and methods from critical geography, visual sociology, education, architecture, and design, Michelle launched the Architecture of Belonging project. The multisite case study examines the role of space in the development of belonging and community in higher education settings. This work has a wide range of theoretical and pragmatic implications, such as offering an unconventional, student-informed approach to examine and address campus climate issues in various educational settings.

Melba Schneider Castro is director for educational partnerships at California State University, Fullerton, where she oversees university, school, and community partnerships focused on enhancing access, college matriculation, and student success. She works in partnership with local schools and school districts to provide educational programs that help students attend college. In addition she oversees five federally funded programs that include Talent Search, Upward Bound, and McNair Scholars, and two GEAR UP programs. Melba has worked with intersegmental educational and community-based partnerships aimed at helping foster student success along the higher education pipeline. Melba's previous experiences include working with foundation and federally funded programs, including Title V Hispanic-serving institutions, FIPSE, Ford Foundation, Kellogg Foundation, and Lumina. She has a BA in political science from the University of California, Berkeley, an MA from Stanford University, and a PhD in education policy organization and leadership from the University of Illinois, Urbana-Champaign.

Lloyd Edward Shelton is a graduate student at the University of Michigan's School of Social Work. He is presently pursuing a master's degree with a focus on community organization. Lloyd's academic interests focus on issues related to identity and society, with a particular focus on masculinity, race, culture, and disability. His interests in these areas stem from his experiences as an African American man living with a disability. Lloyd's long-term goals are to acquire a doctorate in social work and then write, teach, and conduct research. His mission in life is furthering the causes of empowering those with disabilities and those from disenfranchised communities.

Tamara Nichele Stevenson is an assistant professor in the communication and speech programs at Westminster College in Salt Lake City, Utah. Her scholarly interests focus on the intersecting roles of race, gender, and class affecting participation in higher education; issues of access and marginalization relating to faculty and curricular diversity; and the role and function of communication in the teaching and learning process in 2- and 4-year college contexts. Her theoretical approaches to examine these issues include critical race theory, critical communication pedagogy, campus (racial) climate, and racial battle fatigue. Her professional background includes more than 10 years in print and broadcast journalism and corporate communication in automotive, health care, and K–12 and postsecondary educational settings. Her dissertation research examined how African American faculty members contend with racism, discrimination, and an anti-Black sentiment in community colleges.

Marie P. Ting is associate director of the National Center for Institutional Diversity at the University of Michigan. She earned her BA in psychology and MA in higher education from the University of Michigan, and her PhD in higher education policy and leadership from the University of Maryland. Marie has previously worked in academic affairs units at the University of Michigan, where she focused on issues related to college access and the campus climate for diversity. She also worked for several years in the City University of New York system, serving as university director of student affairs and special programs.

Carly Wegner received her MA in higher education from Center for the Study of Higher and Postsecondary Education at the University of Michigan in 2013. She is currently the assistant director of alumni engagement at Albion College. While a graduate student Carly worked at the National Center for Institutional Diversity, developing external funding and communication strategies for the organization. In her free time, she enjoys reading, traveling, tennis, and golf. Carly received her BA from the University of Nebraska in 2012.

Michael R. Woodford is an associate professor with the faculty of social work at Wilfrid Laurier University in Kitchener, Ontario, Canada. His research addresses the social exclusion and inclusion of lesbian, gay, bisexual, transgender, or queer (LGBTQ) people. Specifically, he examines the effects of contemporary heterosexism, including subtle microaggressions. He also studies LGBTQ youth empowerment, heterosexist attitudes, and support for LGBTQ civil rights. Much of Michael's current work explores the relationship between institutional climate, socioecological risk and protective factors, and the health and academic well-being of LGBTQ college students. Part of this research involves exploring the influence of intersecting social identities on these relationships. He is coprincipal investigator of the National Study of LGBTQ Student Success. While a faculty member with the University of Michigan's School of Social Work, Michael was a Faculty Fellow with the National Center for Institutional Diversity in 2008 and 2013.

Eboni M. Zamani-Gallaher is a professor of higher education/community college leadership in the Department of Education Policy, Organization and Leadership at the University of Illinois at Urbana-Champaign (UIUC). She is a faculty affiliate of the Office for Community College Research and Leadership at UIUC. Eboni is past president of the Council for the Study of Community Colleges and director-elect for research and publications for the American Association of Personnel Administrators. Her research has been published in various journals and scholarly texts, including *Equity and Excellence in Education*, *Higher Education Policy*, and *New Directions for Student Affairs*. Eboni has written and edited seven books. She is coeditor of *Working With Students in Community Colleges: Contemporary Strategies for Bridging Theory, Research, and Practice* (Sterling, VA: Stylus, 2014) and *ASHE Reader Series on Community Colleges* (4th ed.; Boston, MA: Pearson, 2014) and is editor of *The Obama Administration and Educational Reform* (Bingley, England; Emerald Group, 2014).

INDEX

abstract liberalism frame, 25–26, 32
  color-blind frames and, 24
  definition of, 25
  structural racism and, 33
academic and nonacademic issues, 103–12, 154
  for African American male athletes, 167–68, 171–75
  on identity development, 68–69
  for LGBTQ, 48, 65–69, 72–74
  Locks on, 122
  precollege on, 118–22
Acorn State, 37
Adams, Henry, 3
Adapting the CIRP to Understand Latin@ Middle School Students' College Going Behaviors, Attitudes, and Algebra Enrollment, 94–95
ADHD. *See* attention deficit/hyperactivity disorder
admissions
  affirmative action in, 32–33
  shaping freshman class for, 7–8
  standardized testing in, 7
affirmative action, 10
  in admissions, 32–33
  African American female faculty and, 192
  anti-, 225
  Jayakumar on, 42
  journalism program, 202–203, 205n2
  legal context on, 48–49
  in Michigan, 205n2
  of 1980s, 207
  to postsecondary access, 49
  race-conscious decisions and, 222
African American faculty, 184
  challenges for, 204–5
  on credibility, 202–205
  as invisible, 186–89, 204
  safe spaces for, 202–205
  at White community colleges, 184, 186, 188–89, 192, 194–96, 203
  White students and, 203–205
African American female faculty, 16
  affirmative action and, 192
  ageism in, 189
  in being silent, 189–92
  campus climate for, 185–93
  colleague interaction with, 189–92
  Colored People's Time for, 189
  in community colleges, 180–96
  competence of, 186–89
  demography, democracy, and diversity of, 181–82
  discrimination patterns against, 195–96
  disrespect of, 186–96
  gender issues for, 187–88
  grievance case and, 180, 195–96
  at HBCU, 182
  identity of, 194–95
  intersectionalities and, 194–95
  as invisible, 186–89, 204
  isolation for, 189, 194
  methodology for, 184–86
  myths about, 186–89
  as overqualified, 188–89
  percentage of, 182–83, 196n3
  in PWI, 186, 188–89
  racial microaggressions towards, 193–97

racism towards, 180–96
RBF in, 184–89, 193–94, 202–205, 205n1
research on, 184–92
safe spaces for, 202–205
sexism and gendered hostilities towards, 180–81, 187–88, 190–93
in STEM, 186–87
stereotypes of, 186–92
structural racism for, 180–81
student expectations of, 187–89
in student success, 181–82
survival of, 188
teaching conditions for, 186–96
tokenism and, 192
at TWI, 182, 192–205
White colleagues compared to, 188–93
in White community college, 184, 186, 188–89, 192, 194–96, 203
White male students and, 180–81, 185, 192
African American male athletes, 15–16, 177–79
academic engagement for, 169–75
on academic self-identity, 167–68, 171–72
athletication of, 166–67
in athletic bubble, 171, 173
of Bowl Championship Series football team, 168
college careers for, 175
faculty towards, 174
false perceptions of, 166–75
grounded theory approach on, 167, 172
identity formation of, 167–69
isolation of, 173
learning environment for, 166–75
on media depictions, 166–74
naturalistic approach on, 168, 172
nonathletes and, 171, 174
prejudices towards, 173

in relationship-building activities, 174
research on, 166–75
social media on, 15–16
sports broadcasters on, 169–71, 174
stereotypes of, 169–73
in university community, 174
African American males
with disabilities, 155–56
in society, 173
African Americans, 196n2. *See also* color-blind ideology; historically Black colleges and universities
Black Student Union for, 119
college access for, 3, 5–6, 118
Colored People's Time for, 189
community colleges for, 184, 186, 188–89, 192, 194–96
disabilities in, 155
discrimination against, 3, 5, 14–16, 23
English vernacular of, 196n5
as exceptional Blacks, 27–28
King, M., 9, 40
me-search principles and, 120–22
plight of, 174–75
positive contributions of, 117–22
precollege outreach programs for, 120–22
president, 223
in racialized space, 202–205
self-segregation of, 30–31
space, White students and, 146
subordination of, 23, 25
in TV and film, 167
women students as, 119
ageism, 191
Agricultural College Act (Morrill Act of 1890), 46
AIDS, 59. *See also* lesbian, gay, bisexual, transgender, and queer
algebra
in eighth grade, 93–103
in tenth grade, 93–94, 103–15

Allen, W. R., 209
Amendments to the Higher Education Act (1965), 90
American Association of Hispanics in Higher Education, 227
The American Community College, 184
American Council on Education, 227
American Indian/Alaskan Native female faculty, 182–83, 196n3
American Psychiatric Association, 59
Americans with Disabilities Act (1990), 148
Anaheim Collaborative for Higher Education, 91
antiracist frames, 37
Antonio, A. L., 224
architectural diversity, 123–39
Arizona, 23
Asian American students
  attitudes towards, 130–32
  at fitness center, 134–37
  intersectionalities of, 134–37
  on physical attributes, 134–37
  in race-space connections, 128–39, 144–47
  racial identity for, 131, 134–37, 144–47
  residence halls and, 129–32, 146
  restrooms and, 129–32
  in space, 124–25, 129, 132–37
  Sticky Rice phenomenon of, 132–33
  in White space, 129–32, 136–37, 146
Astin, A. W., 65–66
athletes. *See also* African American male athletes
  academic achievement in, 166
  African American male, 15–16, 166–75, 177–79
  African American males compared to White males, 166–67
  disability in, 163–65
  White students in, 166–67

attention deficit/hyperactivity disorder (ADHD), 149
axis factor technique, 101–103, 111–12

Banks, J., 155–56
Bayless, Skip, 170–71
biracial identity, 131
Black, 196n2. *See also* African Americans
Black feminism. *See* African American female faculty
Black students. *See* African American male athletes; African Americans; athletes
Black Student Union, 119
Bok, Derek, 3
Bonilla-Silva, E.
  on abstract liberalism frame, 24–26
  on color-blind frames, 14
  on cultural racism frame, 24
  on minimization of racism frame, 24, 26
  on naturalization frame, 24, 26–31
  on Social Attitudes for College Students Survey, 37–38
  theory of, 22–23
Bowen, Howard, 3
Bowl Championship Series football team, 165
Bowman, Philip, 229n1
Bronfenbrenner, U., 69
Brothers of the Academy: Up and Coming Black Scholars Earning Our Way in Higher Education, 178
Brown, R., 209
Brown v. Board of Education, 211
Burcaw, S., 155

California State University (Fullerton), 91–92
campus climate
  for African American female faculty, 185–93
  for disabilities, 149–50

diversity and, 224–25
identity development and, 62–64, 72–74
implications for NCID, 224–25
campus climate research. *See also* Input-Environment-Output; lesbian, gay, bisexual, transgender, and queer
  on African American female faculty, 185
  on experiential climate, 61–62
  identity development and, 62–64, 72–74
  on LGBTQ, 60–62, 73–74
  on non-LGBTQ, 60–61
Career Based Outreach Program, 41
Carter, Courtney
  on graduate advice, 221
  on mandate rhetoric at historically Black colleges and universities, 207–14, 218–22
Carter, Jarrett, 213
caste-like racial inequalities, 41
Castillo, L., 90
Center for Research on Educational Access and Leadership (C-REAL), 88
  GEAR UP collaboration with, 92–93
  work of, 91–93
Chang, M. J., 224
Chesler, M., 37
CIRP. *See* Cooperative Institutional Research Program
cisgender identities, 58, 63
citizenship, 5–6
civil rights
  color-blind racism during, 22–23
  integration during, 8–9
  on social and economic rights, 8–9
civil war, 3
Clementi, Tyler, 85
colleague interaction, 189–92
collectivity
  communities about, 50–51

conscious compared to unconscious, 50–51
college access, 15
  for African American students, 3, 5–6, 118
  for low-income students, 14, 41, 44–51, 54–56, 89–90, 94
  programs for, 121
college attendance, 15
College Board, 166
college careers, 175
College Entrance and Examination Board
  Diversity by Design and, 9
  regarding nontraditional students, 9
college environment, 148, 153–54, 163–65
  for African American male athletes, 173
  for LGBTQ, 69–71
college-going culture, 89–90, 93
college-going process, 118–22
college space. *See* space
College Student Journal (CSJ), 152
Collins, P. H., 194–95
color-blind era, 123
color-blind frames
  abstract liberalism, 24
  African Americans and, 26
  antiracist frames and, 37
  color-blind ideology regarding, 14, 22–23, 36–37
  cultural deficiency, 27–29
  cultural racism, 24
  disconnected power-analysis, 14, 33–37
  minimization of racism, 24
  naturalization frame and, 24
  at TWI, 26
  among White students at HBCU, 22, 26–31
color-blind ideology
  African Americans and, 36–37
  Bonilla-Silva theory of, 22–23

color-blind frames within, 14, 22–23, 36–37
disconnected power-analysis frame and, 14, 33–37
naturalization frame and, 29–31
racial inequality and, 22–25
color blindness, 217–19
color-blind racial primes, 36–37
color-blind racism, 22–23
Colored People's Time (CP Time), 189
coming out, 63–64
community colleges, 193n2. *See also* predominantly White institutions
   African-American female faculty in, 16, 180–96, 203
   for African Americans, 184, 186, 188–89, 192, 194–96
   contributions of, 182, 184
   definition of, 182
   as historically White, 186, 188–89, 192, 194–96
   manifestation of, 5
   research about, 184, 203–205
competence, 186–89
Consortium of Higher Education LGBT Resource Professionals, 64–65
constant comparative approach, 168
Constitution, U. S.
   on census, 226
   on unequal funding, 49–50
Cooperative Institutional Research Program (CIRP) of Higher Education Research Institute, 93–95, 113
Council for Opportunity in Education (TRIO), 46, 91, 121
CP Time. *See* Colored People's Time
C-REAL. *See* Center for Research on Educational Access and Leadership
Cronbach's alphas, 103, 111
cross-disciplinary strategies, 81, 85–86
CSJ. *See College Student Journal*
cultural deficiency frame, 27–29

cultural racism frame, 24

demographics
   of African American female faculty, 181–82
   diversity and, 223–29
   racial, 228
   trends in HBCU, 181–82, 209–10
demography, democracy, and diversity, xiii, xvi–xviii, 46
   of African American female faculty, 181–82
   meritocracy and, 10, 44–45
   shift of, 21
   transformation of, 223–29
   of White males and females, 181–82
Department of Education, U. S., 93
Department of Education's Office of Postsecondary Education , U. S., 150
desegregation, 211–12
Dey, E.
   on faculty of color, 184
   on social ecological approach, 127
The Diagnostic and Statistical Manual of Mental Disorders, Fifth Edition, 193
disabilities
   academic and social barriers with, 154
   accommodations for, 149
   ADHD as, 149
   in African Americans, 155
   in athletes, 163–65
   campus climate for, 149–50
   on diagnosed, 164
   discrimination against, 148, 155
   in diversity, 148, 153
   environment perceptions and, 148, 153–54, 163–65
   faculty and staff perceptions on, 159–57
   faculty and staff training in, 156–59
   faculty positions and, 152, 158

faculty teaching practices in, 157–59
in first generation, 155–56
hidden, 166
identity development and, 154–56, 158–59
inclusive teaching practices for, 157–58
as learning disability, 149
learning styles for, 165
percentage with, 149–50
psychological/mental health, 149, 199
published articles on, 151–53
research on, 150–55, 163–65
top journals on, 151–53
on transitions, 165
visible compared to invisible, 149–50
Disability and Society (DS), 152
disability rights movement, 148
disciplinary norms, 81, 85–86
disconnected power-analysis frame
color-blind ideology and, 14, 21–37
structural racism, power, privilege and, 34–36
discrimination
against African American female faculty, 195–96
against African Americans, 3, 5, 14–16, 23
towards AIDS, 59
with disabilities, 148, 155
HBCU on, 208, 218
against Latin@ students, 49–50
against LGBTQ, 58–59
against low-income students, 49–50
disrespect, 186–96
distributive era, 51
definition of, 45
distributive justice in, 47, 50
inclusion during, 48
low-income students in, 45–48, 50–51
distributive justice, 46–47, 50–51
Diverse Democracy Surveys, 116

diversity. *See also* African American male athletes; historically Black colleges and universities; National Diversity Scholars Network; racial diversity
African American female faculty and, 181–82
African American president and, 223
agenda for, 12, 224
architecture of, 123–39
campus climate and, 224–25
challenges with, 2
citizenship lacking in, 5–6
civil rights and, 8–9
color blindness and, 220–22
concept of, 9–10
contemporary meanings of, 223–29
definition of, 1–2
demography, democracy, discourse and, xiii, xvi–xviii, 21, 181–82, 223–29
disability and, 148, 153
in education and society, 17
on enrollment, 210–11
history of, 1
humanity compared to, 213
inclusion and, 9–10, 213
initiatives for, 207–14
institutional planning for, 226
Ivy League institutions for, 6
King, M. on, 9
meanings of, 11–12
as natural state, 226
nontraditional study of, 123–39, 144–47
organizational missions and, 222
past and present understandings of, 223–29
in PWI, 208, 212–13, 218
racial inequalities and, 41, 223
on racial justice compared to institutional advantage, 207–8
research in, xii–xvii, 12–16, 223–29

in scholarship and educational practice, 224
social, cultural, political contexts in, 1
as state interest, 9–10
structural, 213–14
as term of art, 224
as text and context, 16–19
transdisciplinary understanding of, 227
transformation through, 16, 223–29
of White males and females, 181–82
diversity, demography, democracy, discourse, 12–16
diversity advocates, 210–14
diversity agenda, 224
Diversity by Design. *See* College Entrance and Examination Board; Educational Testing Service
diversity mandate, 210–14
diversity praxis, 118
diversity research, xvi–xvii
Diversity Research and Policy Program, xiii
diversity rhetoric, 212
diversity scholarship, 12, 223–29
of demography, democracy, diversity, xvi, xviii
Gupton on, 54–56
for HBCU, 209–10
Multi-level Engagement Bridging Diversity Scholarship, xvi–xvii
Diversity Scholars Network. *See* National Diversity Scholars Network
DS. *See Disability and Society*
DuBois, W. E. B., 3
Dunn, D. S., 155
Duster, T., 127–28

economic liberalism, 25
Educational Testing Service
Diversity by Design and, 9
regarding nontraditional students, 9
elite universities, 7–8, 47–48, 164, 173, 210, 218
Emancipation Proclamation, 221
empirical diversity scholarships, 209–10
English vernacular, 196n5
enrollment trends, 210–11
environments. *See* space
equality principle, 45
equal protection, 49–51
Equal Protection Clause, 49–51
equity, 41, 223, 228
advancement of social, 84–85
distributive justice and, 51
justice as fairness and, 45
for low-income students, 14–15, 49–50
in regressive era, 51
ethnographic study, 127
evaluation models, 89
exceptional Blacks, 27–28
exclusion
historical patterns of, 11
of Jewish students, 7–8
of LGBTQ, 70–71
during regressive era, 48, 50
of undocumented students, 6
Exodus, Book of, 1
experiential climate, 61–62
exploratory factor analyses
axis factor technique in, 101–103, 111–12
mean substitution in, 101–103

faculty. *See also* African American female faculty
towards African American male athletes, 174
on disability teaching practices, 157–59
female, 196n3
positions on disability, 152, 158
student success and diversity of, 181–82
faculty and staff

on disabilities perceptions, 156–58
in disabilities training, 156–59
familial structures, 95, 100, 111
first generation, 155–56
Fisher v. University of Texas, 49
Fisk University, 212
fitness center
    Asian American students and, 136–37
    in space, 134–37
Flores, Elena, 41
Forman, T. A., 37
foundation-sponsored scholarships, 209
Frankfurter, Felix, 10
freshman class, 7–8
fundamental rights, 49–50

Gaining Early Awareness and Readiness for Undergraduate Programs (GEAR UP), 118
    cohort description of, 93–94
    C-REAL collaboration with, 92–93
    descriptive survey by, 93–94
    about evaluation models, 92–93
    evaluation partners with, 91–92
    for Latin@ students, 15, 88–89
    for low-income students, 90–91, 121
    mission of, 90–91
Gallagher, K. S., 89, 94
GEAR UP. *See* Gaining Early Awareness and Readiness for Undergraduate Programs
gender, 222. *See also* cisgender identities; lesbian, gay, bisexual, transgender, and queer
    African American female faculty on, 180–81, 187–88, 190–93
    campus climate research on, 61–62
    on gender identity, 58, 135–37
    on genderism, 58, 73
    low income and racial, 50–51
    sex compared to, 74n1
    sexuality and, 58

gender issues. *See also* Asian American students; lesbian, gay, bisexual, transgender, and queer
    for African American female faculty, 187–88
Gerdes, H., 155–56
Gibney, Shannon, 180, 195–96
Gibson, J., 155
Girls Round Up Boys (GRUB), 70
graduate advice
    Carter, C. on, 221
    Lombardi on, 164
Gratz v. Bollinger, 10–11, 49
Great Society agenda, 46
grounded theory approach, 167, 172
GRUB. *See* Girls Round Up Boys
Grutter v. Bollinger, 10, 42, 49
Gupton, Jarrett T.
    on college access for low-income students, 54–56
    on diversity scholarships, 54–56
    Pathways to College for Homeless Adolescents by, 55
    on postsecondary access for homeless youths, 54–56
    at University of Michigan, 55
    on value in uncertainty, 54–56
Gurin, Patricia, 42, 229n1

Harrison, K., 166–67
Harvard University, 2, 6–7, 19n3
HBCU. *See* historically Black colleges and universities
HEA. *See* Higher Education Act
health, 65–67, 71–74, 193
hegemonic structures, 40–41
HEOA, 150
heterosexism, 58
    towards LGBTQ, 60, 73–74
    racial, 207–14
higher education, 46, 64–65, 90, 91, 93–95, 113, 1450, 152, 153, 208
    accommodation through separation for, 4

historical roots of, 2–4
land grant institutions for, 5
missions of, 3–4
new student populations of, 4
political/geographic composition and, 5
women in, 3
Higher Education Act (HEA), 1965, 46, 150, 208
Higher Education for American Democracy, 46
high school, 89–90
   for African Americans, 203
   disability transition from, 149
   for Latin@ students, 103–16
   tenth grade algebra, 93–94, 103–15
historically Black colleges and universities (HBCU), 14, 16, 196n4
   African American female faculty at, 182
   on African American students' welfare, 213–14
   as antiracist organization spaces, 212–14
   in being competitive, 212
   on compliance with normative values, 212
   in defining diversity, 220–21
   on demographic trends, 181–82, 209–10
   on diversity, 214n1
   diversity advocates for, 210–14
   diversity challenge of, 209–10
   diversity mandate of, 210–14
   empirical diversity scholarships and, 209–10
   on enrollment trends, 210–11
   foundation-sponsored scholarships and, 209
   on inclusion, 208, 219
   increase enrollment at, 207–14
   institutional legitimacy and, 210–14
   institutional viability and, 210–11
   mandate rhetoric of, 207–14, 218–21
   mission of, 208, 213–14
   National Leadership Institute on Multiculturalism at, 212–13
   in organizational spaces, 218–22
   perceptions of, 218
   on racial discrimination, 208, 218
   racial diversity of, 21, 207–14
   on racial uplift, 208
   relevance of, 212–14
   as role model, 213
   on social responsibility, 208
   in sociology, 220–21
   structural diversity of, 213–14
   traditional agendas of, 213–14
   White students at, 21–22, 26–31, 208–14
historically White colleges. *See* community colleges; predominantly White institutions
Holmes, Oliver Wendell, 11
homeless youths. *See also Pathways to College for Homeless Adolescents*
   challenges of, 55–56
   diverse characteristics of, 56
   postsecondary access for, 54–56
homosexuality, 59
Hossler, D., 89, 94
Hurtado, S., 127

IDEIA. *See* Individuals With Disabilities Education Improvement Act
identity. *See also* African American male athletes; lesbian, gay, bisexual, transgender, and queer; racial identity
   of African American female faculty, 194–95
   for Asian American students, 131, 134–37, 144–47
   gender and, 58

organizational Black space and, 218–19
on physical attributes, 134–37
research on disability, 154–59
safe spaces and, 204
social class and, 50–51
identity development
academic and nonacademic inputs on, 68–69
for African American student athletes, 166–75
campus climate and, 62–64, 72–74
disability and, 154–59
identity pride and identity integration within, 62–64, 68–69
research on disability, 154–59
identity formation, 167–68
I-E-O. *See* Input-Environment-Output
inclusion, 223, 228
of disabled, 149
during distributive era, 48
of diversity, 9–10, 213
HBCU on, 208, 219
for LGBTQ, 57–73
research teaching practices on, 157–58
space for, 138–39
inclusive teaching practices, 157–58
Individuals With Disabilities Education Improvement Act (IDEIA), 149
inequality
Black subordination and, 23, 25
common sense regarding, 24
in integrated spaces, 219
intersectionalities and, 134–37
racial, 22–25, 41, 123, 224
of racial and gender compared to low-income, 50–51
Input-Environment-Output (I-E-O), 65–67, 67–73. *See also* lesbian, gay, bisexual, transgender, and queer
institutional advantage, 207–8
institutional legitimacy

HBCU and, 210–14
legal compliance with desegregation and, 211–12
institutional viability
HBCU and, 210–11
racial diversity and, 210–11
instructional frameworks, 157–58
integration, 8–9
intersectionalities
African American female faculty and, 194–95
of Asian American students, 134–37
identities and, 220–22
research on, 164–65
space and, 125, 134–37
invisible communities
African American female faculty in, 186–89, 204
LGBTQ in, 81–86
isolation
for African American female faculty, 189, 194
for African American male athletes, 173
naturalization frame and White, 29–31
Ivy League institutions
for diversity, 6
Jewish students and, 6–7

Jackson, Andrew, 46
Jackson, Jerlando F. L., 177–79
Jayakumar, Uma M.
on affirmative action, 42
on benefits of diversity, 42–43
on choice, access, and racial equity, 41
mentors of, 42
on social agency and power of resistance, 40–43
on societal hegemonic structures, 40–41
at University of Michigan, 40–43

JCSD. *See Journal of College Student Development*
Jefferson, Thomas, 45–46
Jewell, J. O., 209
Jewish students
　exclusion of, 7–8
　at Ivy League institutions, 6–7
　letter about, 6–7
　after World War I, 8
JLD. *See Journal of Learning Disabilities*
Johnson, Andrew, 46
Johnson, B. J., 181
Johnson, Charles S., 3
Johnson, Lyndon B., 46
Journalism Institute for Media Diversity, 205n2
journalism program, on affirmative action, 202–203, 205n2
Journal of College Student Development (JCSD), 152
Journal of Diversity in Higher Education, 153
Journal of Learning Disabilities (JLD), 151–52
Journal of Postsecondary Education and Disability (JPED), 151–53
Journal of Vocational Rehabilitation (JVR), 152
JPED. *See Journal of Postsecondary Education and Disability*
justice as fairness concept, 45
JVR. *See Journal of Vocational Rehabilitation*

Karabel, J., 6
Kids to College, 91
King, Martin Luther, Jr., 9, 40
Knowles, C.
　on concept of space, 126
　on race-space connections, 128

Land Grant College Act, 46
Latin@ students, 19n1, 113n1, 227
　CIRP and, 94–95

college-going culture for, 89–90, 93
cross-sectional studies on, 94–95, 103–12
discrimination against, 49–50
eighth grade algebra for, 93–103
evaluation partners for, 91–92
familial structures of, 95, 100, 111
GEAR UP for, 15, 88–94
high school analyses on, 111–14
high school aspirations for, 112–15
high school descriptive survey on, 103–12
literature review of, 89–90
middle school analyses of, 100–103
middle school descriptive survey on, 89–90, 93–100
Pew Hispanic Center survey on, 90
SES structures of, 88, 95, 98, 111
social and cultural capital influences on, 89–90
student/academic engagement for, 103–12
tenth grade algebra for, 93–94, 103–15
Lawrence, S. M., 167
LD. *See* learning disability
LDRP. *See Learning Disabilities Research and Practice Articles on Higher Education and Disability*
Learning Disabilities Research and Practice Articles on Higher Education and Disability (LDRP), 152
learning disability
　African American female faculty and, 187
　disabilities as, 149
learning environment, 166–75
learning styles, 165
Lee, "Roony," 3
lesbian, gay, bisexual, transgender, and queer (LGBTQ), 14
　academic and nonacademic issues for, 48, 65–69, 72–74

campus climate research on, 60–62, 73–74
on coming out, 63–64
cross-disciplinary strategies for, 81, 85–86
on developing resiliency, 62–64, 69
discrimination against, 58–59
environment for, 69–71
federal law regarding, 59
hidden identities of, 82
identity and expression of, 68–69, 71–73
identity development for, 62–64
inclusion or exclusion for, 70–71
input influences and, 67–69
as invisible communities, 81–86
legitimacy of, 84
marginalization of, 83
mental health of, 65–67, 71–74, 193
national, state and local socio-cultural-historical context for, 67–73
National Study of LGBTQ Student Success, 63, 68, 74n3
nonacademic experiences of, 68
phobia towards, 60
policies and programs for, 64–65, 67
privilege compared to oppression, 84
protective factors for, 62–64
social/community for, 71–74
support for, 63–64
systems of power effecting, 58–59
trans/bi/homophobia of, 60
violence towards, 59
Lewin, Kurt, xvi
Lewis, A. E., 37
LGBTQ. *See* lesbian, gay, bisexual, transgender, and queer
liberty principle, 45
Lipsitz, G., 128
Liu, Goodwin, 49
Locks, Angela M., 92
on academic and nonacademic issues, 122

in Black Student Union, 119
me-search principles of, 120–22
on methods for observation, 121–22
on positive contributors, 118–22
Lombardi, Allison
on advice for aspiring faculty, 164
on disability, 155–56, 163–65
Lopez-Arenas, A., 90
Lowell, A. Lawrence, 6–7
low-income students. *See also* Gupton, Jarrett T.
college access for, 14, 41, 44–51, 54–56, 89–90, 94
discrimination against, 49–50
in distributive era, 45–48, 50–51
educational choices for, 54–56
GEAR UP for, 90–91, 121
inequality and, 50–51
Obama, B. and M. on, 44
in regressive era, 45, 47–48, 50–51
research on, 46, 54–56
social and legal equity for, 14–15, 49–50
TRIO for, 118
Lumina foundation, 91

majority minority, 228
mandate rhetoric, 207–14, 218–22
Martin, B., 167
Massey, D., 126
Matsumoto, A., 63–64
McDonough, P., 89–90
McGregor, J., 127
MCTC. *See* Minneapolis Community and Technical College
mean substitution, 101–103
media, 205n2
African American male athletes recommendations for, 173–74
depictions of African American male athletes, 169–73
sports broadcasters in, 169–71
mental health

of LGBTQ, 65–67, 71–74, 193
psychological disabilities and, 149, 193
racism on, 193
merit-based scholarships, 47–48
meritocracy
about academic, 48
redefined as, 51
tensions between democracy and, 10, 44–45
test scores and, 49–50
me-search principles, 120–22
Mexican American/Chicano students, 93, 95–112
Meyer, I. H., 67
Michigan
affirmative action in, 205n2
Proposal 2 of, 222
Michigan Society of Scholars Program, xiv
middle school, 89–90, 93–103
Milem, J. F., 224
Minneapolis Community and Technical College (MCTC), 180, 195–96
minority
organizational missions for, 222
sexual, 58–59, 74n2
stress theory of, 67, 69, 83
Moje, Elizabeth Birr, 40
Morgan, D. C., 50
Morrill Act (1862), 46
Morrill Act (1890), 46
Moses, Bob, 40
Multi-level Engagement Bridging Diversity Scholarship, xvi–xvii
multiple regression model, 93–94, 103, 115
Murray, C., 155–56
myths, 186–89

National Center for Institutional Diversity (NCID), xiii–xviii, 2, 229n1
agenda setting of, xiii
on campus climate implications, 224–25
on current views, 224–27
demography, democracy, diversity of, xiii
partnerships with, xiii
research at, 13–16, 224–26
National Collegiate Athletic Association Division I, 163, 166
National Diversity Scholars Network, xiii–xviii, 227, 229n1
exemplary diversity scholars in, xiv, xvi–xvii
partnerships with, xiii
Postdoctoral Fellowship Program of, xiv
National Leadership Institute on Multiculturalism, 212–13
National Study of LGBTQ Student Success, 63, 68, 74n3
Native Hawaiian/Pacific Islander female faculty, 182–83, 196n3
naturalistic approach
on African American male athletes, 168, 172
to research, 168
naturalization frame, 26
color-blind frames and, 24
color-blind ideology and, 29–31
definition of, 24
racial isolation of Whites and, 29–31
segregation and, 29–31
TWI and, 29–31
NCID. *See* National Center for Institutional Diversity
NDSS. *See New Directions for Student Services*
need-based grants, 47–48
Neely, B., 128
Nelms, Charles, 210–11
Nespor, J., 127
New Directions for Student Services (NDSS), 152

New York Police Department (NYPD), 23
Nidiffer, J., 47–48
No Child Left Behind, 93
nonathletes, 171, 174
nonresident alien female faculty, 182–86, 196n3
nontraditional students
  College Entrance and Examination Board regarding, 9
  Educational Testing Service, 9
NYPD. *See* New York Police Department

Obama, Barack, 44, 223
Obama, Barack and Michelle, 44
O'Connor, Sandra Day, 11
Office of Postsecondary Education of the Demonstration Projects, 152, 158–59
Olkin, R., 155
opportunity hire, 192
oppression, 84
overqualified, 188–89
Overton-Atkins, Betty, 9

Parent Institute for Quality Education, 91
partnerships, xvi
  with National Diversity Scholars Network, xiii
  of NCID, xiii
  Woodford, on, 85–86
Pascarella, E. T., 72
Pathways to College for Homeless Adolescents, 55
Paul Quinn College, 212
Pell grants, 46
perceptions, 103–12
  of African American male athletes, 166–75
  on disabilities, 148, 153–54, 156–57, 163–65
  of HBCU, 218

Perna, L. W., 90
Person, Dawn, 92
person-process-context-time model, 69
Pew Hispanic Center, 90
physical attributes
  Asian American students on, 134–37
  in space, 126, 132–37
Pichon, H., 184
Policy Program National Center for Institutional Diversity, xvi–xvii
policy-relevant engagement, xvi–xvii
political/geographic composition, 5
political liberalism, 25
Postdoctoral Fellowship Program, xiii–xiv
postsecondary access, 150–53
  affirmative action and, 49
  for homeless youths, 54–56
poverty argument, 28
Powell, Lewis J., 10–11, 19n3, 48–49, 224
Prado, G., 63–64
precollege
  academic/nonacademic issues for, 118–22
  outreach programs for African Americans, 120–22
predominantly White institutions (PWI), 14, 16, 196n4. *See also* Asian American students; traditionally White institutions
  African American female faculty in, 182, 186, 188–89
  diversity in, 208, 212–14, 218
  diversity rhetoric in, 212
  as historically White, 186, 188–89, 192, 194–96
prejudices. *See* African American faculty; African American male athletes; African Americans; Asian American students; lesbian, gay, bisexual, transgender, and queer
Princeton, 6–7
privilege, 34–35

oppression compared to, 84
structural racism and, 34–36
of White students, 30–32, 36
Proposal 2
of Michigan, 222
Supreme Court, U. S. on, 222
psychological climate, 61–62
Puerto Rican students, 93, 95–112
PWI. *See* predominantly White institutions

qualitative multiple case study approach, 185
qualitative research, 168
quantitative empirical research, 168
queer, 58

race, 15, 225. *See also* African Americans; Asian American students; Latin@ students
affirmative action and, 222
cache, 35–36
color blindness and, 220–22
conscious policies on, 32–33
conscious practices for diversity, 207
in organizational spaces, 218–22
reconstruction of, 220–22
relations and racial structures for students, 193
in space, 124–26, 128–38, 202–203
racial battle fatigue (RBF)
in African American female faculty, 184–86, 193–94, 202–205, 205n1
racialized role strain through, 186
surviving, 202–205
symptoms of, 185
racial demography, 228
racial discrimination. *See also* discrimination
against African American female faculty, 195–96
against African Americans, 3, 5, 14–16, 23
HBCU on, 208, 218

racial disparities, 31
by advancing people of color, 32–33
campus climate research on, 60–62
cultural deficiency frame and, 28
White students and, 27–28
racial diversity, 41
competitiveness and, 212
enrollment challenges and, 207–14
at historically Black colleges and universities, 207–14
institutional legitimacy and, 210–13
institutional viability and, 210–11
interracial interactions compared to, 133–34
promote compared to deter from, 133–34
racially specific mission and, 213–14
in racial spaces, 127–28
rhetoric compared to reality on, 123–24
spatial perspective of, 124
Sticky Rice and, 132–33
racial harmony, 213
racial heterosexism, 208–14
racial identity
for Asian American students, 131, 134–37, 143–47
othering, otherness and, 131, 146–47
physical attributes and, 134–37
Sticky Rice and, 134
racial ideology, 220–22
racial inequality
caste-like, 41
color-blind ideology and, 22–25
within the law, 224
racialization, 123–24, 128, 131, 139n1
Asian American students and, 144–47
in viewing others, 144–47
racial justice, 207–8
racial microaggressions, 193–94, 202
racial politics, 221
racial preferences, 32–33

racial profiling, 23
racial space, 129, 138
　African Americans in, 202–203
　microagressions and, 202–203
　racial diversity and, 127–28
　safe spaces and, 202–205
racial stereotypes, 146
racial tensions, 225
racial theory, new, 123–24
racism. *See also* African Americans; color-blind ideology; cultural racism; historically Black colleges and universities; inequality; structural racism
　towards African American female faculty, 180–96
　institutional, 180–96
　mental health and, 193
　White privilege and, 31–32
racism frame, minimization of, 24, 26–28, 31–32
Rada, J., 167
Rankin, E., 63–64
Rawls, John, 45
RBF. *See* racial battle fatigue
Reason, R. D., 72
reciprocal translation approach, xvi–xvii
Reddick, R. J., 209
Regents of the University of California v. Bakke, 10–11, 48–49, 224
regressive era
　definition of, 45
　equity in, 51
　exclusion during, 48, 50
　low-income students in, 45, 47–48, 50–51
　state funding decline during, 47–48
Rehabilitation Act (1973), 148
Renn, K. A., 63–64
Renn, Kristen, 86
residence halls, 129–32, 146
resistance, 40–43
restrooms, 129–32

Ronald E. McNair Postbaccalaureate Achievement Program, 220–22
Ronald McNair Scholars Program, 91

safe spaces
　for African American faculty, 202–205
　definition of, 204
　identity in, 204
Saldivar, I. M., 90
Samura, Michelle, 128, 144–47
San Antonio School District v. Rodriguez, 49–51
Santa Ana Adelante, 91
Santa Ana Partnership (P-20 Collaborative), 91
scholarship, 206. *See also* diversity scholarship
science, technology, engineering, mathematics (STEM), 186–87
segregation, 29–31
self-segregation
　for African American students, 30–31
　for White students, 30–31
SES. *See* socioeconomic status
sexism, 180–81, 190–93
sexual minorities, 58–59, 74n1, 74n2. *See also* lesbian, gay, bisexual, transgender, and queer
sexual orientation, 74n1, 225. *See also* lesbian, gay, bisexual, transgender, and queer
　examples of, 58
　on gender expression and identity, 58
The Shape of the River (Bowen and Bok), 3
Simpson, Jackie, 86
Sims, S. J., 209
slavery, 2
Smith, Steven A., 170–71
social and economic rights, 8–9
Social Attitudes of College Students Survey, 37–38

social change, 85
social class
  as social identity, 50–51
  as unconscious collectivity, 50–51
social/community, 71–74
social contract theory, 44
  definition of, 45
  shift regarding, 50
social ecological approach, 127
socially marginalized backgrounds, 81–82
social media, 15–16
social responsibility, 208
social work, 82–85, 86n1
society, 170
socioeconomic status (SES), 88, 95, 100, 111, 224–25
sociology, 220–21
space
  for African American female faculty, 202–205
  Asian American students in, 124–25, 128–39, 144–47
  bodies in, 134–37
  built environments in, 125, 128–39
  concept of, 125
  conflicts over, 131
  definition of, 126
  as dynamic, 132
  in education, 127–28
  fitness center in, 134–37
  geographical, 145
  HBCU and organizational, 218–22
  HBCU as antiracist organizational, 212–14
  identity and organizational Black, 218–19
  for inclusion, 138–39
  inequality in integrated, 219
  intersectionalities in, 125, 134–37
  past and present connections with, 128
  physical attributes in, 134–37
  physical compared to social, 126, 132–34
  race in, 124–25, 128–38, 202–203
  restroom in, 129–32
  safe, 202–203
  as social construct, 125, 145
  Sticky Rice phenomenon and, 132–34
spatial approach, 124–25
special education intersectionality, 164–65
Special Services for Disadvantaged Students, 46
sports broadcasters, 169–72, 174
standardized testing, 7
state funding, 47–48
STEM. *See* science, technology, engineering, mathematics
stereotypes
  of African American female faculty, 186–92
  of African American male athletes, 169–70
  on combating, 169–73
  media-propagated, 166–75
  among professors, 170
  research on, 166–75
Stevenson, Tamara Nichele, 205n1
  on community colleges, 203
  on diversity, 204–5
  on RBF and safe spaces, 202–205
Sticky Rice. *See also* Asian American students
  racial diversity and, 132–34
  as racial phenomenon, 134
  as spatial phenomenon, 133
Stone, J., 167
Stonewall rebellion, 59
stress theory, 67, 69, 83
structural diversity, 213–14
structural racism
  abstract liberalism frame and, 33
  for African American female faculty, 180–81

disconnected power-analysis frame and, 34–36
student/academic engagement
  of African American male athletes, 169–73
  for Latin@ students, 104–12
student expectations, 187–89
student learning, 15
student perceptions, 218
  academic self-perception and, 103–12
  African American male athletes and, 166–75
  of college environment, 148, 153–54, 163–65
students, 15, 37–38, 46, 150. *See also* African American male athletes; African Americans; Asian American students; disabilities; Latin@ students; lesbian, gay, bisexual, transgender, and queer; low-income students; White students
  influence on educational choices for, 41, 54–56, 89–90, 94
  Jewish, 6–8
  origins of, 7
  race relations and racial structures for, 15
  undocumented, 6
student services, 151–53
student success
  African American female faculty on, 181–82
  African American male athletes and, 174–75
  for LGBTQ, 63, 65, 67–68, 74n3
subordination, 23, 25
Supreme Court, U. S.
  on fundamental rights, 49–50
  on Proposal 2, 222
  on *Regents of the University of California v. Bakke*, 10–11, 48–49, 224

survival, 185
survivor label, 82

Talent Search, 91
teaching conditions, 186–96
Terenzini, P. T., 72
test scores, 49–50
theoretical framework, 55, 85, 94
  racial space and, 127–28
  research on, 138
theory-based approach, 89
Thompson, C., 184
Tierney, W. G., 46, 54–56
Tinto, V., 67, 70–71
Title IX, 48, 74
tokenism, 192
Towne v. Eisner, 11
traditionally White institutions (TWI), 21–22
  African American female faculty at, 182, 202–205
  color-blind primes and frames at, 26
  naturalization frame and, 29–31
trans/bi/homophobia, 60
transformation, of demography, democracy, diversity, 223–29
transgender. *See also* lesbian, gay, bisexual, transgender, and queer
  campus climate research on, 61–62
  meaning of, 58
  trans/bi/homophobia of, 60
TRIO. *See* Council for Opportunity in Education
Truman, Harry S., 46
Turner, C. S., 153
TV and film, 167
TWI. *See* traditionally White institutions

Understanding Latin@ High School Students' School Engagement, Academic Self-Perception, and Anticipated High School

Extracurricular Engagement and their Degree Aspirations, 103–12
undocumented students, 6
Union Institute, Cincinnati, 8
United States v. Fordice, 211
university community, 171
University of Connecticut, Department of Educational Psychology, 165
University of Michigan, 40–43, 55
   Gratz v. Bollinger case at, 10–11, 49
   LGBTQ research at, 83–84
   Postdoctoral Fellows at, xiv–xv
   reciprocal-translation approach and, xvi–xvii
   scholars at, 223–24
university rankings, 48
Upward Bound, 41, 91

victim label, 82
violence, 59
visual and spatial methods, 134–38, 147

West University, 129, 131–32
White community colleges, 184, 186, 188–89, 192, 194–95, 203
White faculty
   African American female faculty and male, 188–92
   African American female faculty compared to, 188–89, 191, 193
White feminism, 194–95
White plurality, 228
White privilege, 31–32
White space, 129–32, 136–37, 146

White students. *See also* historically Black colleges and universities; predominantly White institutions; traditionally White institutions
   African American faculty and, 203–205
   towards African American female faculty, 180–781, 185, 192
   in African American space, 146
   in athletic world, 166–67
   with color-blind frames, 22, 26–31
   demography, democracy, and diversity of, 181–82
   privilege of, 30–32, 36
   racial disparities and, 27–28
   self-segregation of, 30–31
William and Mary College, 2
Willie, C. V., 208
Winant, H., 123–24
women, 181–83, 196n1, 196n3. *See also* African American female faculty; African Americans; Asian American students; lesbian, gay, bisexual, transgender, and queer
   in higher education, 3
   after right to vote, 5
   in STEM, 186–87
Woodford, Michael R., 81, 83–85
   on partnerships, 85–86
   on social workers, 82
Wulfemeyer, K., 167

Yale University, 6–7
YFCY. *See* Your First College Year
Young, I. M., 12
Your First College Year (YFCY), 93

Also available from Stylus

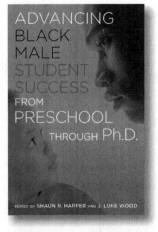

Advancing Black Male Student Success from Prschool through PhD

Edited by Shaun R. Harper and J. Luke Wood

"Harper and Wood have provided a timely and definitive text that offers rich conceptual, empirical, and practical analysis on Black males and education. This book explains the challenges Black boys and men encounter in pursuit of education, and offers meaningful ways to disrupt these troubling trends. It is mandatory reading for scholars, practitioners, and policymakers."—*Tyrone C. Howard*, *Professor and Director, UCLA Black Male Institute*

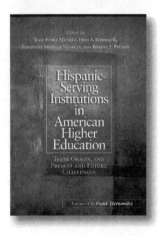

Hispanic-Serving Institutions in American Higher Education

Edited by Jesse Perez Mendez, Fred A. Bonner II, Josephine Méndez-Negrete, and Robert T. Palmer
Foreword by Frank Hernandez

"Readers interested in staying informed about the most pressing current and future issues faced by Hispanic-serving institutions will welcome the ideas and discussions in this book. Policymakers, higher-education administrators, faculty, students, and community leaders will find the content of the book enriching and insightful and will be inspired to act on behalf of these valuable institutions and the students who attend them."—*Frank Hernandez*, *Dean, College of Education, The University of Texas of the Permian Basin*

22883 Quicksilver Drive
Sterling, VA 20166-2102

Subscribe to our e-mail alerts: www.Styluspub.com